Winkelstein

THE MUSIC LOVERS

(Formerly published as "BELOVED FRIEND")
This book is abridged

*The Story of Tchaikowsky and
Nadejda von Meck*

This remarkable account of Tchaikowsky's
turbulent years, which, for the first time, tells
the complete story of the composer's
relationship with Nadejda von Meck, was
Catherine Drinker Bowen's first great success
as a biographer. In reviewing it for ATLANTIC
MONTHLY, John N. Burk wrote:

"The casual listener who at some time has found
himself wondering what really prompted the
abject but shiveringly delightful accents of
melancholy which pour from Tchaikowsky's
'Pathétique' Symphony, the seasoned
musician who has wondered precisely the
same thing and come not a bit nearer to
divining it—these people will find some
enlightenment in this book."

**Ken Russell, producer and director of
The Music Lovers, has made television
documentaries of many famous composers.
His most recent film is the much-acclaimed
adaptation of the D. H. Lawrence novel
*Women in Love.***

D0958891

The Music Lovers

*The Story of Tchaikowsky and
Nadejda von Meck*

Catherine Drinker Bowen
and
Barbara von Meck

HODDER PAPERBACKS

Printed and bound in Great Britain for
Hodder Paperbacks Ltd,
St. Paul's House, Warwick Lane,
London, E.C.4
by Hazell Watson & Viney Ltd,
Aylesbury, Bucks

ISBN 0 340 15154 4

PREFACE

After the death of Tchaikowsky and Nadejda von Meck, their correspondence was by common consent given to Nadejda's favorite grandson, Vladimir von Meck, often mentioned in the letters as Volichka. Barbara von Meck, co-author of this book, is Vladimir's widow. Modeste Tchaikowsky's biography of his famous brother, published in Russian in 1900 and later translated into English by Rosa Newmarch, contained perhaps a fourth of Tchaikowsky's letters to Nadejda von Meck. From these all revelations of intimacy had been cut, and not one letter from Nadejda included.

During the revolution of 1917, all von Meck property was seized, and with it, the correspondence. Barbara von Meck, who with her husband left Russia in 1923 to make her home in New York, heard nothing of the correspondence until the autumn of 1935, when she acquired two volumes published in Russian by the Academie Press (Soviet Government), which included the first six years of the correspondence, entire.

It is from these volumes, therefore, that we have worked. Barbara von Meck, whose knowledge of English is limited, made literal translations of the letters and gave them to me for arrangement and presentation, together with her notes and recollections of the persons and places involved. It became immediately obvious that no further effort of translation could endow these letters with a literary quality they never possessed. Profuse and repetitious as they were, the extremely interesting content had to be dug for, spaded from a mass of detail, of exclamation and nervous ecstasy which, when it reached its fifth consecutive epistolary page, lost for history the emphasis it may have contained for its writers. Therefore I have permitted the material to fall, very often, into narrative rather than epistolary form. All direct quotations are, of course, authentic; and for the narrative text, I have added nothing that was not already there.

C. D. B.

The authors desire here to convey their thanks to Elizabeth Sturgis, who first suggested this book be prepared, and to Frances Woodward Curtis, for her valuable editorial help.

B. V. M.
C. D. B.

I

Rubinstein plays for the Widow von Meck

Nicholas Rubinstein, his fur hat at a careful angle, the skirts of his fur coat striking against his short legs, walked down the steps of his Conservatory and turned northward along snow-lined, dimly-lighted Moscow streets. This was December, 1876, and northward lived, on the Boulevard Rojdestvensky, the richest woman in town—the respected, musical widow of the late equally respected, energetic knight, Karl George Otto von Meck.

Fortunate, thought Rubinstein, that the widow was musical! His Conservatory was ten years old now, but it could not have lived a decade without help—substantial help—from the Boulevard Rojdestvensky. Nadejda Philaretovna had never failed him, the more remarkable in that she was such an unapproachable person. Especially since her husband's death a year ago, she had declared her intention of living as a recluse for the rest of her life; as far as Rubinstein knew, he was the only man the widow received in her house. ... Rubinstein smiled, pressing more tightly under his arm his ever-present portfolio of music; this time it contained a composition of one of his young professors at the Conservatory. Pray the Lord the widow would like this piano transcription of the *Tempest Fantasia*. Peter Ilyich Tchaikowsky, its composer, was all of thirty-seven—only five years younger than Rubinstein himself; but unfortunately Peter Ilyich had not the Rubinstein fingers for picking up money; he was as poor as he was talented.

Men of magic, these Rubinsteins! Anton up in Petersburg, undeniably the first pianist of Europe—the aging Liszt was his only rival—had founded the Petersburg Conservatory, the first music school to exist in Russia, and had thereby revolutionized the status of all Russian musicians. Until then, a musician in Russia had been an ill-paid member of a third-rate theatre orchestra (there were no first-rate orchestras) a liveried servant fiddling in a nobleman's band while the nobleman ate his caviar; or he had been the nobleman himself who could, as an amateur, afford the time-consuming hobby of writing never-to-be-heard operas.

Anton determined to found an institution in which a musician might win the degree of Bachelor of Music, a title similar to that bestowed by the Petersburg Academy of Fine Arts upon painters, sculptors and architects. The Grand Duchess Helena Pavlovna, ever-kind goddess of the arts, approved the scheme, lent her house, gave her enthusiasm and, what was more, her money.

Thus the Petersburg Conservatory was founded, and Peter Tchaïkowsky, a young man of twenty, was one of its first pupils.

The school grew fast, too fast for Anton's taste. The Academy of Fine Arts possessed the privilege of military exemption for its students, and when the Grand Duchess procured a like privilege for the new Music School, young men with not a spark of talent flocked to Anton's door for enrollment. The place became a music factory and Anton was disgusted. He called his younger brother, then a student at the Moscow University, a night's journey to the south. "Nicholas," said Anton, "there is more than one city in Russia. Open a music school in Moscow, and mind you do not repeat my mistakes."

Nicholas went easily now, through the Moscow streets to knock upon the door of the widow von Meck; against the snow his steps were noiseless. Brother Anton, thought Nicholas, would approve this mission; it was Anton who had sent Peter Tchaïkowsky down from Petersburg ten years ago as a candidate for the professorship of musical theory in the new Moscow music school. Trust Anton to know a musician; Nicholas himself was a stern judge of men, but never so scornfully intolerant of mediocrity as his brother. . . .

Dogs barked through the cold dusk; on winter afternoons the dark comes early to Moscow. . . . Dogs barked, chimes from a hundred church steeples boomed beneath the cheerful jingle of troika bells. Horses' hooves were muffled on the snow that, for months to come, would mute all sound. And by this winter-quiet and by these bells and barkings a

8

Muscovite, though blinded, knew himself at home. This was Imperial, Orthodox Russia, every house had its watch dog which sat at the gate before the courtyard; Sharik, Drujok or Sultan, they would descend from owner to owner when the house changed hands. This was Moscow, where one lived in the house one's grandfather lived in, and was served by the sons of one's father's servants. ...

Not that Nicholas Rubinstein had had servants born in his house. Far from it. Nor was he a Muscovite by right of birth; he belonged neither to the rich and respected Moscow merchant class nor to the aristocracy whose quarter of the city he was at the moment traversing. He belonged nowhere, Nicholas Grigorievitch; although born to the Christian religion he was a Jew, essentially homeless. A Jew and a Free Artist, this man, but he loved Moscow none the less, with its pleasant Bohemian artistic life, and felt himself rightfully a part of it. He often told his friends he could never endure to live in that stiff Petersburg atmosphere with his brother Anton. Everybody in apartments instead of big comfortable houses, fog over the streets from November till May, and from Tsar to cab driver, social lines drawn in bands of steel! Here in Moscow everything was different; winter was clear and cold and the snow was beautiful; night and day the streets were gay with sleighbells. Social circles over-lapped here, formed into groups by some mutual interest such as politics or art. In Moscow's famous restaurants —*Praga, The Hermitage, The Yar,* every night friends pledged each other and drank deep, while gypsy orchestras played and sang. ... A toast to the new symphony, or the new play or the new picture! ... Drinking was an art in Moscow of the seventies. So was eating, but then Moscow made an art of everything and, drunk or sober, took its arts seriously. To the Muscovite of that day, a first performance was a vital question; he and his neighbor would quarrel to the death over a symphony or a picture. But there was one cause that could resolve any feud, unite on occasion every social circle—the honor and glory of one's own beloved city against the snobbish and fancied superiority of the Petersburgers. Also, Moscow spoke, literally, one language— professor at the University and cabman in the street—the

9

old Russian, without foreign words, not diluted with affected gallicisms like the bastard Petersburg tongue....

Nadejda von Meck, descending the stairs in a rustle of stiff black silk, was well aware that her visitor had not come this afternoon without a purpose—and Rubinstein knew she was aware of it. These two understood one another, but this did not mean they trusted one another. Too well each knew the world and the hardness of the world. Unlike Rubinstein, Nadejda had been born to wealth and social position—but she was not born to the wealth that supports it. There had been a time when the young wife fed her growing family upon twenty kopeks a day. She was therefore in a sense as self-made as Rubinstein, and her pride, her imperiousness, had fed upon the same fierce necessity, the same restless refusal to remain underdog.

Despots, the two of them, equal as sparring partners. Only one thing could put the widow off her guard: Music! This was a woman painfully reserved yet deeply, passionately musical in the Russian manner that loses itself completely in sound. Music acted upon her with physical force—made her ill, made her well—caused her to tremble from head to foot until she could not stand. But only certain kinds of music.... Rubinstein went to the piano. Would his purpose succeed, he wondered? Would the widow be pleased by *The Tempest*, and help his pupil?—(How Rubinstein loved to gamble!)

Without apology Nadejda moved swiftly away; Rubinstein knew her habit of listening to music from the adjoining room, alone and in darkness. ... The magic fingers touched the keys.

There was a moment's silence after the music ceased, before a rustle and sweep of silk announced the widow's entrance. One hand was against her breast, her eyes as she faced the light were shining, her color high. Rubinstein looked at her, and knew that the day was won. Nevertheless he chose carefully his answers to her eager questioning. Who wrote this music that had color beyond all symphony she had ever heard, and that beyond all symphony seemed so strangely personal to her? It militated nothing against Peter Tchaikowsky for Nadejda to learn that he was a gentleman—not born nor bred to the ranks of professional musicianship. Nadejda had always shown scant sympathy for the jealousies and intrigues of Moscow musical life. Peter Ilyich, Rubinstein told her, was a Petersburger, a graduate of the School of Laws; his father was a government inspector of mines. As a boy, Peter had great love for music and learned to play the piano, but he showed no unusual talent. Even in young manhood his essential quality had not appeared; he was a dilettante in law as well as in art; idle, indeed, to the point of frivolity. He had been twenty-two before, influenced by a musical friend, he entered Anton Rubinstein's newly opened Petersburg Music School. But, once introduced to music, he had seized upon it with an extraordinary grip; he was like a man starving who learns for the first time the name of bread. Counterpoint was bread; musical theory, composition were bread to a young man who until now had thought music meant salon pieces to be played on the piano at evening parties. His progress had been amazing; a year after his enrollment as student at the Conservatory, Peter Ilyich resigned his post at the Ministry of Justice and resolved to become a musician.

A daring step for a young man with no private income! But Anton Rubinstein believed in him; Nadejda von Meck did not need to be reminded that to any young musician, a word from Anton Rubinstein was like a word from God. For the ensuing four years Peter had kept himself alive somehow without asking aid from his father; after all, Ilya Tchaikowsky had bought his son one career—the law—and there remained three younger brothers to educate. Peter found piano pupils, Anton Rubinstein gave him a small post at the Conservatory. But Peter's struggle with poverty had been acute, many times he almost surrendered and returned to the safety of a government law position; once he nearly accepted a post as inspector of meat.

All this, Nicholas Rubinstein told the widow as the two faced each other in her drawing-room on the Boulevard Rojdestvensky. Of course, he added, Tchaikowsky's situation had been easier since he came to Moscow; he, Nicholas Grigorievitch, had seen to it that the young man had a roof over his head and enough to eat. If Rubinstein did not add that he had more than once given Peter Ilyich the clothes off his own back—a dress-coat for parties, a dozen shirts, a new frock-coat from the tailor's—he did not add either that the Conservatory had worked this young man cruelly. Long, grinding hours of teaching musical theory, day after day for ten years; for himself Rubinstein could weather such a life, varied as it was by triumphant concert tours—but unlike Peter Ilyich, Rubinstein was not torn from within, day and night, by a desperate urge to create music of his own. ...

No need, of course, to confess all this to the widow; Rubinstein chose his words well. He told her of the young man's spirit and talent, and of how these things had triumphed over the inconvenience of his birth. It had been by no means easy to induce the directors of the Moscow Conservatory to accept as professor of musical theory a young man—a gentleman at that—with only two years' Conservatory training. What was a mere two years, compared with the youth-long grind of most serious musicians? Also, the Petersburg School of Laws was admittedly a gentleman's school, and what snob, what amateur, ever had under his skin the makings of a serious musician?

Peter Ilyich was a worker and a musician, but he was not a pusher; infernally proud and infernally shy, he would go in rags rather than ask for charity. Would Nadejda Philaretovna, who had helped so many musicians, care to give the author of *The Tempest* a musical commission?

Rubinstein ceased speaking; the widow was on her feet, her dark eyes eager, alight with a glow which those who saw it never failed to remark. ... She shook her head gently, and smiled. "Nicholas Grigorievitch," she said, "I am immensely interested in all you have told me about this young man. But you need not have argued so eloquently in his behalf. His music spoke, before you."

2

Nadejda Philaretovna Frolowsky von Meck

Rubinstein had asked for little. Had he known all that was eventually to be given, had he for a moment suspected the sacrifice this introduction would one day cost his beloved

Conservatory, he would have flung *The Tempest* into Nadejda's porcelain stove rather than let her hear it. For it was Tchaikowsky's *music* with which the widow fell in love and continued in love; let there be no mistake about that. "For several days after hearing your *Tempest*," she wrote Tchaikowsky, "I was in a delirium from which I could not emerge." She never met the man who wrote *The Tempest*, never spoke with him face to face, but for the rest of her life she had only to hear his music to be thrown into all the transports of love.

We do not know what music she first commissioned Tchaikowsky to write that winter of 1876—but we know her reaction to it. Her brief note of acknowledgment is conventional enough in phraseology, but one senses beneath its single paragraph a very volcano of emotion.

Nadejda Philaretovna to Peter Ilyich

Moscow, Dec. 30, 1876

"Gracious Sir, Peter Ilyich:

"Permit me to express sincere thanks for the speedy execution of my commission. To tell you into what ecstasies your composition sent me would be unnecessary and unfitting, because you are accustomed to the compliments and homage of those much better qualified to speak than a creature so musically insignificant as I. It would only make you smile. I have experienced so precious a delight that I could not bear to have anyone find it ridiculous, so I shall content myself with asking you to believe absolutely that your music makes my life easier and pleasanter to live."

The composer's reply:

Moscow, Dec. 30, 1876

"Gracious Lady, Nadejda Philaretovna,

"I am sincerely grateful for the kind and flattering words that you were good enough to write me. To a musician, with all the disappointments and failures that obstruct his path, it is a comfort to know there is a small minority of people like yourself who truly and warmly love our art."

Several months later Peter Ilyich received and executed another commission, and the widow wrote him again:

Moscow, Feb. 27, 1877

"Gracious Sir, Peter Ilyich,

"Truly I do not know how to thank you for your kind indulgence of my impatience. If it were not for my deep sympathy toward you, I should fear that you would spoil me. My great appreciation of your kindness prevents any such reaction.

"I should like very much to tell you at length of my fancies and thoughts about you, but I fear to take your time, of which you have so little to spare. Let me say only that my feeling for you is a thing of the spirit and very dear to me. So, if you will, Peter Ilyich, call me erratic, perhaps even crazy, but do not laugh—it could be funny if it were not so sincere and real."

Peter Ilyich to Nadejda Philaretovna

Moscow, Feb. 28, 1877

"Gracious Lady, Nadejda Philaretovna,

"Permit me to thank you for the generous recompense, too lavish for such a little work.

"Why did you hesitate to tell me all your thoughts? I assure you I should have been most interested and pleased, as I in turn feel deeply sympathetic toward you. These are not mere words. Perhaps I know you better than you imagine.

"If, some happy day, you will do me the honor of writing me what you have so far withheld, I shall be very grateful. In any case, thank you from my heart for the sympathy that I very, very much appreciate."

Tell me all your thoughts ... perhaps I know you better than you imagine. ... Had the widow followed her heart, she would have seized her pen then and there and told her thoughts. But she was a wise woman as well as an ardent one, and she waited three weeks before she permitted herself to answer. A bitter school had taught her the dangers of impulsive action; it was not without reason that she had lately decided upon the life of a recluse.

Nadejda Philaretovna was born in 1831. Her father,

14

Philaret Vasilievitch Frolowsky, was a landed gentleman and a district judge; her mother Anastasia, born Potemkin, was descended from a cousin of that Prince of the Tauride, Gregory Potemkin, famous lover of Catherine the Great.

Like mother, like daughter: Nadejda's mother is described as a woman of great force; her father, according to Barbara von Meck, was a "quiet man who played the violin." The domestic picture is not difficult to reconstruct, but if it was the maternal line—the Potemkin inheritance—that gave almost masculine power to Nadejda Philaretovna, the quiet father gave her something of even more importance to this particular history—a love of music. As a little girl she would listen for hours while her father played his violin; when she and her sister grew older the parts were reversed, Philaret loved to listen while his daughters played duets upon the pianoforte—new and wonderful instrument imported from Germany, and so much more powerful than the harpsichord of his youth!

But when at seventeen the daughter married Karl George Otto von Meck, the unequal domestic scene was not reenacted. Quietness was not a distinguishing characteristic of the tribe von Meck. Proud Teutonic knights of Riga, they were accustomed to command. After her husband's death, Nadejda often expressed herself concerning the institution of marriage; she left no doubt that to her it was a necessary but highly distasteful business. "It is a pity," she once wrote Tchaikowsky, "that one cannot cultivate human beings artificially, like fishes; people would not then need to marry, and it would be a great relief."

But there was nothing artificial about the reproductive capacities of Nadejda and Karl George Otto; twelve children blessed the household von Meck. As antidote for superforceful wives, what more effective treatment could be devised?

Six sons and six daughters—Nadejda did everything with style. And she was far from being daunted by child-bearing and child-rearing; here was a wife who found time for more than that, much more. Tchaikowsky's was not the only career this woman saved. One crucial day, early in their married life, Karl George, talented, powerful visionary that he was, stood hesitant between the paths of safety and adventure.

The risk was great; poverty was plainly ahead and black uncertainty; Karl George went where his wife directed; it was the way of adventure and it was the way of triumph. Let Nadejda tell her own story as she told it later in a letter to Tchaikowsky:

"I have not always been rich,"—she wrote—"the greater part of my life I was poor, very poor indeed. My husband was an engineer in the Government Service, with a salary of 1500 roubles a year—which was all we had to live on, with five children and my husband's family on our hands. Not a brilliant prospect, as you see! I was wet-nurse, governess and dressmaker to my children and valet to my husband; the housekeeping was entirely in my hands; naturally there was plenty of work, but I did not mind that. It was another matter which made life unbearable. Do you know, Peter Ilyich, what it is to be in the Government Service? Do you know how, in that case, a man must forget he is a reasonable being, possessed of will-power and honorable instincts, and must become a puppet, an automaton? It was this I found so intolerable that finally I implored my husband to send in his resignation. To his remark that if he did so we should starve, I replied that we could work and that we should not die of hunger. When at last he yielded to my desires, we were reduced to living upon twenty kopeks a day for everything. It was hard, but I never regretted for a moment what had been done."

Karl George Otto was the eldest son of the most ancient branch of the family von Meck, knights of Riga. A luxurious life ate up his father's patrimony; the estate Zunzel, which had been in the family for centuries, had to be sold. Karl George was a very small boy when his father died, and he was a small boy without a penny. The nobility of Riga, true to their caste, paid for his education, but when he had finished college and wanted further education, it needed another, more inward nobility to carry him on. The School of Engineering was in Petersburg, one hundred miles to the east; Karl George had no money for the fare. But he was a knight of Riga, and he had spirit, and he walked to Petersburg.

16

When his engineering education was completed he was given a position near Smolensk. There he met Nadejda Philaretovna, and Nadejda, eager, at seventeen, to fly the nest, eager—according to her nature—for life—married this northerner. They moved from place to place as the husband's work demanded. Nadejda bore a new child in five new towns before she persuaded her man to abandon the hopeless routine of Government Service. His engineering talent was more than talent, it was vision. His map of Russia, with all the railroads of the future traced upon it according to his judgment and imagination, is even today the pride and treasure of the Kazan Railroad. It existed, at least, at the beginning of the Revolution and the workmen were very proud of it. They would point with their fingers: "You see? As he planned, so has it been built."

Nadejda soon found that with all his talent, her husband was anything but a business man. He was utterly unable to forecast an estimate of work and therefore to bargain a contract. On his first engineering venture he lost every cent of his savings and his wife's dowry besides. This was too much for Nadejda Philaretovna. True daughter of her mother, she seized the reins of government; from then on she managed the business part of her husband's work, leaving him free for engineering designs and projects. With her help he built a railroad from Moscow to Riazan; his sons Vladimir and Nicholas in turn extended it across the Volga to Kazan and eventually still further eastward to the Ural Mountains.

Karl George died in his fifties; he left his wife a large fortune, two railroads and twelve children, the eldest of whom, Vladimir, was twenty-four. One of the roads, the widow sold, the other—the Moscow-Riazan—Vladimir managed with her.

This was her favorite son, her darling, and Vladimir deserved the title. Such a woman could choose as favorite son none other than a creature of sparkle, of vitality and style, with a force of personality equal to her own. Her relationship with this son was to influence not only her own life but Tchaikowsky's.

Karl George's eldest son was as talented as the father, although Vladimir's gifts followed social and executive lines, rather than engineering or map-making. This was the only private railroad in Russia, and Vladimir managed it paternally. He had the dramatic quality possessed by all persons of great charm; what he did, he did with style. His mother, as shy as she was proud, could never, for instance, have equalled his manner of dealing with the arrogant house of Rothschild.

The railroad needed a big loan, and in the Europe of 1870 a big loan was synonymous with the name of Rothschild. Vladimir went to Paris to get the money, and with him went one—just one—bookkeeper from the railroad. The Paris House of Rothschild was extremely snobbish; it dealt not with individuals, but with governments, and it dealt through secretaries. But this being the son of that von Meck who had built and owned a railroad, the banker decided to make exception and grant him an interview. The evening before the day fixed for the audience, Rothschild sent a messenger round to ask how many secretaries Mr. von Meck had brought with him.

Vladimir asked the messenger why he wanted to know, and the man replied that Mr. Rothschild wished to prepare chairs for the audience.

"How many secretaries has Mr. Rothschild?" Vladimir asked.

"Six."

Vladimir did not hesitate. "I have twelve," he said.

Next morning the son of Nadejda Philaretovna walked into the office of the House of Rothschild. He was dressed faultlessly in morning coat and striped trousers, and he was not alone. Behind him walked his bookkeeper and eleven faithful friends, perfect secretaries, who stood or sat as occasion demanded.

And if this man knew how to uphold his authority abroad, against a Rothschild—he carried the banner even higher at home. His manner of living was as lavish as his nature. He knew how to spend money, did Vladimir; he had never lived, as had his parents, upon ten cents a day. Tablecloths to serve a hundred and forty—Barbara von Meck, who inherited them, says they were well-worn from use. He had the first electricity in Moscow, which meant a generator in the house, and an electrician to run it. He had also a very young, very black-eyed wife who could spend money as lavishly as he. When her son Vladimir II was born his mother was only sixteen; to her the baby was but another toy. Fortunately, the baby's grandmother, Nadejda von Meck, adored her new grandson. His young mother would leave Volichka in Grandmamma's great gloomy house and run joyfully to Paris for new gowns. Already she was known as the best-dressed woman in Moscow; she never wore the same dress twice and during a particularly important evening would sometimes go upstairs and change.

But Paris dresses cost money, then as now. The young mother would come home to Russia with ten full trunks and an empty purse; then she would sit down and write to her mother-in-law: "Pay my bills, or give me back my son!"

The bills were always paid.

When Karl George died, his widow did not drift for a day; characteristically, she sat down and mapped her course. Now that wifedom was to make no further social demands upon her, she could indulge her shyness—the furious, uncontrollable shyness of a spirit desperately ambitious. Shielded by a widow's mourning, she kept to her house for the rest of her life, seeing no one but her children. This was, however, no harsh retreat, the widow had as many houses as she had children. Besides her house in Moscow, she owned a huge country estate—Brailov, in the Ukraine, and villas on the French Riviera or wherever she chose to spend the winter season. Since young womanhood she had been subject to colds, by the time Tchaikowsky appeared she was threatened with tuberculosis. She was, therefore, continually on the move, a homesick fugitive from the long terrible winters of her native land. Emotional by nature, subject to alternate fits of exaltation and depression, there is little doubt that incipient tuberculosis, with its frequent colds and racking three-day headaches, exhausted her and deepened her tendency to depression.

When she became acquainted with Tchaikowsky in 1876, an army of people lived in the widow's house; seven of her twelve children were still at home, one had died in infancy. Her married daughter, Countess Bennigsen, often visited her, as did Vladimir—Volichka was not born until 1877.

Nadejda was a Muscovite as all her father's family had been, and she loved her city as Tchaikowsky learned to love it.

Nadejda's shyness cannot be explained wholly by her illness and frequent nervous fatigue. One is tempted to see another reason. She liked to have her own way; indeed, liked is too feeble a word. She *required* her own way, and surrounded herself only with those who would give it to her. She ruled her children's lives in every detail; as they grew up she arranged their marriages, bought houses for them and furniture for the houses; they were not always grateful. She consented to know her daughters-in-law and sons-in-law—but not their respective families. When she invited her married children to visit her, it was a command—and it was obeyed.

An army of servants surrounded this matriarchy; lackeys, footmen, estate stewards, English governesses for her children, German and French tutors—and above all, music teachers. The more she repudiated an ungrateful world, the more feverishly the widow desired music. She always had a musician living in the house to teach her children, or, when the children were away at school, to play duets with her. The list is long, from Danilchenko the Moscow cellist to Claude Debussy himself who came to her from Paris.

We have, thus far, the picture of a woman intense and dominating; let no reader be led into the error of thinking her masculine. She was anything but masculine; her very quality of decisiveness had in it something captious—arbitrarily feminine. She was tall and low-voiced; she moved slowly, with poise and grace—the Russian word "swimmingly" has no English equivalent. Her dark eyes were thoughtful, quick to kindle; her grand-daughter-in-law, Barbara, describes these eyes as the center and soul of Nadejda Philaretovna's personality. Her dark hair was long and abundant; every morning her maid Lucretia combed and brushed it—part of the important ritual of preparing her mistress for the day. No trespassers were allowed in her room until the hair-brushing and facial massage were done —none, that is, until Vladimir II* came into her life.

* Vladimir II, affectionately known as Volichka, was the little boy who would some day, with his wife Barbara, inherit the letters between his grandmother and Tchaikowsky.

Volichka loved to watch the massaging machine, and his grandmamma loved to watch Volichka.

After the hair-dressing and massage were accomplished, Lucretia, who had been with her mistress for many years, would take up her position outside the apartment door in a large armchair, a table beside her. There she would knit, a sentry in bonnet, huge white apron, and shawl. No one could pass unsummoned, not even the mistress' own children—excepting again, the two Vladimirs. Like all despots, Nadejda was shameless in her partiality. Behind this guarded door Nadejda von Meck sat in flowing peignoir and wrote her letters. Her sitting-room, was furnished lavishly, in the French style, and every inch of wall and tables was covered with framed photographs of her family. Over the writing table hung a portrait of Louis of Bavaria, one of Nadejda's correspondents.

Periodically, Nadejda von Meck inspected her house. It was a tour; her eldest servants accompanied her from cellar to roof, and from cellar to roof the household trembled. This was a woman who was never idle; idleness for matrons was not the prevailing fashion, also, idleness was contrary to the habit of her own former active life and to her nature. String was saved for her to untangle and wind, books were bought so that she might cut the pages. She purchased quantities of wool which she would wind into balls and send to her daughter, Countess Bennigsen. And while she did these things, Julia would read to her. Julia had been *summoned* to read to her, and Julia loved to obey her mother's command. Of Julia, her third and favorite daughter, Nadejda Philaretovna demanded everything—and got it.

But a tyrant is lonely. There were many to obey Nadejda von Meck, few to love her. Julia loved her, Volichka her grandson was to love her—to the credit of both Julia and Volichka: love for a tyrant in whose house one lives requires both gentleness and strength. But Volichka was as yet unborn. The widow needed, craved, the love of an equal; so passionate a nature can be satisfied with nothing less. More than an equal; Nadejda wanted a god to worship. Karl George had been her equal, she had made a great man of him, and in the process, had somehow lost her God. She was an atheist; this in itself was not unusual in aristocratic

Russia of the 1870's. Nadejda's atheism and her independence of God and society, so repeatedly professed in her letters to Tchaikowsky, are worth remark as a key to understanding what happened later. Such fury of independence is not always an attribute of the healthy being; genuine independence does not need so much protesting. She liked to call herself a "realist"; Tchaikowsky was nearer the point when he translated her realism as "idealism." Nadejda was a romantic idealist, with all the romanticist's desperate need of a god. The time was to come when this woman would call upon heaven and cringe before man, when a truly pathologic remorse would cause her to break with all that was dearest to her. But just now, and for the ensuing thirteen years, she called upon no one and nothing but Peter Ilyich Tchaikowsky and the music he evoked.

3

Peter Ilyich and the Tchaikowsky family

If, for Nadejda von Meck, the time was ripe for this new friendship, on Tchaikowsky's side the need was no less urgent. Life for Tchaikowsky had reached a crisis, and Tchaikowsky was not the man to seize crisis by the horns and wrestle it into submission. Rather, he was one to let himself be carried along by fate, submitting with a helpless patience very trying to the beholder; the worse things got, the more paralyzed Peter became; he would sit with tortured eyes, waiting for the foe to forget him....

Yet—and for this reason the man's name became history—behind all this passivity, this almost feminine endurance, lay a smoldering fire of nervous strength that wanted only the hand of a friend to touch it to life. And in this most difficult year of Peter's life, the saving hand was to be Nadejda von Meck's.

On that December afternoon of 1876, Rubinstein had told Nadejda von Meck that Peter Ilyich was a gentleman, not born nor bred to the intrigues of a professional musical life. The Tchaikowsky's were indeed gentility, but gentility by virtue of talent, education and bearing rather than birth. Let Peter Ilyich tell his own genealogy as he wrote it to Nadejda von Meck not long after their correspondence began:

"I shall answer your question about my family. I warn you that the description of my dear ones will be an uninterrupted paean of praise, but let me assure you, my sweet friend, nothing is exaggerated in the eulogies that I shall squander on my relatives. The head of my family is my father, an old man of eighty-three. He was for many years a mining engineer, and also for a long time ran the Kamo-Votkin factory in the province of Viatka, where I was born. In 1848 he was retired and lived on the income from the small capital that he had accumulated after many years of service. In 1857 he put that sum in the hands of an adventuress who promised him mountains of gold, and lost all of it that very year, irrevocably. In 1858 he again started to work and was for four years director of the Technological Institute. In 1862 he retired and now lives on a pension in Petersburg.

"My mother died in 1854 from cholera. She was a fine, clever woman and loved her children passionately. In 1865 my father married for the third time. My step-mother, a half-educated but very intelligent and extremely kind woman, succeeded in inspiring us all with a sincere respect for her tender, unselfish devotion to her old husband. We all, I mean my sister and brothers, are devoted to her. My father, once a very clever engineer, has become childish. He is still very alert and healthy in body, but feeble in mind. Only his old love for his children is left, and the angelic kindness that always distinguished him but which is now especially touching. It can truly be said that he cannot hurt a fly. All other activities of his brain and soul have become quite childish. He nearly lost his memory after the dangerous illness he had last year. I have four brothers. The eldest, Nicholas, works on the railroad and lives in Kharkov. He is married but childless. After him I come; after me my brother Hippolyte, who lives in Odessa, married and also childless. Then come those whom you know of, the twins, Anatol and Modeste."

In his biography of Peter Ilyich, Modeste Tchaikowsky lets it be understood that there were no musicians among the family ancestry. He admits that their mother and their aunt and uncles had good voices and liked to sing "romances." (The German *lieder* had not yet become familiar as an art form in Russia.) There was a cathedral Protodeacon in the maternal ancestry, but Modeste in his record chose to ignore him — and with a reason. In the Russian Church, prayers are never said but intoned; therefore, especially in the big city churches, priests with rich bass voices were coveted, but the clergy had no social standing; they were a class in themselves, disliking the nobility and looked down upon, as a class, in return; to Western eyes it seems strange to read of Russian noblemen who boasted they had "no Jewish or clerical blood."

Peter Ilyich, on the other hand, would not have cared had his maternal grandfather been a Tartar or a red Indian. He wasted no time brooding over the bourgeois stamp of his ancestry. "There are a number of Poles bearing my name," he confessed to Nadejda von Meck. "I myself am probably of Polish descent, though I don't know positively who my ancestors were. I know only that my grandfather was a physician and lived in the province of Viatka, and then my genealogical tree becomes lost in darkness. Perhaps Mr. Victor Tchaikowsky and the other fellow bearing the same name as I, who every day advertises in the Moscow News a corn plaster he has invented — are distant relatives of mine."

It is to be doubted if Modeste would have made a like lighthearted admission. Modeste was to be his brother's Boswell — without Boswell's genius. One cannot read memoirs of Russia's musical and literary life of the late nineteenth century without meeting Modeste's name; he was well known in intellectual circles; Barbara von Meck, who knew Modeste, says he had the Tchaikowsky charm. "Every man has his shadow and Tchaikowsky's shadow was his brother Modeste. One cannot name the composer without remembering his brother. Modeste as a demi-genius."

Modeste published a three-volume biography of his brother and for the information contained therein, the world is grateful. But Modeste wrote too soon; writing, he looked about him and saw a living face at every window. Not dismissable faces either; these were prominent people. Modeste shuddered; who now would receive him if he recorded what he knew? Besides, he loved his brother deeply and what better way to prove one's love than by guarding the secrets of the beloved? Also, Modeste never understood Nadejda Philaretovna; he was always rather jealous of the relationship between the two and refused to recognize the intensity of their mutual attachment. How could Petia be so dependent emotionally upon a woman? Modeste did not scruple to change and color his brother's motives to what he considered his brother's advantage.

Modeste is always described as "cultured"; there is no doubt he possessed a sensitive appreciation of literature and art.

"It is remarkable," Peter Ilyich wrote Nadejda, "that I, a musician by instinct, fitted for nothing but music, should be born into a family absolutely lacking in all feeling for music. Both my younger brothers understand music very well because they grew up in my company and through me came into contact with music and musicians. They both love music passionately. Modeste, though quite lacking in any talent for it, has nevertheless developed a wonderfully delicate musical understanding. He plays the piano and is ready to play the whole day long, he loves music so, but still he plays badly and cannot sing at all. The other members of my family do not even like music."

Petia had little to say of Hippolyte in his letters, but he never tired of singing the praises of the twins.

"Without exaggeration," he told Nadejda, "one can say that these two young men are, by virtue of their moral and spiritual qualities, very pleasant persons. I am bound to them by a mutual friendship that is rare even between brothers. They are much younger than I—by ten years; when my mother died, they were only four. My sister was in the Institute. Our eldest brother, a good man but not very gentle, could not take the place of an affectionate and loving mother. Certainly I was no mother, but from the first moment of their bereavement I wanted to be to them what a mother is, because experience has taught me what an indelible imprint a mother's tenderness and caress can leave on the soul of a child. And from that time, between them and me such a bond has grown that I love them more than myself and am ready to make any sacrifice for them, and they are boundlessly devoted to me. They were educated in the School of Laws. Anatol is working and doing well. He is now an assistant attorney in Petersburg. Modeste is very richly talented by nature, but without definite inclination to any special occupation. He has not been very successful; being more interested in books, pictures, music, than in reports. We were all troubled about his future when suddenly a mutual friend had the brilliant idea of recommending him to a certain Conradi who was looking for a tutor for his only son who is deaf and dumb. The matter was arranged, and Modeste soon proved himself a perfect teacher. He spent a year abroad, studying the method of educating deaf and dumb children, and now he is wholeheartedly devoted to his work.

"Although I have two sisters, the eldest (by my father's first marriage) is much older than I—she lives in the Ural Mountains, and I know her only slightly. As to my own real sister (Alexandra Davydoff) I have written you about her. She is an irreproachable and wonderful woman in every sense of the word."

Before Nadejda von Meck came into his life, this sister's estate at Kamenka, near Kiev, was the only real home Tchaikowsky knew. Even without Tchaikowsky, Kamenka is part of Russian history; high tragedy was enacted there, and heroism. Yet when Peter Ilyich knew Kamenka, there was no longer tragedy in its mild monotonous landscape, only peace and the comfortable humdrum of Alexandra Davydoff's busy domestic household.

And Peter Ilyich needed peace; only in quiet surroundings could he do the work that was life itself to him. Living in Moscow with Nicholas Rubinstein was anything but peaceful. Rubinstein thrived upon noise and bustle and much business; during this first year of the Conservatory's life all classes were held in Rubinstein's house. Peter Ilyich was twenty-six when he went, in 1866, to Moscow.

"I have a little room next to Rubinstein's bedroom," he wrote his young twin brothers at their Petersburg school, "and truly I am afraid of disturbing him at night with the scratching of my pen, for only a small partition divides our rooms. I am terribly busy. I sit at home, scarcely ever going out, and Rubinstein who is always rushing about, can't marvel enough at my industry. I have hardly met anyone new as yet except Kashkin, an excellent musician and friend of Laroche's. I have some very low moments, but an insatiable thirst for work consoles me. I have nearly finished orchestrating the overture I worked on last summer and to my horror it is shaping much too long. I have promised it to Rubinstein for a first performance here, then I shall send it to Petersburg."

That first winter away from home (1866) was hard for Peter Ilyich; he was a man who needed roots. To the end of his life, removal from one place to another plunged him into panic. After a month in Moscow he wrote his sister, Alexandra Davydoff:

"Little by little I am becoming accustomed to Moscow, although sometimes I am sadly lonely. To my great surprise my classes are going very successfully; my timidity has completely disappeared and gradually I am beginning to look like a real professor. My low spirits also are disappearing, yet Moscow is still a strange town and it will be a long time before I can face without horror the fact that I shall stay here for years if not forever."

During the winter months, Tchaikowsky over-worked himself; besides teaching twenty-six hours a week, he was writing his first symphony, *Winter Day Dreams*, and by spring he experienced his first serious attack of those nervous symptoms which later were to be his constant companions. Insomnia was one of them, intestinal cramps and throbbing in his head; he often referred to these discomforts as his "apoplectic symptoms." At the end of April he wrote his brother Anatol:

"My nerves are completely out of order. Reasons: (1) The symphony which does not sound right. (2) Rubinstein and

Tarnovsky having noticed that I am easily startled, tease me all day long by devising different manner of shocks for me. (3) The persistent conviction that I shall die soon, before I even have time to finish the symphony. I look forward to summer and Kamenka as to the Promised Land. Yesterday I gave up drinking vodka, wine and strong tea. I hate mankind in general and with pleasure would retire to a thinly populated desert. I have bought my ticket on the diligence for May tenth."

But the diligence went to Kamenka without him. He worked night and day but composition did not come easily: lack of experience meant lack of facility. His nervous symptoms became more and more alarming; real hallucinations, a constant, heavy, nameless fear. Too young to know that this kind of suffering cannot be vanquished by working hard at one's business in life, Peter Ilyich struggled on, ashamed of his symptoms, ashamed also to confess them: Nicholas Rubinstein, with nerves of steel-and-rubber, was hardly the confidant for a homesick young man who wanted badly to tell someone that his head was going to fall off, and would people think it funny if he kept his hand under his chin to hold it on?

By the end of June, 1866, Peter was ripe for a serious nervous breakdown and had it; the doctor said he narrowly escaped madness. For the first time, but not by any means for the last, Peter Ilyich was ordered to "rest, and stop writing music."

4

*Tchaikowsky's music before he was
introduced to Nadejda von Meck*

"Rest, and stop writing music." Futile command! In his letters, Tchaikowsky refers again and again to his persistent need to compose: —"Like a bear in his cave I feed upon my own substance—my compositions, that never cease turning in my head." "I am of no use, except for music . . ." "I must hurry, hurry; I am afraid I shall die with all my music in me" . . . "To compose is for me a kind of musical shriving of the soul" . . .

In the autumn of 1866, rested by his vacation, Tchaikowsky returned to the Conservatory, his first symphony, *Winter Day Dreams*, under his arm. He had sent it to Petersburg during the summer for the criticism of his one-time music masters, Anton Rubinstein and Zaremba, the counterpoint teacher, but to Tchaikowsky's great disappointment the two rejected it on behalf of the Musical Society. They were, indeed, harsh and unsympathetic toward the music, suggested changes which Tchaikowsky made against his will, nor did he like the changes when made. Even as altered, the Petersburg Musical Society consented to perform only the two middle movements of the symphony. These met with a cold reception, and the whole episode embittered Tchaikowsky toward Petersburg and all his former musical associates there, turning his heart toward Moscow, his future home.

All that winter he worked upon his new opera, *The Voyevoda*, and in the early spring both the symphony and the dances from the opera were performed in Moscow. The symphony, *Winter Day Dreams*, from which Tchaikowsky had erased the alterations, was presented in its original form with huge success; the composer was called out; he appeared upon the stage, spectators said, looking definitely untidy, and made an awkward bow. As to the *Voyevoda* dances, Tchaikowsky conducted the orchestra himself, his first experience with the baton — and his last for ten years, owing to the agony he suffered from shyness. Beforehand, to his friend Kashkin, Peter expressed himself as being perfectly calm — not in the least nervous — but from the instant he found himself on the stage, he was a lost creature. Mind fled and with it all sense and sensation save the old conviction that his head would fall off. With one hand Peter Ilyich held firmly onto his chin, while the other hand waved the stick feebly, giving all the leads at the wrong moment to the wrong instruments. Fortunately, the players were well trained, and disregarding the baton entirely, came through quite well.

The concert was important in Tchaikowsky's career because an incident connected with it brought him into contact for the first time with the Petersburg Nationalists, the talented and revolutionary Five: Balakirev, Cui, Moussorgsky, Borodin, Rimsky-Korsakov and their friend and ally, the critic Stassov. The Five had broken—they said—with musical tradition; they believed music could be composed better by inspiration than by rule, that a composer learned by composing, not by working out counterpoint problems. Moussorgsky was the fiercest rebel of them all, and in truth his genius was great enough to justify him had he said music should be written standing on one's head. Borodin also, the chemistry professor, writing his gorgeous tone poems while his test tubes were boiling, could well afford to laugh at rules. As to Rimsky-Korsakov, the other great talent of the Five, the world already knows—and Tchaikowsky's letters will retell—who it was that seduced him from rebellion to the slow and thorny path of traditional musical study.

The Five wished to create Russian music, for Russians, in the Russian language. No French words in their songs, no Italian libretti for their operas! The fount at which they drank was the deep well of Russian folk-song; fiercely they disclaimed all "foreign" influence, the French, the German, and more particularly the Italian operatic tradition to which Russian music had been enslaved for the past fifty years. Glinka was of course their forerunner, Dargomisky their immediate inspiration. The Five were especially scornful of Bach. "The old man is beginning to grind flour," Stassov would say when he heard one of the huge five-voiced fugues begin to roll up its giant momentum.

The Rubinsteins were of course regarded by the Five as hopelessly *passé*; not only did the Rubinsteins teach their pupils by the old despised conservatory régime, but more sinister still, the two of them laughed frankly at nationalism and would as soon write an opera around an Italian libretto as a Russian one.

And Tchaikowsky was as bad as a Rubinstein, if not worse —so thought the Five. Was he not a pupil of both Rubinsteins, first Anton and then Nicholas? Dangerous conservatives, all three, teaching music by rote in their "music factories," as the Five dubbed the Petersburg and Moscow Conservatories. And the suspicion was mutual; to Tchaikowsky the Five were not only dangerous radicals, they were dilettantes who toyed with a serious art, repudiating the hard preliminary study necessary to musical composition, repudiating Tchaikowsky's musical heroes, above all, his god, Mozart. But Tchaikowsky knew none of the Five personally, that is, until 1868 when his own *Voyevoda* dances were played in Moscow on the same concert program with Rimsky-Korsakov's *Serbian Fantasy*. A review of the concert appeared afterward in *The Entr'acte*. Tchaikowsky's music was highly praised while Rimsky-Korsakov's work was dismissed as "lifeless and colorless." During rehearsals, Tchaikowsky had learned to respect not only Rimsky-Korsakov's music but the composer himself; consequently he wrote a fiery reply to *The Entr'acte* which created a sensation both in Moscow and Petersburg and brought the Five from hostility to immediate friendship. At Easter when Tchaikowsky went up to Petersburg to visit his father, he was received with much cordiality by the Invincible Band, as the Five called themselves, and although neither Tchaikowsky nor the Five (excepting Rimsky-Korsakov) ever compromised concerning their respective musical philosophies, from this time onward their personal relationship remained cordial. During the next five years, three of Tchaikowsky's best compositions were dedicated to members of the Band. The symphonic poem *Fatum* and the *Romeo and Juliet* overture to Balakirev, who had suggested the latter as a subject—and to Stassov the symphonic fantasia which plays such a large part in our history, *The Tempest*.

During the winter of 1868–69 Tchaikowsky had what he liked to refer to as a "love affair" with the singer, Désirée Artôt, who came to Moscow for a few weeks with an Italian opera company. Peter wrote glowing letters to his brothers about his goddess, and then quite suddenly found himself engaged to marry her. He seems to have floated into the entanglement quite lightheartedly—and floated out again long before there was danger of complete submersion. From first to last the affair was shaped by events rather than by Tchaikowsky himself. This was characteristic of the man. He had heard Artôt sing and admired her intensely as an artist; later he met her at a musical party. "She expressed surprise," he wrote his father, "that I had not called. I promised to do so, but I should never have gone (because of my shyness with new acquaintances) if Anton Rubinstein, in passing through

Moscow, had not dragged me there. Since then I have had numerous invitations from her and drifted into the habit of going to her house every day."

Tchaikowsky's friends, he went on to tell his father, tried their best to prevent a marriage. Nicholas Rubinstein especially, advanced arguments which Ilya Tchaikowsky countered in a return letter to his son:

December 29, 1868

"You ask my advice, dear Petya, upon the most important decision of your life. Truly, my friend, marriage is not a step to take heedlessly; it is a gambler's risk, it is the hazard of the brave. As a father I rejoice; Désirée is surely worthy because my son Peter loves her, and my son Peter is a man of taste and talent who would naturally select a wife with like qualities. The two years difference in your ages means nothing.

"You are both artists, both make capital from your talents, but she has already won money and fame, whereas you are only beginning, and God knows if you will go as far as she. Friends and sympathizers fear that your career will be sacrificed to this marriage; I disagree. You who for your talent's sake gave up a career in the Government Service surely will not, at the first momentary disappointment, cease being an artist. What musician but is unhappy at the start? Pride makes it bitter for you to depend financially on your wife — but if you both work you will forget this jealousy. Go your way and let her go hers, but let neither of you give up your vocation until you have saved enough money to say, 'This is ours, this is our mutual victory.'

"Let us analyze these words: "As husband to a famous singer you will be a piteous slave, following her over Europe, fattening on her money and becoming too lazy to work on your own behalf.' — But if you love each other sincerely, maturely, this is a nonsensical picture. Happy marriage is based on mutual respect; you would never ask your wife to be your servant, nor will she demand lackey's service from you. As for travelling with her, that is your duty; but can you not compose on the road, seizing every opportunity to have your compositions performed abroad? With such a companion, your talent should grow rather than diminish.

Suppose your mutual passion cools, leaving only 'wounded vanity, melancholy and ruin.' Why should this be? I lived with your mother twenty-one years, and all that time I loved her as ardently as a youth, respecting and venerating her as a saint. You resemble your mother; if your beloved has your mother's qualities, all these fears are vain.

"I question only one thing: Are you both quite sure of your love? 'To marry is not to cross a field'; would it not be wise to try your love—not, for heaven's sake, by jealousy, but by time? Wait a little longer and then decide, having asked God's help. Meanwhile describe your loved one to me truly, my darling."

Tchaikowsky had barely time to digest this affectionate advice when the question was taken out of his hands: in Warsaw, whither she had gone to sing, Artôt, without a word of warning to anyone, married a Polish baritone. Tchaikowsky was far from heartbroken.

Artôt jilted him that winter of '68; his opera *Voyevoda* was a failure; the libretto was insipid; Tchaikowsky had managed to cut from it every scene that might have proved good musical material. All his life he was to choose unfortunate subjects for his operas; his sense of the theatre was by no means his strong point. *Voyevoda* was a failure, so was the symphonic poem *Fatum* which followed it. Tchaikowsky tore up the score of *Fatum* and plunged into a new work, the three-act opera, *Undine*. *Undine* was finished in seven months but was never performed in full. Tchaikowsky destroyed this score also, except for an aria and a wedding march which he used in later compositions. None of these failures seemed to depress the composer unduly, and so it was all his life; by the time one work was ready for performance he was always engrossed in a new composition; buoyed up by faith in the new work, he sailed over the head of failure, merely pausing to remark that he had been chagrined, yes—but what a lot he was learning!

Even the *Romeo and Juliet Overture-Fantasia* for orchestra, written in 1869 and now considered one of Tchaikowsky's finest works and the beginning of his career as an important composer, when performed in Moscow early in 1870, attracted no notice at all. Nicholas Rubinstein conducted;

the players must have been very clumsy indeed to conceal the power and the poetry of this composition. Perhaps the composer knew his music was good, for a few weeks after the performance he wrote his brother Modeste:

March 26, 1870

"I congratulate you on leaving school. Thinking over my life since my graduation from the School of Laws, I see with some pleasure that the time has not been lost. I wish the same for you. . . ."

During the next five years, Tchaikowsky's life was not especially remarkable. He taught, he wrote music, he travelled, he enlarged slowly but steadily both his fame and his personal circle of friends. After *Romeo and Juliet* his next big work was an opera, *The Oprichnik*, which had its first performance at Kiev in 1874, and was a success in spite of the fact that the Censor—that figure so devastating to the Russian Imperial Theatre—forbade the *Oprichnik's* hero, Ivan the Terrible, to appear upon the stage. The opera has since found oblivion.

During the four weeks before Christmas, 1869, Tchaikowsky wrote his first opus of original songs—Opus 6. One of these, *Nur wer die Sehnsucht Kennt*, is the best known of the 117 songs he was destined to publish. The First String Quartet, in D major, was written soon afterward. It contains the famous *Andante Cantabile* that has wrung tears from so many listeners, a tune that, lovely as it is, has become tiresomely representative of the name of Tchaikowsky; like Handel's *Largo*, the world sometimes forgets its composer wrote anything else. The famous *Andante* is based on a folk-song Tchaikowsky heard at his sister's estate in Kamenka. He was in his room working on the orchestration of *Undine* when a gardener outside his window sang the song through to Russian words.

That summer of 1870 Tchaikowsky wrote his *Manual of Harmony*, for use in his courses at the Conservatory. The book is thorough and concise, abounding in those musical illustrations for which Tchaikowsky was famous as a teacher. Scanning it, one is faintly surprised that Peter Ilyich could have written anything at the same time so complete and coldly impersonal. Many a great composer of the 1870's and '80's struggled through this merciless little book, among them Rimsky-Korsakov who in his memoirs has confessed the hard work Tchaikowsky's counterpoint exercises cost him.

The Second Symphony, in C minor, was written in 1872 (later drastically revised). This year also saw the completion of music to Ostrovsky's poem, *The Snow Maiden*. Tchaikowsky himself did not think much of this; it has since been totally eclipsed by Rimsky-Korsakov's ballet music for the same story. *The Tempest* was begun that year and finished in the summer of 1873. Then came the Second String Quartet, in F major, and an opera, *Vakoula the Smith*. (This opera was remodelled in 1885; produced in America in 1922 as *Oxana's Caprice*, it was pronounced by the critics "extremely humorous, delightful and fantastic.") Numerous songs and piano pieces followed the composition of the opera, and in 1874 Tchaikowsky composed one of his major works, the brilliant B Flat Minor Piano Concerto. The principal theme of the first movement of this concerto was also heard at Kamenka; Tchaikowsky wrote Nadejda von Meck that he first heard it sung by blind beggars at the village fair.

As soon as it was written, the composer took the concerto to Nicholas Rubinstein for criticism. Four years later, Tchaikowsky wrote an account of the episode to Nadejda:

To Nadejda von Meck

San Remo, January 21, 1878
"In December, 1874, I wrote a piano concerto. As I am not a pianist, I needed a virtuoso's opinion as to what was technically impractical, difficult, unplayable, and so on. I needed a serious but friendly critic, but only for the pianistic aspect of my composition. Rubinstein is not only the first pianist of Moscow, but is truly a perfect pianist; knowing he would be deeply offended if he thought I had ignored him, I asked him to listen to the concerto and give me an opinion on the piano part, although some inner voice protested against my selecting him as judge. It was Christmas Eve of 1874. We were both invited to a Christmas tree that evening at Albrecht's, and Nicholas Gr. suggested that we go to one

of the class-rooms at the Conservatory beforehand. And so we did. I arrived with my manuscript, and after me Nic. Gr. with Hubert. Have you any idea, my friend, what the latter is like? He is very kind and clever, completely lacking in independence, very talkative, needing a whole preface to say yes or no, incapable of expressing an opinion in a simple way, always backing the one who at the moment expresses himself bravely and decisively. I hasten to add that it is because of lack of character, not servility.

"I played the first movement. Not a word, not a remark. If you only knew how disappointing, how unbearable it is when a man offers his friend a dish of his work, and the other eats and remains silent! Well, say something—scold, in a friendly way, but for God's sake, one sympathetic word, even if uncomplimentary! While Rubinstein prepared his thunder, Hubert waited for the situation to clarify so he would know which way to jump. The point was that I did not want a verdict on artistic merits, but advice as to piano technic. Rubinstein's eloquent silence had great significance. As much as to say—'My friend, can I speak of details when the thing as a whole disgusts me?' I armed myself with patience, and played it through to the end. Again silence. I stood up and said 'Well?' Then from the lips of N. G. R. poured a torrent of words, first quiet, then more and more the tone of Jupiter, master of the thunder-bolts. It appeared that my concerto is worthless, impossible to play, the themes have been used before, are clumsy and awkward beyond possibility of correction; as a composition it is poor, I stole this from here and that from there, there are only two or three pages that can be salvaged, and the rest must be thrown away or changed completely! 'For example, that—well, what is that?' (And he plays the place indicated, exaggerating it.) 'And that? Is it possible!' and so on. I cannot convey the tone in which it was all spoken. An outsider, dropping into the room, would have thought me a madman, without talent, ignorant, a worthless writer who had come to annoy a famous musician with his rubbish. Noticing that I was obstinately silent, amazed, and shocked that a man who had written a great deal already, and who is teaching the course of free composition in the Conservatory, should be subjected to such a reprimand, to such a humiliating sentence, without appeal—a sentence such as one should not pronounce even on a pupil of little ability without first looking through his work with care—Hubert started to explain N. G. R.'s opinions, not differing from him, only softening what His Excellency expressed so unceremoniously.

"I was not only astonished but offended by the performance. I am no longer a boy, trying his strength in composition—I no longer need lessons, especially lessons expressed so sharply and in such a hostile manner. I need, and will always need, friendly criticism, but this was nothing like friendly criticism. It was a decisive, blanket condemnation, expressed in such a manner as to touch me in a sensitive spot. I walked out of the room without a word and went upstairs. I was speechless with excitement and fury. Rubinstein appeared soon after, and seeing my disturbed state of mind, called me to another room. There he repeated that my concerto was impossible, and, having pointed out many places needing radical change, told me that if I would alter the concerto according to his wishes by a certain date, he would do me the honor of performing it at his concert.* 'I won't change a single note,' I replied, 'and will print it exactly as it is now.' And so I did.

"This is the incident that caused Rubinstein to look on me as a *frondeur*, a secret enemy. He has grown colder toward me since then, though it has not prevented him from repeating on all occasions that he is terribly fond of me and ready to do anything for me."

This letter, written four years after the event, is very little exaggerated, and quite true in essence. As long as Tchaikowsky remained subservient, Nicholas Rubinstein looked upon him with greatest affection, but from the beginning, both Rubinstein brothers maintained an inexplicable, two-sided attitude toward Tchaikowsky. They recognized in him a great musician, yet they could not bring themselves to accept his music the first time they heard it; extreme caution characterized all their criticisms, often enough they never retracted this original harshness. Anton especially, while urg-

* Rubinstein later played this concerto all over Europe, and with greatest success. This and the violin concerto remain the most popular of Tchaikowsky's works for solo instrument.

37

ing Tchaikowsky from the very beginning to embrace a musical career, greeted his successive compositions with scorn, or ignored them. After these bouts Peter found it an enormous comfort to take his bruised ego to Nadejda von Meck; her faith and her indignation proved balm and nourishment for any wound. . . .

As to the B Flat Minor Piano Concerto, after Rubinstein's condemnation Tchaikowsky scratched the word Rubinstein from the dedication and replaced it with the name of the famous German pianist and conductor, Hans von Bülow. Bülow had for some time been an admirer of Tchaikowsky and was pleased with the compliment; he became more than ever a champion of Tchaikowsky's music in Europe. But Rubinstein's strictures must have had more eventual influence than von Bülow's praise, for fifteen years later Tchaikowsky revised the piano part completely, and the concerto, "that duel between piano and orchestra," became once and for all one of the most popular of virtuoso piano concerti.

By the time the B Flat Minor Piano Concerto was written, Tchaikowsky had already effected somewhat of a separation from Nicholas Rubinstein; that is to say, he no longer lived in Rubinstein's house. Rubinstein had been married, earlier in life, but his wife had proved unsympathetic toward his professional musical life; especially, she had objected to concert tours. Anyway, Rubinstein left her, but he could not bear to live alone. Tchaikowsky came to his house in 1886 and stayed six years, and for Tchaikowsky it was not an easy situation. He was forced to adapt his daily schedule strictly to his host's—and the two kept entirely different hours. Unable to endure the noise of Rubinstein's pianoforte classes, Peter Ilyich used to take his music paper to a nearby student café in the mornings, and write there amid the empty tables. When he first came to Moscow, Rubinstein's rooftree had been a welcome shelter. As Peter acquired more money he tried several times to leave Rubinstein and set up independent quarters, but Rubinstein would have none of it. Six years passed before a friend appeared who was willing to substitute as a Rubinstein guest. Tchaikowsky moved into a tiny three-room flat and for the first time in his thirty-two years, found himself alone and master of his days.

By this time he was earning 3000 roubles a year; 2000 roubles from his salary at the Conservatory and the sale of his published works, 500 from his newspaper and magazine articles. This latter work had begun with his defending Rimsky-Korsakov in the *Entr'acte* in 1868. Many of Tchaikowsky's critical articles have been preserved and published in English, but they are not to be compared in value or interest with his creative musical output. To write words was a burden to Tchaikowsky and he did it only when in need of money. In a letter to Modeste, written just after the completion of the B Flat Minor Concerto, the composer describes his difficulties with both kinds of composition, literary and musical. That winter he had written a great many newspaper articles on music.

To Modeste Tchaikowsky

Moscow, January 6, 1875

"Your newspaper article about the Kiev opera pleases me greatly. You complain that writing is hard and that one must ponder over every phrase. But how can you believe that anything completes itself without work and effort? Sometimes I sit for hours biting my pen, wondering how to begin my article. I feel sure it will be badly done, and then afterward people praise it and say it reads easily and fluently. Remember the trouble Zaremba's counterpoint exercise gave me, remember that summer of '66 at Miatleff's house when my nerves got so upset because my symphony would not work out as I wished. Even now I pace my room, bite my nails and smoke huge numbers of cigarettes before I can invent the main theme of my composition.

"Sometimes, on the contrary, the music writes itself with marvelous ease; ideas struggle and tumble over one another. All depends on one's mood, one's state of mind. But even lacking the right mood, one must force oneself to work. Otherwise, nothing will be accomplished."

Between this letter and the year that elapsed before Nadejda von Meck gave him her first musical commission, Tchaikowsky wrote his Serenade in B minor for violin with orchestral accompaniment, and his ballet, *The Swan Lake* —

neither work showing the power or charm of the B Flat minor Piano Concerto. The Second String Quartet, in F major, dedicated to the Grand Duke Constantine, had already been written and played; it is not to be compared with the melodious First Quartet nor the Third and last of Tchaikowsky's string quartets, written early in 1875. This is the E flat minor Quartet with the brilliant and popular *Scherzo*. As an admirer — really an adorer — of Mozart, Tchaikowsky liked string quartet music and often said so. His genius of course was pre-eminently orchestral, the fury of his emotions needed the sweep of many instruments; nevertheless no one can study his last quartet without a sense that the composer had a sound feeling for this difficult creative medium. It is a great pity that he ceased, after only a third attempt, to develop it.

During this same year, 1875, Tchaikowsky wrote *The Seasons*, twelve pieces for piano. They are utterly unimportant and Tchaikowsky knew it. He wrote them on commission for a Petersburg musical journal, tearing one off every month and then forgetting about it until his servant, under orders to do so, appeared next month and asked mildly, "Peter Ilyich, isn't it time to mail that package to town?" By mailtime the package was always ready.

Early in 1876, Tchaikowsky wrote the now almost notorious *Marche Slav* for orchestra, letting himself go in his most purple manner and earning for himself those Tchaikovskian adjectives that will forever cling to his name. And then came from his pen a piece of music deserving very different adjectives, a piece mature and masterly, the symphonic fantasia for orchestra, *Francesca da Rimini*. Tchaikowsky could not have chosen a subject more suited to his musical and emotional temperament; together with the *Overture-Fantasia Romeo and Juliet*, *Francesca* deserves a place by the side of his last three symphonies. With no resort to musical trickery, no bells ringing or horses' hooves galloping, the composer here achieves the very perfection of the romantic ideal of program music.

Thus Tchaikowsky's life moved on. Petersburg heard *The Tempest* without enthusiasm except in the camp of the Five, who reported upon it most favorably. Saint-Saëns came to

Moscow to play some of his own music, and he and Tchaikowsky became instant friends.

Other events of the year were the successful performance of the Third Symphony in Petersburg and of the Third String Quartet E flat minor in Moscow. Exhausted by his winter, Tchaikowsky went abroad again for the water cure, and thence to Bayreuth. Here he was surprised to find himself received as a distinguished visitor. "It appears," he wrote home, "that I am not so unknown in Western Europe as I had thought." Consequently his days in Bayreuth were one long confusion of hospitality. "After the final note of the *Gotterdämmerung,*" the letter finished—"I felt as if freed from poison. Perhaps the *Nibelungen* is in truth a great creation, but surely no music was ever so tediously long-drawn."

Such then, was the Peter Tchaikowsky to whom Nadejda von Meck, in the winter of 1876, gave a musical commission. Small wonder that the widow, accustomed in the Muscovite manner to accord honor to art, addressed Peter Ilyich with respect and even some timidity; already he was a far from inconsiderable figure in the musical world. But, forging steadily ahead musically, in other directions Tchaikowsky was for the moment blocked, halted completely; he needed emotional support as badly as he needed money. And the widow, whose active personal life had come to a standstill and who lived now only in the lives of her children (a program totally inadequate to her nature), needed Tchaikowsky as greatly as he needed her.

5

Peter's pension. The Fourth Symphony and Eugene Onegin *begun*

December—January—February—and between Peter Ilyich and Nadejda von Meck four letters have passed. Peter wrote the last one, a short note, but friendly enough to break down all the widow's reserves—or nearly all. A sensitive creature, this Tchaikowsky; already he has felt Nadejda's reserve and tells her frankly that with him, she need not be on the defensive. Why, he asks, does she fear he will laugh if she tells him all her thoughts? "I feel deeply sympathetic towards you," he writes. "These are not mere words" . . .

Nadejda's reply is in essence, touching; the difficulty is that Nadejda's letters are apt to be as long-winded as they are sincere, her emotions as unskillfully rendered as they are intensely felt. It was fortunate that from the beginning, Tchaikowsky saw nothing ludicrous in the widow's extravagantly ornamental style. Also, it is interesting to remark, in this third letter she wrote Tchaikowsky, that already Nadejda sensed the strange fact that between herself and this man, physical presence and the spoken word would never be necessary; wise woman that she was, did she sense further that physical intimacy would be impossible, and the very hint of it would send Tchaikowsky flying in horror?

Nadejda Philaretovna to Peter Ilyich

Moscow, March 19, 1877
Monday

"Gracious Sir, Peter Ilyich,

"Your kind answer to my letter gave me an intenser pleasure than I have experienced for a long time. But you know human nature—the more one receives, the more one wants. I have promised you not to become spoiled, but now begin to doubt my own strength, for I dare ask you a great favor, a favor which will seem perhaps strangely unconventional.

"A person who lives, like me, the life of a recluse, naturally grows to feel that what people call conventions, social laws, decency—are but sounds without meaning. I do not know your opinion about this, Peter Ilyich, but from what I have heard, I believe that you, less than anyone, will hold it against me if I am mistaken. Say frankly 'No,' if you wish, without explanation—Give me your photograph. I have two now, but I want one from you. I want to search your face for the thoughts and feelings that inspired you while writing music that sweeps one into a world of emotion, hope and insatiable yearning. How much joy and sadness is in your music—sadness that one does not wish to relinquish. In it man feels his highest powers, his greatest hopes, and a hap-

42

piness that reality cannot grant. The first of your compositions I ever heard was *The Tempest*. It is impossible to describe the impression it made upon me. For several days I was as one in a delirium from which I could not emerge."

The widow's critical acumen, ordinarily alert for any symptom of insincerity, any display of musical fireworks unauthorized by the innate musical idea of the piece, was apt, where Tchaikowsky's music was concerned, to be dulled by adoration. *The Tempest*, the second of Tchaikowsky's three overture-fantasias for full orchestra, was not up to the mark of *Romeo and Juliet* and *Francesca da Rimini*. On the other hand it was a vivid piece of musical tone painting, original for its day and definitely branded with that Tchaikovskian mark which would always bring Nadejda to her feet. Nadejda never pretended to be a musical critic, and indeed she was to be something far more valuable to Tchaikowsky —a person who upon first hearing, invariably understood and sympathized with the emotional content of his work.

"Let me confess," her letter continued, "that I am incapable of separating the musician from the man; and in him, servant of such a great art, more than in other people, I look for these human qualities I revere. My ideal man is a musician, but only when character equals talent does he make a deep and true impression. If, on the contrary, in the musician there is no man, the better his compositions musically, the more he seems to me a living lie, a hypocrite, an exploiter of simple people. I think of a Musician-Man as one of the greatest creations of nature. Even after many mistakes and disappointments, I cannot change my opinion. That is why I feel such intense interest in musicians, and why I immediately wanted to know, after my first great joy in hearing your music, what the man was like who created such a thing. I began looking for opportunities to know more about you, never permitting means of such news to escape me. I am interested in everything about you; I should like at all times to know where you are and approximately what you are doing. From all I have observed or heard about you, favorable and unfavorable, a great sense of fellow-feeling and enthusiasm has grown. I am happy that in you, musician

43

and man unite so beautifully, so harmoniously, that one can give oneself to the full charm of your music; it expresses fineness and truth. You have not written for the crowd but to express your own feelings and ideas. I am happy that my ideal can now be realized, that I need not abandon it and that, on the contrary, it grows more precious and dearer. If only you knew what I feel, listening to your music, and how grateful I am for those feelings!

"There was a time when I wanted to meet you. Now, the more I am charmed, the more I fear meeting. I could not talk to you. If somewhere accidentally, we should come face to face, I could not look upon you as a stranger—I should give you my hand, but only to press yours wordlessly. At present I prefer to think about you at a distance, to hear you in your music and in it to feel with you. It is too bad that I have not yet heard your *Francesca da Rimini*. Impatiently I await the time of its publication for piano.

"Forgive me, Peter Ilyich, for saying all this—you do not need it—but do not regret giving to one who is drawing near the end of her life, who is indeed practically dead, the opportunity to feel alive, for a moment, in such a beautiful way.

"I have one more favor to ask, Peter Ilyich, that may seem odd. I don't know how people feel about such things, so please feel free to refuse without ceremony. It is this: in your *Oprichnik* there is a passage that drives me distracted. Oh, what music! One could give one's life for it. I should like to die hearing it. So, from these themes, Peter Ilyich, make me if possible, a *Marche Funèbre*. I enclose the opera with the parts marked that I should like to have in the march. If you can, I beg you to arrange it for four hands. If you find my request inconvenient, refuse. I shall be disappointed but not offended. But if you consent to do it, please, Peter Ilyich, do not try to do it quickly, for it is a favor to which I have no right and I am ashamed to take this advantage. Allow me to print the transcriptions you did for me. Shall I have them done at Jurgenson's or at Bessel's? And finally, Peter Ilyich, permit me in writing you to drop such formalities as 'Gracious Sir' . . . Truly they do not come naturally to me. And in your letters to me, please do the same. Surely you will not refuse?"

Nadejda Philaretovna to Peter Ilyich

Moscow, March 30, 1877

"Thank you, thank you, without end, Peter Ilyich, for the photograph, for your sweet picture. It made me very, very happy, made my world glow and my heart light and warm. May life be always as beautiful for you as it was for me at that moment. I rejoiced to see you, and also that you had granted my wish, for I must confess that I was beginning to be afraid, not knowing how you had received my request. In your letter, so dear to me, only one thing worried me, and that was your explanation of my fear of meeting you. You think I am afraid of not finding the unity of Man and Musician of which I dreamed. But in you I have already found it! Before I was sure of this, I might indeed, as you say, have feared that you could not personify my ideal in all its attributes, that you could not be the recompense for all my disappointments, mistakes and disillusionments. Yet now, had I happiness in my two hands, I should give it to you. My fear of meeting you has now quite another reason behind it, quite another feeling.

"Your *Marche*,* Peter Ilyich, is so beautiful that it lifts me, as I had hoped, into that mood of blissful madness in which one can forget all that is bitter and offensive in the world. It is impossible to describe the chaos that reigns in my head and heart when I hear it. A shiver runs through my nerves—I want to sob, to die, I long for another life, but not the life that others believe in and look forward to, a life that is different, intangible, indescribable. Life, death, happiness, pain, all merge. I soar above the earth, my temples throb, my heart beats wildly; mist darkens my eyes and I hear only the enchantment of that beautiful music. One loses the outer world, feeling only the beauty within, and dreads awakening. *Dieu,* how great is the man that can impart such moments to another soul! How I wish I could enter into your soul when you listen, for instance, to *Francesca,* or one of the others. Oh, what a joy *Francesca* is! What better portrays the horror of hell and the charms of love, and all the emotions that belong to the rarer levels of feeling! How can

* The *Marche Funèbre,* never published, was lost.

45

Wagner, with his realism, compare with you? He profanes the art, though unhappily he has great talent.

"Your promise to give me another photograph pleased me enormously, and please forgive me if some day I remind you of it. I understand and sympathize with your dislike of having them taken. Since you have decided to have it done, however, please pose so that your eyes look straight at one, as I dislike pictures that turn from me.

"Excuse me, Peter Ilyich, for writing such long letters. As you always find something to say in music, so I always have something to say when I write to you—and yet I leave much unsaid. Thank you again, many times, and remember sometimes your,

> "Cordially devoted,
> "Nadejda von Meck"

Having made such a beginning, from now on the two showered one another with a very prodigality of photographs. Nadejda was never satisfied with her Tchaikowsky gallery; again and again she asked for new pictures; desiring not only photographs of Peter Ilyich but of his sister, his twin brothers and all the Davydoff family, father, mother and grandmother. The photographs of Tchaikowsky's pretty Davydoff nieces she had done over in color in the prevailing rather horrifying fashion and professed herself immensely pleased with the result. In return she sent numerous pictures of herself, taken with various of her children. The two derived enormous satisfaction, even some little excitement, from this exchange—especially Nadejda. Their accompanying comments and explanations of photographic features reached a length and profuseness impossible of quotation.

Nadejda Philaretovna to Peter Ilyich

Moscow, May 12, 1877

"How lonely I was, not hearing from you, Peter Ilyich, and how happy now that I have heard! Had I the right, I should ask your permission to write you at any time I wish—by so doing I would always know where you were, especially in the summer, when I have no other news of you. Your letters are not only a pleasure, but truly good for me. So, dear Peter Ilyich, even though I have no claim on you, if you will say 'yes' to this desire of my heart, you will make me unspeakably happy.

"Yesterday I returned from Petersburg. I am unlucky—again I missed your *Vakoula*, for they did not give it. I shall have to recompense myself somehow, so I ask you, Peter Ilyich, be good enough to write me a composition that might express, and be called *Reproach* (for violin and piano). I have a short composition by Kohne, called *Le Reproche*, also for violin and piano. I like it, but it does not say what I want, and also seems to be about some one person. My *Reproach* must be impersonal. It can depict Nature, or Fate, to me, but not to anyone else. It must be the expression of unbearable weariness of spirit, like the French phrase: *Je n'en peux plus*. In it must be the broken heart, faith trampled on, hurt pride, lost happiness, all, all that is dear and sweet to man and that is mercilessly taken from him. If you ever have lost what you loved and held dear, you will understand that feeling. In this *Reproach* must be heard the longing of unhappiness, the surrender to despair, the impotence of the soul, and, if you think proper, death. It is possible in music to find the solace that life does not give for the asking. Oh, yes, in the *Reproach* must be heard too these memories of happiness of which one has been robbed. Nothing can portray such a spiritual mood so well as music, and no one could understand it better than you. And so I bravely hand over to you my feelings, my idea, my desire, and I am sure that this time I surrender my dearest possession into the right hands.

"I cannot write briefly to you. I have so much to say! It is because I feel so near you in spirit that I have this impulse to open my soul to you. I know you will judge not from the ordinary point of view, but from your own. Your standards and ideals are rooted in musical earth, but thank God, they have not grown in a stereotyped musical environment, which is the reason they are so honorable and high. These are not mere words and compliments, but are a small expression of the feeling and enthusiasm you arouse in me.

"*Au revoir*, I don't want to say 'Good-bye,' because I don't want this letter to end.

"Devotedly yours (devoted from my soul)
"Nadejda von Meck"

Peter Ilyich was not the man to balk at a commission; he was a professional artist and he could write to order. But *The Reproach* was too much for him. *He* had not lost what he held dear; let Karl George Von Meck rest in peace. Peter Ilyich had written one funeral march and did not, apparently, feel like writing another : —

Moscow, May 13, 1877

"Dear Nadejda Philaretovna,

"As always, I shall be very glad to fulfill your request, and to put into my composition as nearly as possible what you want to hear. But I shall have to ask you to wait longer this time than you had to wait for the other compositions. I am very busy just now and don't know if I can find a moment and the appropriate mood. I will write you in detail one of these days. *Au revoir*, my dear Nadejda Philaretovna."

Tchaikowsky must have sent this by the bearer of Nadejda's letter and then gone back to his desk and written another long one; anyway, they are both dated May 13th. The long letter he kept until he saw how Nadejda received his refusal of her commission. She received it with graciousness; womanlike, she decided his nerves were upset:

"I am sending you, Peter Ilyich, the book of Kohne's *Études Characteristiques*, in which you will find *Le Reproche*. Judging by what you write me and what I already know, I think, Peter Ilyich, it would be wiser to postpone the work I asked for until summer, when the Conservatory examinations are over and you are quite free.

"And now I want you to do another, less important work for me — arrange your first quartet for the piano, four hands. I do want this very much."

Tchaikowsky replied instantly:

"Dear N. Ph.

"Yesterday I wrote you a letter which this morning I dedecided not to send. But your letter of today definitely convinced me that I was right in the reasons on which I based mine of yesterday. I am sending it, then, and if it seems tact-less, please excuse and forgive.

"Yours devotedly,
"P.T.

"P.S. The arrangement of the quartet for four hands is already in the printing press."

Peter Ilyich gave the portentous letter to Nadejda's messenger and then, like many a man who has launched a letter—sat down and worried about what he had written. Actually, he had asked Nadejda von Meck for 3000 roubles—a request flagrant enough to make a man less sensitive than Peter Ilyich pace his room while awaiting an answer.

On the face of it, a request for 3000 roubles was, to say the least, surprising, coming from a gentleman whom Nicholas Rubinstein had described as too proud to ask for charity. The sum exactly equalled Tchaikowsky's current income; $1500 a year was, in those days, sufficient for a man who cared nothing for luxury; why then had the composer need to ask for more? Simply because, as regards money, Peter was and would always be, utterly without sense. The possession of ten dollars was to him riches and security; when in 1866 his salary—his total income—had been raised to $600, he wrote home to his brothers that he had "money enough to spare." Whenever there was money in his pocket, Tchaikowsky was extremely pleased and said so, but he instantly spent it or, more likely, gave it away; when it was gone he was surprised, as though suddenly in the midst of sunshine, rain had begun to fall. Toward the end of his life he earned enough, from his operas and published writings, to be more than comfortably off, but he never seemed to have money in reserve.

During his whole life, Peter Ilyich gave away about half his income—but there was one thing he never gave away, and that was his musical integrity. Nowhere is this better illustrated than in this first of financial letters between him and Nadejda von Meck. The letter that the widow opened in her bedroom on the Boulevard Rojdestvensky on that cold spring morning of 1877 was daring, but never servile—and above all, it was honest:

"Dear Nadejda Philaretovna,

"In spite of the most emphatic denials on the part of our mutual friend,* I have reason to believe that I owe to his friendly scheming the letter I received from you this morning"—(commissioning Peter Ilyich to write music for *The Reproach*)—"Your former musical order had already given me the idea that you were guided by two motives; first, you really wanted one or another of my compositions; second, you wished to help me. The too-generous payment with which you rewarded my little work convinced me of it. This time I am quite sure that you are guided by the second reason only. That is why, reading your letter, in which I glimpsed between the lines your tact and kindness, your touching sympathy for me, I felt an uncontrollable distaste for beginning the work and hurried in my brief answer to put off the fulfillment of my promise. In my relationship with you, I do not want any of that falsity and insincerity which would inevitably appear if I should not wait and listen for the inner voice and inspiration which are necessary to create what you wish. Should I not wait, I would hurry to create something, send the 'something' to you and get from you undeserved payment. In which case you could not help feeling that I was willing to dash off all sorts of musical works, the result of which would be little hundred-rouble papers. Would it not then occur to you that if you were poor, I should refuse your requests?

"This is a delicate matter; every time I receive an envelope from you, money falls out. It is assumed that an artist is never humiliated by receiving remuneration for his work. But in creative work such as you now demand, there must be a certain mood, so-called inspiration, which is not always at one's disposal. I do not wish to be artistically dishonest for the sake of improving my circumstances, and by taking advantage of my technical skill, give you false metal for true. Yet I am in great need of the despised metal! It would take

* This was Kotek, a young harmony pupil of Tchaikowsky's who for some time had been coming regularly to Nadejda's house in the capacity of violinist; he adored Tchaikowsky and was always ready to sing his praises and relate to the widow those details of the composer's life that she was avid to hear.

long to explain how and why a man, earning enough for more than a comfortable living, has managed to get so into debt that it often poisons his life and paralyzes his inclination to work. Just now, when the time before leaving for the summer is short, and when, before going, I must find means for returning, I have involved myself in a most disagreeable financial difficulty, from which I cannot extricate myself without help.

"For that help I have decided to ask you. You are the only person in the world from whom I am not ashamed to ask money. First, you are kind and generous. Second, you are wealthy. What I should like to do is to put all my debts in the hands of one generous creditor, and with his help, free myself from the clutches of the money-lenders. If you would be good enough to consent to *lend* me enough for this, I should be immensely grateful. The sum of my debts is large—approximately 3000 roubles. I could repay in three ways: first, by making for you musical arrangements and transcriptions such as I have already made for you; second, by giving you the royalties that I get from the Directory for my operas; third, by paying part of my monthly salary. As to the first—you can ask me for that type of work at any time, without any fear of inconveniencing me. The experience of many years has taught me that these arrangements such as you have already ordered, cost me little effort; so if for twenty years you should ask me to do one every day, I should not think it equal in value to the help for which I am asking you.

"Quite another thing—about that composition, *The Reproach.* The necessary mental attitude is not always possible. For instance, I am now busy with the symphony I started this winter (No. 4) which I want very much to dedicate to you, because I think you will find in it an echo of your innermost feelings and thoughts. Any other composition at this moment would be difficult—I mean work that needs the creative mood. Secondly, I am in an anxious, nervous and irritated frame of mind just now, very bad for composing, so that even the symphony progresses very slowly.

"It will pain me very much if my request seems tactless to you. One reason I decided to make it was that, once for all, it would exclude from our relationship the element of money, very embarrassing when it has to come up so often. I think that without it our friendship would be easier and more sincere. A correspondence in which every letter means payment and the reception of money, cannot be absolutely frank. Anyway, I am sure that this letter will not alter your opinion of my honesty. In case it displeases you, please forgive me. I am very nervous and upset these days, and tomorrow I shall probably regret having sent it.

"Very sincerely yours,
"P. Tch.

"P.S. Positively I shall write *The Reproach*, but when I cannot say. When I decide my summer plans, I will write you. Please send me the Kohne piece."

Nothing could have pleased Nadejda more than such an appeal. Instantly she replied:

"Thank you sincerely, Peter Ilyich, and with all my heart, for the confidence and friendliness you have shown in addressing me on such a matter. What I appreciate especially is that you have come straight to me and I beg you always to do so as to a close friend who loves you sincerely and deeply. As to paying me back, please, Peter Ilyich, do not worry. I myself will find ways for that.

"You have not yet answered me concerning my writing whenever I want to hear from you—which means that I want to write you from inner impulse rather than upon business. However dilute their religion may have become, the devout need saints and prophets. I need you, the pure prophet of my greatly beloved art. So, if you have no reason to say no, Peter Ilyich, save my sinless musical soul for earthly musical happiness—beautiful though not eternal—by allowing me to correspond with you. For this, some Lord Apostle will forgive you one sin.

"As to your dedicating your symphony to me, you are the only person from whom such an honor would be pleasing and valued.

"Sincerely, devoted with all my soul
"I am your friend,
"N.v.M."

Peter Ilyich wrote two replies on the same day; in the first one he did not address the lady by name. Perhaps he feared the straying eye of a pupil.

To Nadejda Philaretovna

Moscow, May 15, 1877

"I am in my class at the Conservatory, and that is why it is impossible to answer at greater length, and to thank you properly. You have helped me very, very much, dear N. Ph. Thanks to you, I am going to live a peaceful life, and it will surely have a good effect on my musical work.

"Today or tomorrow I shall write you further."

May 15, 1877, Moscow

"Dear N. Ph.

"I have lived through one of the most difficult days of my life. I was ashamed. At the bottom of my heart, I knew that you would take my letter as you did. I knew it was not right to ask favors from a person like you, who would not know how to refuse. I reproached myself for exploiting your kindness, generosity, and delicacy. Vainly I invented all sorts of excuses for myself—an inner voice continued to reiterate my guilt. But your letter today is full of such sincere friendship, such warm wishes for my welfare, that the consciousness of having demeaned myself by asking for material help, no longer detracts one iota from the simple fact of my gratitude. Fear that it might be otherwise has been really painful. The kind and friendly tone of your sweet letter has persuaded me that I have done exactly the right thing.

"So I am doubly grateful. Not only have you rendered me invaluable service, but you have known how to defend me from the inner pricks of conscience. I know I express myself badly. Even the sincerest gratitude can impose a heavy yoke. In order not to impose that yoke, when granting such immense material gifts as you have granted, one must possess infinite tact and delicacy.

"You ask if I would find it agreeable to have you write me any time you feel inclined. Please, dear Nadejda Philaretovna, never doubt this. Correspondence with you can never be other than a pleasure; to discuss music with you is a joy. I have told you already of my deep feeling of sympathy toward you.

"Once more I thank you, kind N. Ph. Remember that you have helped me out of a very, very bad situation, and I shall never forget the delicacy with which you gave such great help. Before you leave Moscow I hope you will write once more and give me your summer address. I shall be glad to keep up an active correspondence with you."

Nadejda replied happily. She was going soon, she said, to her estate in the Ukraine. She wished Peter Ilyich could share beloved Brailov with her. She was worried to think of him in the Caucasus. "I am afraid of war. And if there is no danger from a regular war, there is always danger of a descent of the 'children of the Turk.' Please be careful. In August, if there is no war with Austria, I shall go abroad—where, I have not decided."

. . . Peter Ilyich answered immediately; the letter dated May 27, 1877, was to be his last for more than a month. There was good reason for the delay: the "something" that bothered him so much was Antonina Miliukoff, who, innocent but determined young woman that she was, would very shortly play a part in this man's life far too sinister to be referred to merely as a bother.

Peter Ilyich to Nadejda Philaretovna

Moscow, June 8, 1877

"Thank you for your sweet, kind and friendly letter, dear Nadejda Philaretovna. It meant much to me, especially because before it came, my conscience had begun to torture me again for fear I had taken advantage of your wonderful kindness and generosity. Well, let us say no more about that. Know only, N. Ph., that my gratitude to you will never end; always I shall remember how much I owe to you.

"The examinations are nearly over. I am very tired of them and also of other worries connected with my departure. Then there is something else that bothers me greatly. I can't write to you at present about it, but surely in my next letter I shall be able to explain what the matter is and how it will end. It was great good fortune that material worries did not confuse my spirit or I should have fallen ill. On Sunday I am going to the country place of K. S. Shilovsky, a very agreeable man who with his equally agreeable wife and family lives on his estate near the New Jerusalem Monastery. I shall have a house and a piano at my disposal; I want to start steady work on the opera. Shilovsky, under my supervision, is doing the libretto which is taken from the poem of Pushkin, *Eugene Onegin*. Isn't this a brave idea? The few people to whom I have spoken about writing such an opera were first astonished and then enthusiastic. The opera will certainly not contain much action but the setting should be interesting. What poetry it contains! For instance, the scene of Tatiana and the nurse. If only I can find the peace that is so needed for composition, I feel that Pushkin's text will inspire me.

"I have finished the symphony—I mean the outline. Toward the latter part of the summer, I shall orchestrate it. I have heard, N. Ph., that you never before consented to have a composition dedicated to you; I am very grateful that in my case you made an exception. But if you do not wish to have your name on the symphony, we can omit it. Let you and me alone know to whom the symphony is dedicated.

"I wish you happiness, health and all good fortune, kind Nadejda Philaretovna."

6

Plans for marriage

Peter Ilyich was thirty-seven when he wrote to Nadejda, complaining that "something" was bothering him. He was thirty-seven, he was an established musician making 3000 roubles a year. High time for something of the kind to bother him. High time, indeed, for him to take a wife and settle down. The frivolity of his youthful days had, it is true, disappeared, but it had been replaced by what his father considered an almost unnatural nervous intensity.

Ilya did not know what lay at the bottom of that nervous

intensity and frequent distressing hypochondria of his son's. Peter's sister knew it and so did one or two friends; artistic circles in Moscow suspected it. Peter had a dark secret to hide, and the urgent necessity for this concealment was to him a source of unremitting torment. For a man whose outstanding characteristic was sincerity in all personal relationships, such a secret was enough to cause more than hypochondria; it might well have caused—and would soon be on the brink of causing—madness.

Peter Ilyich was a homosexual. This fact has hitherto been strangely ignored or covered up by his biographers; we exhume it, not to rattle the old bones of scandal but because it was in truth the very structure and architecture of the man's personality. Had Tchaikowsky been possessed of lesser genius his abnormality might well have been his whole existence and we should never have heard of him; had he been a man of less self-control we should have heard of him in a blaze of notoriety. His brother Modeste was a homosexual and also the nephew Bob Davydoff, Tchaikowsky's heir, who killed himself. All others of this large family were normal, and except for the paternal grandfather's "fits"—which may or may not have been epileptic—there is no ancestral history of degeneracy, disease or genius. Only Tchaikowsky's attitude toward his affliction—for so he considered it—inclines one to the belief that homosexuality, like genius and hypochondria, was forced upon him by nature rather than chosen as a way of life.

Not until Peter Ilyich planned to marry, did he give posterity any overt proof of this dark secret which he never named outright but referred to in his letters always as *The*. Proof is lacking, not by accident but by design; Tchaikowsky's friends and family destroyed every bit of evidence they could lay hands on, and because the man did not live notoriously, he and his brother Modeste managed to cheat posterity of much gossip. And they had a right to such deception. The facts are not of nearly so much interest as are the inferences to be drawn from the facts. What concerns us here is Peter's psychologic and spiritual reaction to his trouble, his own view of it, its enormous and poignant influence upon his character and indirectly, upon his music.

Ilya Tchaikowsky was eighty-three when son Peter announced that he was to be married, and at eighty-three the news, wrote the old man to his son, made him ready to jump for joy.

But Peter did not tell his father about his marriage until ten days before it occurred in July, 1877; long before this—in August, 1876, he had mentioned it to Modeste. This letter to Modeste is the first written news we have of Tchaikowsky's "intentions"; obviously, he looked upon marriage as a major operation, painful but necessary.

"I have now," he wrote, "to pass through a critical moment in my life. By-and-by I will write you about it more fully; meanwhile I must just tell you that I have decided to get married. This is irrevocable . . ."

During the four years beginning in 1872 when he left Rubinstein and set up housekeeping for himself, Tchaikowsky had been growing more and more dissatisfied with his Moscow life. He was popular in society, he had many friends, but essentially he was lonely. He longed for some close tie, some intimacy that would extend to every detail of his daily life; again and again he expressed this wish and this unhappiness in letters to his brothers. In March, 1875 he wrote Anatol from Moscow:

"Fate, the Mocker, has arranged it so that for the past ten years all whom I love most in the world are far from me. I am extremely lonely in Moscow, not from lack of company but from lack of my dear ones. Perhaps you have already observed that my friendship with Rubinstein and the other Conservatory people is based only on the fact that we work in the same place. I have no one to whom I can pour out my soul. Perhaps this is partly my fault. I do not make friends easily. Anyhow while I was suffering from attacks of hypochondria, the lack of intimate friends was very hard. Nearly all winter I was constantly unhappy, sometimes to the very edge of despair; I longed for death. With the coming of spring these attacks have ceased, but I know that every winter they will return, stronger than ever. Therefore I have decided to keep away from Moscow all next year. Where I shall go I don't yet know, but I must have a change of place and surroundings."

Tchaikowsky seemed convinced that his hypochondria was due to loneliness; later events point to another cause. Indeed, the entire testimony of his life proves that solitude held no terrors for this man, provided he could write music. Wandering in Europe by himself, living quite alone in the country, he was happy as long as he was composing. But let any outward event, any person or circumstance, interfere with his hours of work or with his creative flow, and he was instantly black with melancholy. In the four years prior to his marriage, his creative powers were approaching their zenith; the voices in his head were becoming more powerful, more insistent—and his Conservatory duties gave him little or no time to listen to the voices. Knowing himself exhausted and rendered unfit for composition, Tchaikowsky was, very naturally, torn within himself. In proportion as he became conscious of his creative powers, he resented a world that seemed to conspire against the realization of those powers. But why he should have thought marriage a solution is one of those perversities to which genius seems especially prone.

And now we come to the second reason for Tchaikowsky's marriage: the first was his belief that marriage would stabilize his life so that he could do better work. The second reason does not make nearly such pretty reading—the man lived in mortal terror lest his homosexuality should be discovered by the world. This was a time and a place, be it remembered, that gave no quarter to this kind of sinner; a decent citizen would step off the sidewalk in passing rather than be contaminated by touching the garment of a homosexual. Peter Ilyich lived in continual terror, stalked forever by a horrid phantom—and a like shadow pursued his beloved brother Modeste. No wonder Peter Ilyich clung to Modeste; with each other, these two could drop the rigid and exhausting mask they were forced to present to a world of normal men. When the brothers parted even for a month, they wept and were not ashamed of weeping.

Three weeks after writing Modeste that first excited but rather vague announcement of his matrimonial plans, Peter Ilyich wrote more fully:

Moscow, September 22, 1876

"I have been thinking much, these days, about myself and my future. The result of all these thoughts is that dating from today, I shall make a serious effort to marry, legally, anybody. I am aware that my inclinations are the greatest and most unconquerable obstacle to happiness; I must fight my nature with all my strength. . . . I shall do everything possible to marry this year, and if I am not brave enough for that, at any rate I shall conquer my old habits for once and all."

October 4, 1876

"There are people who do not despise me for my vices only because they began loving me before they suspected I was only a man with a lost reputation. Among them for instance is Alexandra" (Peter's sister). "I know that she guesses everything and forgives everything. So it is with many of those I respect and care for most. Is it not a bitter thing to be pitied and forgiven when, truly, I am in no way guilty? So it has been a hundred times, and will be a hundred times more. In a word, I should like to marry, or by some known liaison with a woman, shut the mouths of all despicable gossips, for whose opinion I do not care a bit, but who can hurt people close to me.

"Fulfillment of my plans is not as near as you think. I am so confirmed in my habits and tastes that to throw them away as one would an old glove, is impossible. And then I have far from an iron will. . . ."

Almost on the same day he wrote Anatol:

"Tolia, I live to see you again. I am bothered because I fear that in Moscow I was not thoughtful of you and did not let you see the real depth of my love for you. If you noticed this, realize (surely you know it already) that if I did not treat you kindly it was not because I did not love you, but because I was annoyed with myself. When I am annoyed with myself it always looks as if I were angry with others. I was annoyed with myself because I felt I had lied when I told you I had decided to make a thorough change in my life. Truly I have not made this decision at all! I only have it in view, though seriously; I wait for something to force me into action. Meanwhile I must admit that my cozy little apartment, my solitary evenings, the peace and quiet of my life has for me an especial charm. When I think that I must give it up—and to marry one must give it up—'the frost pricks my skin....'"

To Alexandra Davydoff, the sister he mentioned in the letter of October 4th, Tchaikowsky wrote under date of October 6th:

"Please, my angel, don't worry about my getting married. First, I don't expect to take such a step soon, certainly not within the school year. During these months I only want to look around and prepare for matrimony, which for many reasons would be a very good thing for me."

This was October. The winter was busy, and matrimonial plans, which so far had fixed upon no particular lady, were for a while in abeyance. Only now and again when captured by severe melancholy, did the idea of a wife recur to Tchaikowsky. It will be of value therefore, to follow him briefly through the winter and see what were the events that preceded his final decision to marry.

Late in November his opera *Vakoula* had its first performance in Moscow—characterized by the composer as a "brilliant failure." "I alone am to blame," he wrote Taneyeff. "*Vakoula* is not good opera style—it has neither movement nor breadth." In Vienna, Tchaikowsky's symphonic overture, *Romeo and Juliet*, was played and, as he himself recorded, "triumphantly hissed." But in Western Europe of the time, hisses were by no means a criterion of musical value. Russian music was not regarded seriously. In Paris the popular conductor, Pasdeloup, attempted the overture, but his orchestra played it so badly—according to Tchaikowsky's faithful friend Taneyeff, who was there—that the intrinsic quality of the music was by no means evident. Tchaikowsky tried in vain to raise funds to have it played properly by Colonne's famous Paris orchestra—the same orchestra which was to be Nadejda von Meck's vehicle for hearing Tchaikowsky's music.

Just before the Christmas holidays—at about the time Nadejda was writing to thank him for executing her first musical commission—Tchaikowsky became acquainted with Leo Tolstoi. Tchaikowsky had always admired Tolstoi's writings and characteristically, whom he admired, Peter Ilyich adored. He regarded Tolstoi as a demigod, and said so. On his side, Tolstoi had heard Tchaikowsky's music and expressed a desire to meet him; so. Nicholas Rubenstein arranged a musical evening at the Conservatory during Tolstoi's Moscow visit. Included in the program was the *Andante* from Tchaikowsky's D major String Quartet. "In all my life as a musician," wrote Peter in his diary, "I don't believe I was ever so flattered and touched as when Leo Tolstoi, sitting by my side, listening to the *Andante* of my first quartet, started to cry."

When Tolstoi returned to Yasnaya Polyana, he wrote Tchaikowsky as follows:

"I send you, dear Peter Ilyich, the songs. You will make of them a wonderful treasure, but for God's sake, arrange them after the Mozart-Haydn style, not the artificial Beethoven-Berlioz style that tries only for effect. How much I left unsaid to you! There was not time for all I had to say; I was simply having a good time. That last day in Moscow will remain a cherished memory. I never had such precious reward for my literary labors as on that wonderful evening. How charming Rubenstein is; thank him again for me. I liked him so much, and those other priests of the highest art in the world who sat with us around the board—they left with me such a pure and serious impression. All that was so kindly done for me in the round room I cannot remember without a shiver of emotion. Tell me which of the men in the quartet do not own my works and would care to read them. I should like to send them each a book.

"As yet I have not looked over your things, but shall. Whether or no you desire my opinion I shall write it frankly, because I already have learned to admire your talent. Goodbye, I press your hand.

"Yours,
"L. Tolstoi"

To this Tchaikowsky replied:

"Count — I thank you sincerely for the songs. I must tell you frankly that they have been taken down by an inexperienced hand and therefore retain no more than traces of their original beauty. The chief defect is that they have been artificially forced into conventional rhythm. Only the Russian choral dances have regularly accented rhythm; the Bylini (legends) have nothing in common with the choral dances. Also, most of the songs have been forced into the key of D major, unsuitable for the true Russian folksong, which nearly always has an indefinite tonality, more like the ancient church modes. The songs you sent cannot be treated systematically, that is, they can never be made into a published collection of folksongs. That would require the most authentic research, an exact transcription of the original songs as sung by the people. This would be a very difficult task, demanding the most refined musical sensitivity and profound historical knowledge; except for Balakirev and perhaps Orokunin, I know of no one who could do justice to the work. But your songs are symphonic material—very good material, and I shall certainly make use of them some day.

"How glad I am that the evening at the Conservatory remains a pleasant memory with you! Our quartetists played as never before. Which proves that one pair of ears, if they belong to an artist as great as yourself, can inspire musicians more than a thousand ordinary pairs. You are one of those authors beloved for themselves as well as for their work. As for me, I cannot tell you how happy and proud I was that my music could touch and charm you.

"Fitzhagen cannot read Russian, but all the other quartetists know your work. I know they would be very grateful if you gave each of them one of your books. For myself, I should like best to have *The Cossacks*, if not now, then next time you are in Moscow—a day I shall look forward to with much impatience. If you send your photograph to Rubinstein, do not forget me too."

The friendship with Tolstoi went, however, no further; it ceased indeed, with some abruptness. In his biography of Peter, Modeste Tchaikowsky blames this upon his brother's constitutional shyness; Peter felt uneasy in the presence of so great a man. An extract from Tchaikowsky's diary, written ten years later, confirms this, and with an extremely significant addition. The trouble was more than shyness; Peter had reason to dread the probe of a great man's eye; he was quite convinced that anyone who could write so inspired a book as *War and Peace*, had only to clap eyes on Peter Ilyich Tchaikowsky to know him for the outcast he was.

"When I met Tolstoi," wrote Peter Ilyich, "I was possessed by fear and a feeling of uneasiness. It seemed to me that this great searcher of hearts could pierce at a glance every secret of my heart, that before him a man could not hide the nastiness that lurks in the lowest depth of every soul, nor could a man put the best side upon it. I told myself that if Tolstoi proved kind (which he surely would) then purposely, like a physician with his scalpel, he would delicately probe my wound, seeing instantly the sorest spots and avoiding them —and this very avoidance would prove that nothing was hidden. Or, lacking compassion, he would lay his finger on the very center of pain. I was terribly afraid of these two things. Neither occurred. He who in writing is so astute, so great a searcher of hearts, in conversation proved simple, sincere, wholehearted, making no parade of the omniscience I had feared. He did not regard me at all as a subject for dissection, he simply wanted to chat about music, which interested him at the time."

During January and February of this year—1877—Tchaikowsky seemed in high spirits. His symphonic fantasia, *Francesca da Rimini*, was beautifully performed under the baton of Nicholas Rubinstein in Moscow, and met with heart-warming success. Tchaikowsky began to sketch out his Fourth Symphony—the one he had proposed to dedicate to Nadejda von Meck. All seemed merry and normal enough —and then suddenly, for no reason except perhaps, the fatigue attendant upon the end of a long winter—Tchaikowsky walked into blackness. Suddenly, life was not worth living. To his friend Klimenko he wrote under date of May 8th:

"Since last we met I am very much changed—especially mentally. Not a kopek's worth of fun and gayety is left in me.

Life is terribly empty, tedious and tawdry. My mind turns toward matrimony or indeed any other steady bond. The only thing that has not changed is my love for composing. If the conditions of my life were different, if my desire to create were not balked at every step—for instance by the Conservatory teaching which every year I find more irksome—I might write something really decent. But alas! I am chained to the Conservatory."

Fallow soil this—a young man, lonely, overworked, depressed, in search of a remedy for life. Ground prepared—and onto it, surrounded with all the persuasive panoply of spring, walked Antonina Miliukoff, young, pretty, good-natured, and madly in love with Peter Ilyich.

7

Two women and one man

Poor Antonina Miliukoff! We do not know where she first saw Tchaikowsky, but we know that from first sight she was violently in love. Antonina, ten years his junior, was utterly obscure both as to background and talent. The Miliukovs were not, as a family, attractive people; they were lower middle class, with none of the sturdiness of the class just below them nor the imagination of the class just above. They were, in short, haphazard and commonplace—the last persons for a Tchaikowsky to choose as life companions.

Antonina was pretty, she looked, according to Peter Ilyich himself, twenty-three rather than her real age of twenty-eight. She was blonde, with a pleasing figure and a beautiful, clear complexion. The testimony of those who knew her leaves no doubt that at the time Tchaikowsky became acquainted with her, Antonina was an attractive person—and this same testimony leaves no doubt also that she was temperamentally as impossible as a woman could be. Those who saw her a fifth and sixth time testified that while her appearance at first deceived the beholder, in the end it made her stupidity only the more irritating; she was decidedly subnormal in intelligence. Her persistent delusion that the world of men was in love with her, was a symptom of something far more sinister than stupidity. In the first letter we have that she wrote Tchaikowsky, this tendency is evident, although as yet it is only a tendency, and would be in no way remarkable did we not know to what appalling proportions the tendency was to grow. Antonina Miliukoff ended her days in an insane asylum. It is only fair to Tchaikowsky to state this now, at the beginning, and to state also that Tchaikowsky was not responsible for her loss of sanity. She suffered great unhappiness at his hands, nor is his treatment of her easy to condone. But with or without Tchaikowsky, hers was a nature that could never have achieved happiness; she proved that she could not live with anyone, husband or lover or her own family. Her type of insanity is well known to psychiatry: a sexual delusionary madness that can develop without provocation.

From the beginning, Antonina showed herself irresponsible and capricious beyond the normal actions of a woman of twenty-eight. She did not seem to know the difference between a lie and the truth, nor did she seem able to recognize this as a fault in herself. It was this characteristic more than any other that made her so difficult. There was no harm in Antonina and no meanness; beyond a natural resentment at humiliation, there was no desire to hurt her enemies. A woman who, writing a letter to the man she loves, drops blood upon the page from nails bitten to the quick, is a woman to be pitied. But we must be careful, in pitying her, not to cherish a corresponding resentment for the man who received the letters. Let us remember that Antonina bit her nails to the quick habitually, letters or no letters, and that this is not a normal trait, and let us remember also that although Tchaikowsky failed most lamentably in his relationship with her, almost anybody would have failed.

The first letter we have from Antonina to Peter Ilyich is dated May 6, 1877. Unfortunately for historical justice, all his letters to her were destroyed. When she wrote this letter, Antonina had seen Peter, had written to him and had a reply, but the two had not met except in the company of other people.

Moscow, May 16, 1877

"I see it is time for me to make myself over, as you your-self suggested in your first letter. Now that I don't see you, I console myself with the idea that we are in the same city. In a month, perhaps even sooner, you will be sure to leave town, and heaven knows when I shall see you, as I don't expect to stay in Moscow. But wherever I go, I shan't be able to forget you or stop loving you. What I like in you I shall not find in anyone else—in short, I don't want to look at any man but you. And yet a week ago I had to listen to the declaration of a man who has been in love with me almost since school days, and has been faithful to me for five years. It was hard to listen to him, and I realized then that it can-not be easy for you to read my letters, not having anything encouraging to answer me, and with all the good will in the world, not being able to show more than absolute indiffer-ence. For a whole week I was in agony, Peter Ilyich, not knowing whether or not to write you. I see that my letters begin to annoy you.

"But is it possible you may drop the correspondence be-fore meeting me even once? No, I am sure you won't be so cruel! God knows, perhaps you think me a fickle, infatuated girl, and because of that don't trust my letters? How can I prove that what I say is true? Surely in such matters one cannot lie. After your last letter I loved you twice as much, and your faults mean absolutely nothing to me.

"Perhaps if you were perfect I should have remained quite indifferent to you. I am dying with unhappiness and sorrow because I want so terribly to see you, to sit and talk with you, yet I fear that at first I should not be able to say one word. There is no fault that could make me stop loving you. It is not the love of a moment but a feeling that has been growing for a long time. I simply cannot, and will not, destroy this feeling now."

There is no question that this was an affecting letter; the frank fierce avowal of a girl helplessly in love, is always affecting. Even now, after fifty years, one feels sorry for Antonina. And how natural and indeed, flattering he must

66

have thought the girl's statement about the suitor she had had to turn away. Impossible for Peter to see in that simple statement the future hint of madness, of a delusion that was to inspire a hundred such little stories—whether or not this particular one was true. Impossible, indeed, for anyone, to have divined it, and this very impossibility, this innocence of Peter's in the face of oncoming, implacable fate is, from the vantage point of history, an awful thing to watch.

Antonina wrote again only two days later; reading her mention of his "frankness," how one longs to know what Peter Ilyich had said! Had he told the girl what he was to reiterate so often—that he might return her love by affection, but that she must never expect more than affection?

Antonina to Peter Ilyich

May 18, 1877

"I sent you a letter today, by messenger, and was much surprised to find that you are not in Moscow, which made me more unhappy. I sat at home the whole day, wandering from one corner to another like a half-mad person, thinking only of the moment when I may see you. I shall be ready to throw myself on your neck, to kiss you—but what right have I to that? You would think me bold. You were frank with me and I owe you a like frankness, but I must add that it would be very unfortunate if you should misinterpret this confession of my feelings. I can assure you that I am a girl of good reputation. I have nothing to hide from you. My first kiss will be for you and for nobody else in the world. Good-bye, my dear. Don't try to disillusion me about yourself, because you will only waste your time. I cannot live without you and so, perhaps I shall soon make an end of myself. Let me look at you and kiss you so I may carry that kiss into the other world.

"Good-bye,
"Eternally yours,—"

"Don't try to disillusion me about yourself," said Antonina. Peter Ilyich never indulged in mock humility or coyness; he knew his worth and he knew his weakness; there is not much doubt about what he was trying to tell Antonina.

67

Certainly, he was frank about it before he married her. But such confession could not be put to paper—even with one's brother one must be careful to refer to one's shame by hieroglyphic. The genuine homosexual is never ashamed of his homosexuality, but if he be an honest man—and Peter Ilyich was an honest man—he is bitterly ashamed of the disguise he must wear and the lies he must tell. As to the suicide threat in Antonina's letter, it was the most effective move the girl could have made. Peter Ilyich, who knew so little of women, took it quite seriously. It was a bad business all round, this Antonina affair, and how on earth had it developed so rapidly? True, he had told Modia and Tolia he was planning to marry, but heaven knows, he had had nothing specific in mind in the way of a wife. Bachelors are always saying they have decided to marry. On the other hand, his father wanted him to settle down, and here was this girl, ready to kill herself for love of him. How easily, with what few words, he could turn her misery to joy!

Peter Ilyich met the girl as her letter requested; he listened to what she had to say but refused to call on her in her rooms. She wrote him again at the end of the month:

Antonina to Peter Ilyich

June 7, 1877

"Let me know ahead, please, when you will come to see me, because Tuesdays, Thursdays, and Saturdays I am not in Moscow. Now that I cannot see you, I look at your picture, but Panoff has made you so terrible that I am indignant for you. Here I have finished my letter and still I do not know what to do with myself, I am so crazy with unhappiness. I hope you enjoy your stay in the country.

"It is three days since I wrote my letter, but I kept it until today, understanding you are not yet in Moscow. Once more, I implore you, come to me. If you knew how I suffered, surely you would have mercy and grant my desire. Having only one room at my disposal I shall have to apologize for such an uncomfortable way of receiving you—but I trust you will not think less of me because of it. It was my own wish to work and be independent. Tomorrow, Thursday, I must go to Hovrino, by the Nicholas Railroad, and I shall look for you all day Friday.

"I kiss and embrace you ardently, ardently.
"A.M."

And on the very same day that Antonina wrote this letter, another lady sat down to write to Peter Ilyich.

How long—wrote Nadejda—how very long since news had come of Peter Ilyich! Nevertheless she must write anyway, to congratulate him on his approaching name-day. She wished him the health, joy and happiness that she knew he deserved; she would drink his health and her heart would be with him. . . . About the Fourth Symphony now in process of composition and Peter's request that he might dedicate it to her—she had never given such permission before, and even this time she could not say yes until she asked one question:

"Do you, Peter Ilyich, consider me your friend? Because of my understanding of you and boundless desire for your good, I have reason to call myself your friend. But as you have never called me by that name, I do not know whether you recognize or consider me so. If you can say yes to that question, I should be most pleased if you would dedicate the symphony to your 'Friend' without mentioning the name. If you cannot do so, forget, Peter Ilyich, what I have said, and be sure my feeling for you will not change one iota. I shall await news from you with impatience."

The widow had a long time to wait. All through June, no word came. Nadejda was at her southern estate, Brailov, in the Ukraine, before she had her answer. And what she read in it was indeed news—"For God's sake, dear Nadejda Philaretovna," Tchaikowsky wrote from Moscow on the third of July, "forgive me for not writing before. Briefly, here is the story of what has lately happened to me.

"In the latter part of May, to my own great surprise, I became engaged to be married. This is how it happened . . ."

"The story of what happened to me" . . . Not, be it observed, the story of what he himself had done, but passively, of what had happened to him. Patently, Peter Ilyich had no

easy time writing this letter. From day to day he had put it off; before breaking the news to Nadejda, he broke it to his brothers, his sister Alexandra Davydoff and his father. He wrote them all on July 5th, and with his wedding day fixed for July 18th, he knew well enough that nobody would have time to advise him or come to his wedding. Then, on July 15th—only three days before the fatal step was taken —he wound himself up to the task of confessing to Nadejda —for between these two an intimacy had been established that could declare the inclusion of another woman by no lesser ceremony than confession.

Moscow, July 15, 1877

"For God's sake, dear Nadejda Philaretovna, forgive me for not writing before. Briefly, here is the story of what has lately happened to me.

"In the latter part of May, to my own great surprise, I became engaged to be married. This is how it happened. Some time ago I received a letter from a girl whom I knew and had met. From it, I learned that she had honored me with her love for a long time. It was written so sincerely and warmly that I was led to do what in such cases I had always carefully avoided—to answer. Although my answer did not give any hope that the feeling could be mutual, the correspondence started. I will not tell you in detail about it, but the result was that I consented to go to see her. Why did I? I now feel as if Fate had drawn me to that girl. When I met her I again explained to her that I felt no more than sympathy and gratitude for her love. And when I left I began to think over all the giddiness of my behavior. If I did not care for her, if I did not want to encourage her, why then did I go to see her, and how will it all end?

"From her next letter I found that if I should suddenly discontinue all relations with her after having gone so far, I would make her most unhappy and drive her to a tragic end. So I had a difficult alternative—to save my freedom at the price of the girl's ruin (ruin is not an empty word—she really loves me to distraction)—or to marry. I could not do otherwise than choose the latter. One thing that helped me to a decision was the fact that my eighty-two year old father and all my relatives live in the hope of having me marry.

So one fine evening, I went to my future wife, told her frankly that I did not love her, but that I would be a devoted and grateful friend, described my character in detail, my irritability, my variable temperament, unsociability, and finally my circumstances. Then I asked her if she would be my wife. The answer, of course, was 'yes.' I have no words for the feelings I experienced during the days following that evening; it can only be imagined. Having lived thirty-seven years with an antipathy for marriage, it is hard to be goaded by circumstance to the role of a fiancé completely indifferent to his bride. It means altering one's whole life, thinking of the welfare of the person to whom one is united. All this, for an egotistical bachelor, is not easy.

"In order to think it over and adjust my mind to such a future, I decided to go to the country for a month, according to my original plan. The quiet country life, surrounded by pleasant people and beautiful nature, had a beneficial influence. I decided that I could not avoid my destiny and that Fate itself had decreed my meeting with this girl. Also, I knew from experience that very often in life, what frightens and appalls results in good, while on the contrary, the very happiness we have longed for and worked for, disappoints us. Let what is to be, be.

"Now let me tell you a little about my future wife. Her name is Antonina Ivanovna Miliukoff. She is twenty-eight. She is rather attractive. Her reputation is irreproachable. To be independent and free, she supports herself. She has a loving mother. She is quite poor, educated not above the average (she was educated in the Elisabeth Institute) and seems to be very kind, capable of giving herself without reservations.

"You ask whether I call you friend. But how can you doubt it? Have you not read again and again between the lines of my letter how deeply I care for your friendship, and that my tenderness for you is very true and warm? How I should like to prove sometime, not by word but by deed, all the strength of my gratitude and sincere love for you! Alas, I have only one way, my music. Well, in that way, I am always ready to serve you; so why don't you write about the work you wanted me to do? If I cannot always satisfy your wishes as to the composition of one or another piece, because I cannot always be in the mood that is needed for composition, I can always do any other type of musical work. I even urge you, order such things from me as often as possible so that I can, little by little, pay my debt to you.

"I shall write on the symphony, 'Dedicated to My Friend,' as you have desired.

"And so good-bye, my dear, good, sweet friend. Pray that I shall not break under the approaching change in my life. God knows I am filled with the best intentions regarding my future help-mate, and if we are unhappy, it will not be my fault. My conscience is clear. Though I am marrying without love, I do it because circumstance would permit no other course. I giddily accepted the first declaration of love she sent me; I should not have answered her; but once I had encouraged her love by responding and visiting her, I had to do as I did. Anyway, I repeat, my conscience is clear. I have not lied or pretended. I have told her what she can expect from me and on what she must not count. Please do not tell anybody what has led to the marriage. Except you, nobody knows."

It was two years before Nadejda Philaretovna told Peter Ilyich what his "news" had really done to her; her confession is to be found in a later letter in this volume.

On that summer day in Brailov when Nadejda received her letter, she sat down instantly and replied—and she wrote like a lady and a sportsman. Also, she wrote like a woman. Cautiously but clearly she leaves open a double road for future correspondence—it can be personal, or it can confine itself to music:

"With all my heart"—(how this opening phrase must have reassured Peter Ilyich, and how little he deserved reassurance!)—"I congratulate you, my dear friend, on the new step, a step that is always a gamble. In your case it rejoices me, because it would be a sin for a man with so golden a heart, so delicate a capacity for feeling, to bury such treasures. You have given happiness to someone and so you will be happy yourself, and in all justice, who should be happy if not you, the giver of such great joy to others? In this you have acted with the honor and delicacy that is always yours.

You are good, Peter Ilyich, and certainly you will be happy.

"I cannot find words to express how deeply and sincerely grateful I am for the confidence and frankness shown in your letter. They are precious to me as happiness itself. Be sure, Peter Ilyich, that I appreciate your trust, and can be silent when necessary.

"With all my heart I thank you for the dedication—the symphony will always be a light to my life.

"I am sure, my dear, good friend, that in your new life, or under any circumstances, you will not forget that you have in me a deeply loyal friend, and will, regardless of all the fabrications and errors of public opinion, always see in me a soul that is devoted and true to you. You will write me everything about yourself, frankly? Indeed, my dear Peter Ilyich, nothing that concerns you will ever be a bother to me.

"I shall hope to hear in your next letter that you are satisfied with the new life and that you are happy. May Heaven send you every good thing.

"From my heart, I press your hand. Do not forget one-devoted-with-all-her-soul,

"N.v.M."

8

Marriage. A growing breach and a growing friendship

Quite different in tone from his confession to Nadejda were the letters Tchaikowsky sent his brothers and father concerning his marriage. These were rather in the nature of announcement, the mood calm and affectionate. Peter Ilyich was in the country when he wrote them—the first sentence would seem to indicate that Anatol had a keen nose for trouble.

To Anatol

Glebovo, July 5, 1877

"Dear Tolia,

"You guessed rightly that I was hiding something from you, but you were wrong as to what the 'something' was. At the end of May something happened that I planned to keep for some time from all my near and dear ones, so that you should not be anxious for fear I was acting unwisely. I wanted to finish the matter entirely and then make full confession. I am going to be married. At the end of May I became engaged, planned to marry early in July and announce it to you all afterward. But your letter has changed my mind. First, knowing I shall see you, it would be hard to invent a whole drama of lies to explain why I can't go with you to Kamenka. Second, it would be wrong to marry without Father's blessing. Give him the enclosed letter. Please don't worry about me. I have given the matter much consideration and I take this important step quite calmly; you will believe this when I tell you that with marriage so near, I could write two-thirds of my opera." (*Eugene Onegin*.)

"The girl I am marrying is no longer very young, but quite honest and possessing one great attraction—she is in love with me. She is quite poor. Her name is Antonina Ivanovna Miliukoff. So I not only announce my future marriage but invite you to it. You and Kotek will be the only witnesses. Ask Father to be sure not to tell anyone, and the same to you. I myself will write Sasha" (Tchaikowsky's sister Alexandra Davydoff) "and the other brothers."

Once more, Tchaikowsky banishes what he has done somehow—somewhere—outside of himself. Something has happened, he writes Anatol, as though he himself had sat passively watching. As to his working hard and sketching out a new opera, this was a usual state with Peter before he took an important active step, good or bad. It would seem that the emotional turmoil necessary to propel his external life forward, was equally effective inwardly: emotional suspense was for Peter a state of balance as well as tension. Only when action occurred did the scales tip—and tip horridly—and Tchaikowsky's world went sliding into chaos.

The letters between son and father are cheerful and easy —the last untroubled words that Peter Ilyich will put to paper for many a long day. Except for his solicitude lest his father be shocked by the suddenness of his news, Peter writes like a little boy who, before leaving the house for a party, comes to show himself to his parents, all dressed in his party clothes:

To Ilya Tchaikowsky

Glebovo, July 5, 1877

"My very dear Father,

"Your son Peter has decided to marry; he asks you now to bless him on the threshold of a new life. My future wife is poor, but a pleasant, worthy young girl who loves me devotedly. Dear Father, you know that at my age a man does not marry without forethought, so do not be anxious on my behalf. I am sure my future wife will add greatly to my peace and happiness. . . . Keep well, my darling, and answer me at once. I kiss your hands."

Ilya Tchaikowsky's reply

Pavlovsk, July 9, 1877

"My sweet Son Peter,

"Tolia gave me the letter in which you ask my blessing upon your marriage. It made me so happy I crossed myself and jumped for joy. The Lord be praised, and His blessing be upon you! I don't doubt that your intended deserves the same blessing that your old father of eighty-three and all his family bestow upon you; not only your father but all who know you. Is this not true, my dear Antonina Ivanovna? From now on, permit me to call you my beloved, heaven-sent daughter, and to bid you love your chosen bridegroom, for indeed he deserves your love. Tell me the day and hour of your wedding. I will come myself—(may I?)—to bless you, and for the purpose I will bring the ikon with which you were blessed by your own godmother, Aunt Nadejda Timothevna, a kind and clever woman."

Poor Ilya Tchaikowsky! Not even the ikon of Aunt Nadejda—kind and clever though she may have been—could bring blessing to this union. Anatol knew it and rushed to Moscow—but he was too late; he could do no more than stand by and try to conceal real grief as he saw his brother plunging into a situation he knew would be disastrous. One other person witnessed the ceremony; Kotek the violinist, Tchaikowsky's young pupil who in the beginning had acted as go-between for Tchaikowsky and Nadejda von

Meck. That same evening Anatol saw the bride and groom off to Petersburg for a week's "honeymoon." The wheels of the train were scarcely in motion before the bridegroom was assailed with a thousand misgivings, a thousand inner questionings. . . . Marriage! . . . He was married; he had rushed into a serious, lifelong relationship with no more consideration than one would give to the acceptance of a dinner invitation. All his life he had suffered from a wound, his real motive in marrying, he knew now, had been to cure this wound.

Two days after his marriage, Tchaikowsky wrote the first of those frightened letters to his brothers that were to continue for two months, wavering sometimes between fear and a temporary hopefulness, but rising always toward the dark climax of September.

To Anatol

"I should lie to you if I said I was already quite happy, quite accustomed to my new position. After such a terrible day as the eighteenth of July, after that ghastly spiritual torture, one cannot recover quickly. I suffered intensely to see how you were afflicted for me, yet you were responsible for the fact that I fought so bravely with my agony. When the train started I was ready to scream; sobs choked me. But I had to entertain my wife with conversation as far as Klin to earn the right to lie in the dark in my own armchair, alone with myself. My only consolation was that my wife did not understand or realize my ill-concealed unhappiness. She has looked quite happy and satisfied all along. *Elle n'est pas difficile.* She consents to everything and is satisfied with everything. We have had conversations that have made our mutual relationship clear. She consents absolutely to everything and will never raise any objections. She needs only to fondle and take care of me. I have kept my full freedom. . . . I have so arranged matters that when my wife and I once become used to one another, she will not really bother me. I don't deceive myself. She is very limited, but even this is good. A clever woman would scare me. With this one I stand so high and dominate her to such an extent that I feel no fear of her."

76

There is no doubt that Peter Ilyich was trying hard, was "doing his best." During these first days, the kindly dispositions of both bride and groom served to conceal the true state of affairs. In spite of his nervousness, Peter had always been an easy-natured man—alas, too easy!—and it was impossible for him not to answer smile for smile. As for Antonina, she was both good-natured and extremely stupid. There is small doubt but that she disbelieved entirely her husband's declaration of his homosexuality and considered that to win him over would be only a matter of time and proximity.

To Anatol

July 23, 1877

"Truly I am going through a hard time. Yet I feel that little by little I am becoming used to my new position. It would be quite insufferable and inexcusable if I should mislead my wife in any way, but I told her long ago that she could expect only my brotherly love. Physically she has become absolutely repulsive to me. . . ."

At the end of this first week of marriage, the pair returned to Moscow. Peter hurried to the Conservatory and found there what he hoped to find—a letter from Nadejda von Meck. It was in answer to his of July 15th wherein he had announced his impending marriage. Nadejda's letter, we will remember, had spelled reassurance with the first words: "With all my heart, I congratulate you on the new step . . ."

And now we come to a difficult task; Tchaikowsky's reply is not grateful reading for a biographer who is fond of his subject. Barely had Peter Ilyich read Nadejda's friendly words when he sat down and asked her for money.

Peter Ilyich to Nadejda von Meck

Moscow, July 27, 1877

"Yesterday I came to Moscow and found your letter at the Conservatory, dear Nadejda Philaretovna. In my present excited state of nerves, your friendly words and warm sympathy were very helpful.

"Nadejda Philaretovna! Strange and crass though it appears, I must again ask you for material help. This is what has happened: Out of the sum you know of, there was enough left to go to the Caucasus and live quietly during the summer without worrying about expense. On the scene comes my marriage. All that money went for the wedding and for the expenses connected with it. I did not worry, because my wife had inherited from her father a stretch of forest land in the district of Klin, worth approximately four thousand roubles. Just before the wedding, she decided to sell it and had every reason to think a sale had been arranged; indeed, she had been assured it would go through. We planned to use the money for our living in Moscow before leasing an apartment, for the furnishing of our future home, and afterward for my trip to Essentuki. As often happens with impractical people—she was misled, the forest was not sold. So we are badly in need of ready funds. We have nothing to live on, we can't take an apartment, I can't go to Essentuki. And yet I need to go away, far away, to be alone, to rest, to think things over, to be treated, and lastly, to work. I desperately need rest from the excitement I have been through. Because of all this, I must ask you to augment my debt by one more thousand. I make no further apology.

"It is hard for me to write you this; I do so because only you can give me a helping hand, only you will not consider my request troublesome or misread my motives, only you can save me from an intensely disagreeable situation. Tomorrow or the day after I go with my wife to meet her mother, who lives in the country. We shall stay about five days and then return to Moscow. I don't know what will happen after that. I know ahead that you will again help me. If I am not mistaken, you are a person who does not know how to refuse. Nadejda Philaretovna, let me postpone the story of all I have lived through these last days until I write again. I am so nervously upset that I cannot speak of it calmly or in detail; moreover, I do not yet well understand what is happening to me. I can't decide whether I am happy or not. I am sure of only one thing—I cannot work. It is a sign of an excited, abnormal state.

"Good-bye, my dear sweet friend. Whatever happens to me, the thought of you helps me, quiets me. Your friendship will always be the joy of my life."

The world of music lovers owes a debt to Nadejda von Meck for the brief note she wrote Peter Ilyich from Brailov in July, 1877, and for the accompanying fact of money—the first of those *lettres chargées* that were to grace the composer's mail so often. "Go to the Caucasus," she wrote, "and go quickly." Nadejda knew she need not add, *Go alone.* There is small doubt also, that she was not sorry to be the instrument of his going "alone"! . . . "Think of me sometimes," she continued. "Enjoy nature, be quiet and happy. I hope your next letter will explain more fully, and that from it I shall know all, all."

What a strong weapon is patience, for womankind! Had Nadejda demanded to know all—and surely, she had a right so to demand—she might never have progressed another inch with this difficult creature. But from Peter Ilyich the widow did not, then or ever, demand; she merely "hoped," and her hope was rewarded.

His brief reply is one long gasp of fear and tension; one feels it written in the very act of fleeing, of escape, the writer casting a terrified glance now and again over his shoulder. His pursuers—Antonina, and all the world that sympathizes with Antonina—will it catch up before this last hour is over and he shall be gone from Moscow?

"Thanks, Nadejda Philaretovna, thanks! I am afraid to say anything that would look like a formality, so I add nothing to that word. I am leaving" (Moscow) "in an hour. I shall stop for some hours in Kiev for the special purpose of writing you a long letter and pouring out my soul to you. If I emerge from this struggle victorious, it will be due to you and you alone. A few days more and I swear I should have gone mad. Good-bye, my dearest friend, my Providence. In three days you will have my letter with the details.

"P.T."

And in three days she had it:

"Nadejda Philaretovna, here, briefly is the story of all I have lived through since the eighteenth of July, the day of my marriage.

"I wrote you that I married, not because affection urged me, but because of a chain of circumstances inexplicable to me, which forced a hard alternative. I had either to jilt an honest girl, whose love I had carelessly encouraged, or marry. I chose the latter. At first I thought surely that I would fall in love with a girl who was so sincerely devoted to me; also, I knew that my marriage was fulfilling the dreams of my old father and others close and dear to me. The instant the ceremony was over and I found myself alone with my wife, realizing that our fate was henceforth to live inseparable and together, I knew suddenly that I felt for her not even simple friendship, but that she was abhorrent to me in the full sense of the word. There came to me the conviction that I, or rather the best and perhaps only good part of the being that is I—music—had perished forever. My future life seemed mere vegetable existence—a dreary, unbearable comedy.

"My wife is in no way guilty. She did not ask for marriage. To make her feel, therefore, that I do not like her, that I look on her as an insupportable nuisance, would be cruel and mean. All that is left is to pretend. But to pretend all one's life is the height of torture. How could I ever work? I felt desperate, especially as there was no one to turn to for support and encouragement. I wished terribly to die. Death seemed the only way—but death by my own hand was out of the question. I care deeply for some of my family, my sister, my two youngest brothers, and my father. I know that to decide on suicide and carry it through, would be to deal them a death blow. There are many other people, dear friends, whose love ties me to life. And then, I have the weakness (if one can call it a weakness) to love life, love my work, love my future success. I have not yet said all I have to say, all I want to say before the time comes to migrate to Eternity. Death does not come to me of her own accord. I shall not and cannot go to her, so what remains?

"I told my wife that I shall travel through August for my health, which is truly impaired and needs radical treatment.

No sooner had I said it than my trip began to take on the aspect of freedom from prison—though temporary; the very thought that the day of departure was not far away, gave me the strength to endure. After a week in Petersburg, we returned to Moscow. There we found ourselves without funds, as a certain Kudriavseff who had promised to sell her forest, had duped her. So began a new series of anxieties and tortures.

"Then I had to visit my wife's mother. Here my torments increased. I have an antipathy for the mother and the whole *entourage* of the family I have entered. Their ideas are narrow, their opinions wild, they are all at swords' points. My wife (perhaps it is unjust) hourly became more abhorrent to me. It is hard to describe, Nadejda Philaretovna, the spiritual agonies I experienced. Before going to the country, in a desperate effort to find a way out of the terrible situation and longing to get away, I applied to someone well-known to you, a sweet and dear friend, living at present at Brailov. The thought that she would help me, the certainty that she would free me from these awful bonds of sorrow and madness, bore me up. But would my letter reach her? The idea that the letter might go astray tortured me. We returned to Moscow.

"At last, one happy evening, a letter came from Brailov . . . I began to feel more cheered. The intervening days were occupied in preparations for departure and arrangements for future lodgings, and on Tuesday, at 1 P.M., I left. I don't know what the next step will be, but I feel as if I had waked from a terrible, painful nightmare, or rather from a long illness. Like a convalescent from fever, I am still very weak. It is difficult to think consecutively. It was very hard to write even this letter. But what a sensation of sweet rest, what a drunken feeling of freedom and solitude!

"If my knowledge of the way I am constituted does not deceive me, it is very possible that, after resting and calming my nerves, returning to Moscow and the routine of occupation, I shall look upon my wife quite differently. Truly, she has many qualities that can make for my future happiness. She sincerely likes me and does not desire anything more than my peace and happiness. I pity her.

"I am staying in Kiev for a day. Tomorrow I go to my

sister, and from there to the Caucasus. Forgive the incoherence and inconsecutiveness of this letter, Nadejda Philaretovna. My nerves, my whole spirit, are so tired I can hardly put two thoughts together. Yet, exhausted though my spirit may be, it is not so broken that it cannot glow with the most unbounded and profound gratitude to the hundred-times-dear-friend-without-price that is saving me. Nadejda Philaretovna, if God gives me strength to live through the horrible present, I will prove to you that this friend has not helped me in vain. I have not said one tenth of what I want to say. My heart is full. It wants to pour itself out in music. Who knows, perhaps I shall leave after me something truly worthy of the fame of a first class artist! I have the audacity to hope so. Nadejda Philaretovna, I bless you for all you have done for me. Good-bye, my best, my dearest, sweet friend.

"P.T."

His next letter is from Kamenka, his sister Alexandra Davydoff's country home, where he was to pass six blessed weeks without a wife. Whatever may seem false in the above letter—such as Tchaikowsky's intimation that he was trapped into marriage by concern for a girl's broken heart—one thing rings true throughout. He loved life, loved his work, loved his future success. And the three were, for Tchaikowsky, synonymous; the awful mistake of his marriage was to prove this to him irrevocably. He had made the gesture of trying to live as other men live, he had taken a wife, tried to shape his life about a central intimacy, a personal responsibility: what, as a result, was happening to him?

He did not know as yet, he could not define this fear and this *malaise*; after two weeks of marriage Peter knew only that he was vastly bewildered and vastly distressed. Perhaps rest and the shelter of his sister's household would enable him to order his thoughts once more and take stock of what his life was to be. Here at Kiev as he paused to write Nadejda, he knew that already a great gain had been made; twenty-four railroad hours away from his wife, and he felt once more the blessed urge to write music, the inspiration that alone spelled manhood and self-respect.

But it was fickle in its visitations, this urge to create music. Arrived in Kamenka, finding himself surrounded by people who had known him since his youth, the tension of desperation relaxed and with it, for a little time, musical inspiration.

The letter goes on to ask whether Nadejda has received his long letter from Kiev, and soars suddenly into a paragraph concerning the soul—Nadejda's soul in particular—a dithyramb which for want of better qualification we can only describe as Russian.

"Dieu!" cries Tchaikowsky, "what kind, beautiful souls live on this earth! Meeting such people as you on the thorny road of life, one grows to feel that humanity is not as selfish and wicked as the pessimists say. There are wonderful exceptions sometimes; among a million others, if such a one as you appears, it is enough to save a man from despair. I know I express myself badly and stupidly. But I am sure you will not read empty phrases where I want to express the deepest and sincerest love for you."

There is no doubt now of what was happening to Peter. In despair of his relationship with Antonina, he was turning to another woman, a being as far removed from Antonina, in character and position, as woman could be.

This man had never wanted a wife; he had wanted, in company with all homosexuals, a mother, someone at the same time intimate and remote whom he could worship and who would in turn worship him—always at a safe distance. And who, among womankind, could fill the role so beautifully, so convincingly, as Nadejda von Meck? Had she not, in almost the first letters she wrote him, declared him her ideal, and in the same breath had said she did not wish to meet him or to speak with him in the flesh?

And on her side, Nadejda had cause for rejoicing. She had asked for this man's complete confidence and she knew now, that she had won it. She wrote from Brailov that she had received his letter from Kiev, and that she was relieved because he had not gone to the Caucasus; nobody could ever tell how far that ancient enemy, the Turk, would venture. Also, her dear friend was now among people who not only *cared* for him, but *understood* him. . . . (How shrewdly and how blandly a Madame von Meck could dispose of an Antonina Miliukoff!)

"Thank you deeply, my best of friends," the letter continued, "for telling me all that has happened. How I suffered for you, how I pitied you when I read that letter, I can never say. Several times, tears filled my eyes. . . . What would I not give for your happiness! But I hope as you do, that after some rest, some time passed among people with whom you have so much in common (if you only knew how I am drawn toward them!), you will regain your strength, and find things not so bad as you thought. I am not an optimist—I do not lay false colors upon the bad things in life—but I find there are conditions to which one must *se résigner*, or, more exactly, in Russian, at which one must wave one's hand, make peace with, and grow accustomed to. Truly, resignation is stupid, but what can one do? One cannot torture oneself by constant fighting. From my heart, I implore heaven to give you joy again, pray that all your past unhappiness may be but payment for future good, because no good thing can be had for nothing.

"You have understood my moods, you would like to make my life gayer—already you are making it easier. Your music, your letters, give me moments when I can forget all the trials, all the misfortunes that everyone must have, no matter how fortunately placed in the world. You are the only person who gives me such profound, such great happiness; I am infinitely grateful, and only hope that what inspires it will not end or change, because such a loss would be unendurable."

Tchaikowsky's reply showed much improvement of spirit; he was again at work upon the Fourth Symphony, hereafter referred to, in writing Nadejda, as "your symphony," or "our symphony."

"I feel very much more at peace. The pleasant society, the quiet and tranquillity, together with the water cure that I started last Saturday, have made me over. I must confess that I showed terrible cowardice in my trials and a complete absence of strength. I am ashamed that I let myself go to such an extent and gave way to that sinister nervous excitement. Please forgive me for disturbing and alarming you. I am sure I shall emerge from this situation a victor. I must fight this feeling of alienation toward my wife, and learn to give her good qualities the appreciation they deserve. There is no doubt that she has them.

"I have so far recovered as to work a little on your symphony. One of my brothers—the twins—whose opinion I greatly respect, liked the part I played to him. The orchestration of the first movement will take a good deal of effort. It is very complicated and long, but is, I think the best movement. The other three are very simple and will be great fun to orchestrate: The *Scherzo* will demonstrate a new instrumental effect from which I hope much. First, only the strings play, *pizzicato*; in the *Trio*, the woodwinds enter for a solo passage; they are replaced by a group of brasses also playing alone; at the end of the *Scherzo*, all three groups call to one another in short phrases. I think it will be an interesting musical effect. I hope you will like it. That is the most important thing of all."

Tchaikowsky's life at the moment is moving too rapidly for us to stay and draw a picture of him at Kamenka as Uncle Petia; during these days of self-condemnation and nervous distress, no doubt the kind Alexandra was more thoughtful than ever toward the wayward and talented brother. She had feared for his sanity, those first few days. But since he had begun to work again, the life had come back to his face and after a morning with his new symphony he would actually run from his room to the garden, shouting to the children with his old gayety....

"Our symphony," Tchaikowsky wrote Nadejda, "is advancing a little." And forthwith he went on to mention the "new instrumental effect" of the *Scherzo*, from which he "hoped much." That his hopes were not too high, every conductor who likes to play Tchaikowsky will testify; the effect is tense and brilliant. So brilliant, in fact, that ambitious conductors are tempted to take the movement too fast, and sacrifice melody to show off their orchestral control.

Nadejda found this letter in Vienna, on her way to Italy; her impatience to have it in her hands had made the forty-three hours in the local train between Brailov and Vienna, interminable. She was of course delighted that Peter Ilyich was working, and pleased to have him call the symphony "ours." "I like *pizzicato* very much," she wrote. "It runs like an electric current through all my nerves." But, if the symphony was so nearly finished, what next? "How," asked this indefatigable woman, "is your opera coming along, Peter Ilyich?"—(*Eugene Onegin*) "How far have you gone with it?"

This was characteristic of Nadejda. From first to last, Tchaikowsky's music was not an excuse for this relationship, it was the basis and foundation stone on which the whole matter rested, and the widow never let Tchaikowsky forget it. To her, his music *was* Peter Ilyich, if his music prospered, *he* prospered; this man's music was his growth, the kernel his life fed upon; if she sent him money, it was to feed this life that she knew was so well, so very well, worth nourishment.

Tchaikowsky's reply was gloomy. He had been a month in Kamenka; it was high time for him to go. Had he known what in truth awaited him, he would have dreaded Moscow with something more than the nostalgia he felt now. . . . His letter is, however, concerned mostly with Nadejda's question about his opera. It is plain that at Kamenka Peter Ilyich had buried himself in Pushkin and Pushkin's *Eugene Onegin*. And this was peculiarly fitting, because Pushkin was one of the traditions of Kamenka; as a friend of Vasili Davydoff (the Decembrist) Pushkin had often visited Kamenka. In the grand days of Kamenka—fifty-odd years ago—the grotto above the west garden had been used as a banquet hall. Alexander Davydoff had it built as a cool place to eat his Lucullan suppers in summer; while he and his friends feasted, an orchestra of servants sat on the roof and played. . . . Now all this grandeur was vanished. But Tchaikowsky loved the grotto; dreaming in its shade on warm summer afternoons he saw the creatures of Pushkin's glorious verses pass across the grotto's mouth. . . . Striding through the sunlight—to sweet and melancholy music—Onegin, that arch-swaggerer. And clinging to his arm—

lovely, young and tragic—Tatiana, with a song upon her lips . . .

Indeed, it was in the grotto that old Elizabeth Davydoff, Siberian born during her father's exile, bred in the old régime, sat through the whole night with Peter Ilyich, beseeching him not to do the sacrilege he had planned with Tatiana, not to have her leave her husband and run off to illicit, joyful love with Onegin. In his verses, Pushkin had not let her run off. Sitting bolt upright, a frail tiny figure in her old-fashioned grey gown and pelisse, Elizabeth implored. . . . And as the sun rose, Tchaikowsky agreed against sacrilege, so that the generations of opera-goers may sigh over the melancholy triumph of Tatiana's sinful love denied.

But grottoes and delicious old Davydoff ladies could no longer have part in Tchaikowsky's life and he knew it. Something was awaiting him in Moscow, something of his own shaping which had small relation to innocence.

To Nadejda von Meck

Kamenka, Sept. 11, 1877

"I am writing in a gloomy state of mind, dear Nadejda Philaretovna. The fields are bare and it is time for me to go. My wife writes that our apartment will soon be ready. It will be hard for me to leave. But anyhow I shall go from here a healthy man, with strength to fight my fate. I know there will be hard moments, but then habit will assert itself, which as Pushkin says, 'is given to us from above in place of happiness.' For instance, I became accustomed to my duties at the Conservatory, that in anticipation had loomed as the direst misfortune.

"You ask about my opera—it progressed very little here, but I have orchestrated the first scene of the first act. Now that the primary enthusiasm has gone and I can look on it impartially, I think it is condemned to failure and indifference from the public. The story is simple, there are no stage effects, the music has no splendor or brilliance. Nevertheless it is possible that some of the elect, listening to this music, may be moved to the emotion that moved me when writing it. I am not trying to say that my music is so beautiful; merely, I know it is not within reach of the vulgar. In a word, I am unable to write for the express purpose of pleasing either the crowd or the elect. I think one must, in writing, submit one's instinctive bent, without thought of pleasing one camp or the other. I began *Onegin* without any particular purpose, but the way it has developed, the opera will not be interesting theatrically. So those for whom the first condition of opera is dramatic action will not be satisfied, but those who can see in an opera the musical interpreation of simple human feeling, far removed from the theatrical and dramatic, can (I hope) be satisfied with mine. In short, it is written sincerely, and on that I rest my hopes.*

"Good-bye, my sweet friend."

Tchaikowsky did not leave Kamenka until September 11th, but history possesses only one more letter written from there. Perhaps, with Moscow and Antonina drawing ever nearer, he feared to write Nadejda; even when writing to Anatol, he tried to reassure himself as to the horror that awaited him by referring to it with such light words as "indifference" and "annoyance":

To Anatol, in Petersburg:

Kamenka, September 23

"Only when thinking of a loved one far removed can a man realize the full strength of his love. Tolia! I love you terrifically. But oh, how little I love Antonina Ivanovna Tchaikowsky! With what deep indifference does that lady inspire me! How little does the prospect of meeting her cheer me! Yet she does not frighten me—she is simply an annoyance."

Nothing, here, about *Onegin*; no mention of music, no eager words concerning *pizzicato* or Tatiana's lyrical soliloquy. It will be some time, indeed, before we see Peter Ilyich once more as we love to see him, in that guise that was his best self, his only real self—the guise of an honest work-

---

* His hopes were not too high. The simple lyricism of *Onegin* still enchants audiences the world over.

man. He is leaving Kamenka and his friends, he is about to enter that particular hell which Fate reserves for persons of enormous emotionality, enormous sensitivity, and weak will—the hell of terror and remorse over crazy, futile actions for which the subject well knows he has no one to blame but himself.

9

Disaster

Peter Ilyich to his brother Anatol, the day after Peter's arrival in Moscow

Moscow, September 24, 1877

"My wife came to meet me . . . I know you are wondering how I feel now. Tolia! Don't ask me—I am frightened—that is all I shall say. I was too happy in Kamenka, maybe that is why the contrast seems so sharp . . ."

Upon his arrival in Moscow, Peter found a brief note from Nadejda Philaretovna, in which—strangely enough, she did not mention Peter's troubles, but expressed herself as lost in profound depression, a pessimism that seemed to have no foundation, no source and no endings. The creation of man—wrote the widow—this life that ends in death and a handful of dust—is it not a grim and hideous joke perpetuated by someone upon us helpless victims here upon earth—?

Thus Nadejda, from the depths of her Russian nature. Peter Ilyich responded in kind—but with one essential difference. The widow's gloom had neither object nor reason, it was a kind of oriental resignation, a black shrug of the shoulder, a turning away from life. Peter Ilyich, on the contrary, has the devil at hand, here, over his shoulder. And Peter will not turn to the devil and face him down. Peter does not desire to fight the good fight. He desires but one thing, and his face is turned toward it—Flight! Escape! "To run away, somewhere—how—when—?"

89

Twice, on that morning after his first night alone with Antonina in the new home, Peter sat down and wrote Nadejda:

To Nadejda Philaretovna

Moscow, Sept. 24, 1877
9 A.M.

"Yesterday I arrived in Moscow and found your letter from Lago di Como, dear Nadejda Philaretovna. Your profound and poignant unhappiness is at one with my own spiritual condition since I left Kamenka, and which today is hopelessly low—beyond words or any describing. Truly, death is man's greatest blessing, and I pray for it with all my soul. To describe my feelings, it is enough to say that my only desire is for the chance to run away somewhere. But how and where? It is impossible, impossible, impossible!

"Forgive me for not restraining this confession of misery when you have enough troubles of your own.

"I haven't been to the Conservatory as yet. My classes start today. As to our new home, my wife has done everything possible to please me. The apartment is comfortable and nicely arranged; everything is clean, new and attractive. And yet I look upon it all with hatred and resentment."

Same day, 11 o'clock

"Two hours ago I decided I could not send you those lines. Now I have reconsidered. I want to write you; I cannot leave you without an answer and I cannot write you anything but the truth. Very probably, the black mood will soon pass. I realize that difficult moments lie before me—I foresaw them and armed myself to meet them. But I was weaker than I thought. God, how hard and bitter life is, and what a price one pays for the few happy moments! When I sat down to write this letter, I wanted to help you with your own distress. I wanted very much to console you but all I can do is tell you of my great sympathy. Nadejda Philaretovna, look for solace and reconciliation with life through the contemplation of nature. The privilege of wealth is that it gives one the opportunity to run away from people and to be alone with nature, which in Italy is finer and more lavish than anywhere.

"I have orchestrated the first movement of the symphony. Now, after a few days devoted to adjusting myself to the new life, I hope to work. When I feel a necessity for work (the first sign of mental recovery) I shall begin orchestration of the opera or the last movement of the symphony, depending upon which I think more urgent. In any case the symphony will be finished before winter."

For the ensuing two weeks, from September 24th to October 6th, Tchaikowsky stayed with his wife. He attended his classes at the Conservatory and during the first week even went a little into society. Kashkin, the close friend whose brief memoirs constitute the only record we have of these two weeks, testifies that upon returning to Moscow from his own vacation, he was invited to Jurgenson's house to dine — Jurgenson was Tchaikowsky's publisher — and there he was astonished to meet Peter Ilyich — *and his bride!* The news was out at last, and Kashkin was not the only Muscovite to be astonished.

And while Moscow was gossiping over Tchaikowsky's marriage, shrugging shoulders, perhaps, and smiling a bit — in Venice Nadejda von Meck was organizing her cumbrous household for the return trip to Russia. The gloom and despair of her last letter may have been due to the cold she had contracted in Naples; these repeated colds were a serious matter for a woman threatened with tuberculosis. But whatever the cause of her despair, she found Tchaikowsky's reply more than adequate. And with this letter of his from Moscow urging Nadejda to find recuperation for her spirit in communication with nature, their positions were for the moment reversed. Tchaikowsky became cheerer and adviser, Nadejda, the lost soul seeking help. In her reply is to be found a remark she will reiterate often — "My life is nearly over." At forty-five, still handsome and vital, Nadejda quite genuinely considered herself an old woman, ready for chimney corner and lace cap.

It was late in October when Nadejda wrote from Venice. How she would like, she said, to follow Peter Ilyich's advice — run away from the world and live with Nature — but he has overlooked the fact that escape requires more than money. Freedom cannot be bought at a price. Eleven children drag her back to Russia, to the cold she hates. "I draw near my end" (Nadejda had sixteen years ahead of her) "but my life has nothing to give the world, whereas you, dear friend, deserve consideration." And Nadejda goes on to tell Peter Ilyich what she never tires of telling him—of his great worth to herself and to the world. All her concern for him is selfish, she says; he alone, prophet of the art she worships, can make her life happy. If he will permit her to send him away somewhere to rest, all the gratitude will be on her side.

It was unfortunate that three weeks elapsed before Peter Ilyich received this letter. For if ever man needed cheer, needed the prop of a woman's love and understanding, that man was Tchaikowsky—although it is to be doubted if even Nadejda could quickly have repaired the psychological damage of two weeks in the little flat with Antonina. It was such a small place, the flat—intimate. "Cozy," was the word people used to describe it. There was no escape from this tiny place, from the strong, all-pervading femininity of Antonina. Tchaikowsky's piano was set up in a corner of the sitting-room, and during those first days he tried to work, so he told Kashkin.

But the evenings! With Antonina always at hand, laughing, chattering, gossiping. And she was so *close* to him, there in the little room! Why could she not sit apart—so—against the other wall? Beads of sweat stood on Tchaikowsky's brow. . . . But if he got up and walked away, she would question him . . . Where are you going, Petia? Petia, do you want anything . . . ? She would follow him to another room; behind him he felt the horror of her reaching hands and knew with ill-concealed shudder this physical presence that he afterward described—and described repeatedly—as "unbearable torment."

But Peter did not describe it now. At least he wrote no letter, and if his diary gave him any relief of expression, we shall never know because those pages were burned. Something of what he suffered during those two weeks we know through Kashkin, in whom Tchaikowsky afterward confided. When on these evenings, the tension engendered by

Antonina's presence rose within him to the frightening point, Tchaikowsky would go quickly from the room and the house, and wander for hours through the Moscow streets.

On one such night, Tchaikowsky, almost delirious, found his way to a lonely place on the banks of the Moscow River and under cover of darkness, waded into the water up to his waist. It was almost October, a hint of snow was in the air and the slow waters of the river were icy. Peter stood there as long as he could bear the intense cold; the water was not deep enough to drown a man, but perhaps, reasoned Peter, sobbing, muttering to himself—perhaps a man might catch pneumonia and die without the final obloquy of suicide? Battering his way home, through empty streets, his icy clothes heavy against his legs, Peter, sobered for the moment by his act, knew well that tonight he had not played the part of a hero: a half-suicide is always a subject for ridicule, open to the suspicion of self-dramatization and self-pity, not desperate enough in his grief to deserve even the forgiveness accorded a suicide.

So when he got home, Peter told Antonina he had joined a fishing expedition and fallen into the water, and except for Kashkin, no one ever heard the truth. Even Nadejda never learned of that foolish and ineffective gesture. But what he had done frightened Tchaikowsky still further; he knew himself scarcely sane now; only a thread held him from utter irresponsibility. And when that thread should snap, when once he slipped into that black labyrinth, there would be, he knew, no return. . . . And most horrible of all was this irrational and dangerous hatred for Antonina that he felt growing within him. After all, the girl was blameless. Tonight, for instance, when he came in she had run to him, exclaiming over his wet clothes. She had knelt to help him off with his boots and the most horrible, ghastly impulse had come over him. He wanted to lift his foot and smash the girl in the face; he wanted to reach down and take that white neck in his hands and twist it until the breath was gone from it. . . . He had thrust his hands behind him and groaned aloud, and Antonina had looked up, startled. . . .

On the morning of October 6th, Tchaikowsky appeared at the Conservatory, records Kashin, looking "strangely agitated. He said he had been summoned to St. Petersburg by

Napravnik" (the orchestral conductor), "and took hasty leave of his colleagues." What really happened was that Peter Ilyich had written Anatol to telegraph him in Napravnik's name to come to Petersburg, and Anatol had complied. It is not unlikely Anatol had been expecting something of the kind.

But Anatol was not prepared for what he saw early next morning. Hurrying through the gate of the Nicholas Station and along the cold platform, he searched for his brother's face and quick familiar figure among the travellers descending from the Moscow train—all of them a little pale, perhaps, and dishevelled from a night of travel. One white face he saw that might be his brother's, but Anatol turned quickly from it. That huddled figure standing by the train steps was too old, too haggard and helpless for Petia. . . .

Anatol drew nearer, and looked again. He spoke his brother's name and a pair of frightful eyes were lifted to his—

Somehow, Anatol got his brother into a cab and to the nearest hotel, where after a dreadful nervous attack, the manifestations of which Anatol never disclosed, Peter became unconscious and remained so for forty-eight hours. The doctor feared for his life, and as soon as the patient became conscious and the crisis was passed, told Anatol that the only chance for his brother's recovery lay in a "complete change of life and scene." Complete change of life and scene meant, of course, complete separation from Antonina, so Anatol went down to Moscow and making what excuses he could, delivered Antonina into the arms of her mother and sent the two of them to Odessa. At the Conservatory Nicholas Rubinstein was sympathetic, and the lifted eyebrow was not in evidence. Definitely, though, Rubinstein made it clear that he hoped the recovery would be rapid and the Conservatory would soon see its best professor reinstated in the classroom. The two agreed concerning the desirability of spreading a proper story: Tchaikowsky was ill and going abroad; his wife would follow as soon as she could arrange it.

"I remember very little of my stay in Petersburg," Peter Ilyich afterward told Kashkin. "I remember cruel nervous attacks. I remember Balinsky, my father, my brothers, and them only."

94

In eight days from the time of his arrival in Petersburg, Tchaikowsky was well enough to attempt a journey. His brothers got him up and onto the Berlin express; Anatol was to make the journey with him. Neither Peter nor Anatol knew their exact destination, nor how long they would stay; but one thing they both knew, and Modeste, waving good-bye from the station platform, knew it too: A vast relief to be increasing the distance between Peter Ilyich and the woman known as Antonina Ivanovna Miliukoff Tchaikow-sky.

10

The Refugee

From Berlin, the brothers hurried to Switzerland. Clarens, on the shore of Lake Geneva, was a favorite resort for Russians.

A few days after his arrival in Clarens, Tchaikowsky wrote a long letter to Nadejda von Meck. A month had passed since his last word to her, written the morning after that first night in the Moscow flat with Antonina. "Death," he said, "is in truth man's greatest blessing, and with all my soul I pray for death." The very next line, however, had naively revealed that Tchaikowsky's prayer was not for death so much for death's sister—escape. "My one desire is to find a chance to run away somehow, somewhere..."

The letter from Clarens is more consistent in tone than any Tchaikowsky has written since his bachelor days. It is not only more consistent, but it is honest—always, with Tchaikowsky, a symptom of mental health. He is still frightened, but he writes frankly and naturally, making no excuses:

Clarens, Oct. 23, 1877

"Nadejda Philaretovna, you will be surprised to get this letter from Switzerland. I don't know whether you have had the letter written soon after my arrival in Moscow and addressed to you at Naples. I have had no answer to it. This is what has happened since.

"I spent two weeks with my wife in Moscow. Those two weeks were a series of the most unbearable mental agonies. I saw right away that I could never love my wife, and that the *habit* on which I had counted would never come. I fell into despair and longed for death, which seemed the only way out. I had moments of madness in which my whole being was filled with such terrific distaste for my poor wife that I wanted to strangle her. I could not carry on my work either in the Conservatory or at home. My mind began to go. Yet I knew I alone was to blame. My wife, whatever she may be, is not responsible for my encouraging her and bringing us to the point of marriage. My lack of character, my weakness, blundering and childishness were responsible for everything. In the midst of it I had a telegram from my brother telling me to come to Petersburg for another production of *Vakoula*. Happy to escape even for a day from the whirlpool of lies, pretense and hypocrisy in which I was caught, I went to Petersburg. At sight of my brother, all I had hidden in my heart during those endless two weeks came out. Something terrible happened, what, I do not remember. When I began to recover I found that my brother had had time to go to Moscow, talk to my wife and Rubinstein, arrange matters so that he could take me abroad and send my wife to Odessa, of which last nobody will know. To avoid scandal and gossip, my brother agreed with Rubinstein to spread the rumor that I was ill, that I was going abroad, and that my wife was to follow.

"Now I find myself in the midst of beautiful country, but in a most dire mental state. What will happen next? I cannot return to Moscow. I cannot see anybody. I am afraid of everyone. Finally, I am idle, unfit for any occupation. There is no place in Russia where I can go. I am even afraid of Kamenka. Besides my sister's family—and she has a grown-up daughter—Kamenka houses Leo Davydoff's mother, his brothers, many people who are working in the plant, and others. How are they going to feel about me? How could I defend myself? I am not yet fit to talk to anybody about anything.

"I must stay here for a time, rest, and let the world forget me. I must arrange for my wife's comfort and think over my future relations with her.

"I need money again, and again I can ask no one but you. It is terrible, it is painful and lamentable, but I must do it, must again have recourse to your infinite kindness. To bring me here, my brothers procured a small sum by telegraph from my sister. They are far from rich; to ask them again is impossible. And money had to be left for my wife, various kinds of bills had to be met, the trip here paid for, and as if by design, our exchange is low. I had hoped Rubinstein would be able to forward a sum, but my hope was vain. In a word, I am spending the last of my small means and have only you in view.

"Oh, my good sweet friend, in the midst of my tortures in Moscow when I thought there was no way out but death, when I gave way to unlimited despair, there were times when I felt that you could save me. When my brother came abroad with me, I realized I could not exist without your help and that again you would come forward as my saviour. And now as I write this letter, tormented with shame before you, I still feel that you are my real friend, a friend that can read my very soul, in spite of the fact that we know each other only by letters. I should like to tell you a great deal, to describe my wife in detail, explain to you why a life together is impossible, why all this happened, and what brought me to the conviction that I could never adapt myself to a life with her. But it is impossible as yet for me to tell a calm story.

"Why have you not written to me from Naples? Were you ill? It troubles me very much.

"Good-bye, Nadejda Philaretovna. Forgive me. I am very, very unhappy."

And while Peter Ilyich was writing this letter, Nadejda von Meck was leading her retinue—her four children, her servants and governesses and the faithful Julia—across the continent northward to Moscow, whither she arrived some days after Tchaikowsky's departure. Not having heard from him in nearly a month, Nadejda had no idea Peter Ilyich had left either Russia or Moscow; no doubt she looked forward eagerly to being in the same city with him now that winter and the Conservatory term had begun. She loved to be able to send and receive quick letters by messenger, and surely, thought she, the young wife would not prevent

97

this, would not come between them now. On the contrary, Peter Ilyich seemed more than ever to need counsel and friendship.

It was truly a blow to find her friend vanished from Moscow and Russia—and no word to tell her of his whereabouts. Surely, he might have left a message for her! Horrible rumors reached her. . . . His letter from Clarens did not arrive for several days and the widow, painfully anxious, had recourse to the nearest source of information. How cannily the interview with Rubinstein was conducted, will be seen from the widow's own account:

Nadejda to Peter Ilyich

Moscow, Oct. 29, 1877

"How glad I was to have your letter, my sweet, dear friend! When I came to Moscow, I was so frightened to find you gone that I truly did not know what to think, nor could I understand why I had not known about it before. Now I know everything that has happened, my poor friend. It makes my heart ache to think of your suffering and of how your life has been spoiled. Yet I am glad that you have taken a definite step—it was necessary, the only thing to do. I did not let myself tell you before what I truly thought, because it would have seemed like gratuitous advice, but now I believe I have the right, as a person so close to you in spirit, to give you my real opinion. And I repeat, I am glad that you escaped from the hypocrisy and lies—not for you, these things, and not worthy of you. You tried your best for another's sake, you fought to the end of your strength, certainly without profit to yourself; a man like you can perish in such circumstances, but he can never reconcile himself to them. Thanks be to God that your nice brother came in time to save you, and that he was so energetic.

"As to my feelings toward you, my God! Peter Ilyich, how can you think for a moment that I despise you when I not only understand all that has happened, but feel it as you feel it; I myself would have done the same, only I would surely have taken the step of separation earlier, because it isn't natural to me to make such a sacrifice as you have made. I live in your life and your sufferings; everything you feel and do is comprehensible and precious to me. Dear Peter Ilyich, why do you vex and offend me by torturing yourself with the material side? Am I not close to you? You know how I love you, how I wish you well. I think that not blood and physical ties, but feeling and spiritual kinship give one the right to help, and you know what happy moments you grant me, how deeply grateful I am for them, how indispensable you are to me, and how I need you, exactly as you are; therefore it is not you I help, but myself. Agonizing over it, you spoil my joy in taking care of you, making me seem no more than a stranger. Why do you do it? It hurts me. If I needed something from you, you would give it . . . ? So then, we are quits, and please do not interfere with my taking care of your affairs, Peter Ilyich.

"Nicholas Gregorievitch" (Rubinstein) "has just been here to tell me he had a letter from you, and that you are in Clarens. He came because when I arrived in Moscow and was so shocked to find that you had gone abroad, and was told such horrors, I was desperate and wanted to know where you were. I asked my brother to inquire of Rubinstein. N.G. said, Geneve, Poste Restante, but the next day I had your letter, and the third day he came to say that the address is Clarens. I don't know how you feel, Peter Ilyich, but I prefer not to have anyone know of our friendship, so with N.G. I talked about you as one about whom I was quite indifferent. As though I knew nothing and with ingenuous interest. I asked him for how long you had gone abroad and why. I had the impression that he wanted to awake warmer sympathy for you, but I kept within the cold limits of a simple admiration for your talent. He told me some of his plans for you which I imagine you must know, and also that your nerves are in bad shape. But you are better now, Peter Ilyich, are you not? With God's help you will soon recover, you will take up work on our symphony, music will again interest you and fill your life. Oh, how I desire all to be well with you! You are so dear to me. All will be well—you will rest, recover, and all the suffering you have lived through will seem a dream that can never repeat itself."

"The cold limits of a simple admiration for your talent. . . ." There are times when social training and the privileged "distance" of aristocracy stand a lady in good stead. "Some" of Rubinstein's "plans" no doubt referred to the proposition that Tchaikowsky be appointed delegate to the Paris Exhibition in January, a scheme very dear to Rubinstein's heart because Tchaikowsky's name would advertise the Moscow Conservatory abroad. Also, the position would carry a substantial salary, and when Anatol had gone down to Moscow and asked for an advance of money to take Peter Ilyich abroad, Rubinstein had been forced to refuse. Rubinstein was genuinely fond of Tchaikowsky, but the Chief (as the members of the Conservatory called Rubinstein)—preferred to keep his friendships on the debit side; this attitude—and especially the Exhibition plan—was soon to cause a serious quarrel between himself and Tchaikowsky. Nadejda must have discerned something of the kind; anyway she was careful not to call Rubinstein's plans by name.

But before Tchaikowsky had Nadejda's letter, a note came from Rubinstein, a friendly missive. "Calm yourself," he wrote. "Take care of your health and don't fear anything or anybody. You are too highly estimated as a musician to be compromised by anything outside of music."

Tchaikowsky wrote back immediately, reporting that he was at work on his opera. "Friend Petia," Rubinstein replied. "I am very glad you are recovering and have begun to work a little. Soon I shall have to kill the fatted calf for the prodigal's return. I am extremely interested in what you say about *Eugene Onegin*. Please assign the parts. Even if we have to change the casting a bit, it is most important to know your preferences. Can I count on the symphony too? I saw Frau von Meck and we had much to say about you. She will probably send you another commission, or money direct."

She did. She sent him the letter of October 29th from Moscow describing Rubinstein's visit, and she enclosed what the Chief so aptly called money direct—in the shape, not of a casual gift, but the first instalment of what was to be an annual allowance of 6000 roubles. But Peter did not receive it immediately; their letters crossed; he received, instead, Nadejda's letter from Venice written on October 8th, promising to forward a sum large enough to enable Peter to stay abroad for a few months and rest. What Peter wrote in reply is what he will write Nadejda many times in the future: an expression of gratitude and love, of shame, a reminiscence of terror as though by telling his nightmare, a man could disperse it. Lastly, his letter expresses that nervous restlessness which will cause him to wander from country to country, from scene to scene, in search of a peace no scenery can ever afford to one whose nature must forever deny peace, forever repudiate it even as the search seems ended. The letter of November 1st has a vagueness of tone that is somehow irritating to the reader; in this mood, Peter Ilyich is not at his best.

To Nadejda von Meck

Pension Richelieu, Clarens, S.
Nov. 1, 1877

"Today I received several letters from Moscow, forwarded after I left there. Among them was yours from Venice, dear Nadejda Philaretovna. How I have come to rely on your friendship, how I believe in you as an instrument of Providence sent to save me in this miserable period of my life! Your every letter shows an excess of generosity and kindness toward other people's mistakes. Have you ever reproached me for all my madness? You understand and forgive everything, Nadejda Philaretovna. You offer me means to rest. In my last letter, which you have by now, I anticipated your offer; I asked your help once more. How hard it is! The more generous and kind you are, the more shameful is a further appeal to you. Your letter today has relieved my mind. If you only knew how very, very much you do for me! I was standing on the brink of an abyss; the only reason I did not plunge into it was because I put my hope in you. I owe my salvation to your friendship. How shall I repay you? Oh, how I hope that sometime I may be of use to you! What would I not do to express my gratitude and love. I shall stay here until I receive from you the means to go to Italy, which attracts me strongly. It is very agreeable here, very quiet, but a little depressing. The first days I could not get my fill of gazing on the mountains. Now those same mountains begin to frighten and oppress me. I long for space. Some three days ago it started to rain, the sky is hopelessly grey, the sun hidden from morning to evening.

"You write that one cannot buy freedom at a price. In truth entire freedom cannot be bought. Yet the limited freedom I have now is for me a supreme delight. At last I can work. Without work, life has no meaning for me. And to work with a person near me outwardly so close, inwardly so far removed, was impossible. I went through a terrible ordeal, and think it a miracle that I emerged with my spirit not destroyed, only deeply wounded.

"My sister, as clever as she is kind, writes that she went to Odessa, found my poor wife and took her to the country. My sister has promised to talk with my wife about our future relationship, and here my wife's wonderfully placid disposition will come in very handy. She who, by threats of suicide, forced me to come to her—endured my flight, our separation and the news of my illness with an indifference simply incomprehensible to me. Oh, how blind and mad I was!"

And now came Nadejda's letter written in Moscow after she had seen Rubinstein, and enclosing not merely a casual sum, but the promise of an annuity. To Peter Ilyich, 6000 roubles a year spelled more than riches; it spelled freedom, peace, easement from fear. It meant that he could choose his life, it removed the menace of home and Moscow. In a word, it released him from the intimacies of marriage. Antonina could never pursue him across a continent. If his daily bread was not dependent upon the Conservatory, he need never have less than five hundred miles between himself and that girl. She would forget him; one of her colonels would come along—surely some of them must be real? Next day, after he had read her Moscow letter, Peter sat down and wrote Nadejda again—words that must have made the recipient very happy:

"I doubt if the opportunity will ever come," wrote Peter Ilyich, "for me to prove my readiness to make any sacrifice for you—you will never be able to ask of me a great enough service. And so I have no recourse but to serve you with my music. Nadejda Philaretovna, from now on, every note that comes from my pen will be dedicated to you. When desire for work renews itself with redoubled strength, it will be owing to you, and when I am working, never, never, for one second shall I forget that it was you who gave me the chance to go on with my career. Much, much remains for me to do. All false modesty aside, everything I have written up to now seems weak, unfinished, in comparison with what I can and must do. And I will do it."

Warm words, and heartfelt. And how quickly, how instantaneously warmth is gone—turned to ice with the first mention of Antonina! Nadejda had asked for a word-portrait and Peter gave it at some length, with an obvious effort at objectivity which broke down at the end of every sentence, no matter how charitably begun.

Antonina was blonde, wrote Antonina's husband—without, however, once using Antonina's name. It is noticeable that Tchaikowsky never wrote Antonina's name to Nadejda, referring to her at first as "my wife," later in vaguely legal terms as "the known person," and still later, to his brothers, in epithets more specific and less attractive.

"In her head and heart," went on Peter Ilyich, breaking down completely, "is absolute emptiness. After having assured me that she had been in love with me for four years and that she was a good musician, can you believe that she knew not one note of any of my compositions, and that on the day I left, she asked me what piano pieces of mine could be had at Jurgenson's? It was this above all else that made me feel our life had run into a blind alley and could progress no further. I was no less astonished to find that she never went to the concerts and quartet performances of the Musical Society, where she knew surely that the object of her four years' devotion could be met, and where she could so easily have come.

"You wonder, perhaps, how we passed the time when we were alone? She is very talkative, but everything she said led inevitably to: The numberless men who loved her (which she repeated continually), most of them generals, nephews of famous bankers, well-known actors, or members of the Imperial family. The vices, baseness and detestable behaviour of her relatives—with all of whom she is at swords' points—were described with the strangest fury, most of it being aimed especially at her mother."

Whether or not the nineteenth century had words for nymphomania and persecution complex Tchaikowsky, more shrewdly than he knew, had selected for characterization, traits that were more than merely irritating; they were dangerous.

"Nevertheless," continued Tchaikowsky to Nadejda, recapturing objectivity with an effort, only to lose it before the sentence came to a stop— "It is fair to add that she tried in every way to please me, sincerely desired my love, never opposed any of my plans or ideas and lavished her caresses on me to satiety.

"After this you must be amazed that I could have bound my life to such a strange companion. I myself cannot explain it. Some madness must have come over me. I imagined that I would surely be affected by her love for me, in which I then believed, and that on my side I could learn to love her. I know now that she never loved me. But one must be just—her wish to marry me, she mistook for love. And then, I repeat, she did everything she could to make me love her. Alas, the more she tried, the more she alienated me! I vainly fought this feeling; I knew she did not deserve it, but what could I do with my unruly emotions? Dislike grew not by the day, the hour, but by the minute—little by little becoming a huge, ferocious hate such as I never before felt and of which I did not think myself capable. At last I lost the ability to control myself. What happened next you already know. Just now my wife is with my sister, and soon she will choose a permanent place to live.

"Yesterday my brother had a letter from her in which she appears in an absolutely new light. From a gentle dove, suddenly she turns into a very ill-natured, demanding person, a liar. She levels many reproaches at me, the gist of which is that I have shamelessly duped her. I have written to her explaining that I do not wish to start any argument, because it will lead us nowhere, and taking all guilt on myself. I begged her to forgive me the wrong I had done her, and said that I yield beforehand to whatever decision she may make, but that live with her I never shall—this I said positively. Certainly it is understood I will see that she is not in need, and I asked her to accept means of support from me.

I await an answer. I have sent money enough to take care of her for some time.

"This is all I have to tell you about my relations with my wife. Looking back on the short time we lived together, I have come to the conclusion that the 'beau role' is entirely hers, not mine. She acted honestly, sincerely and consistently. She deceived herself by her love, and not me. She was sure, I imagine, that she loved me. As for me, though I had carefully told her that I bore her no love, yet I had promised to do everything I could to love her, and as I arrived at a somewhat contrary result, I was guilty of deluding her. Anyhow she deserves pity. Judging from yesterday's letter, offended pride has awakened, and has decidedly begun to speak.

"Little by little I have started to work, and I can say definitely that our symphony will be finished not later than December, and then you shall hear it. Let this music, so closely connected with your image, tell you that I love you with all my soul, my best friend, my friend-above-all-friends."

Peter Ilyich put down his pen and all that day rejoiced with his brother over his new good fortune. But by next morning he could contain himself no longer; he must share this wealth. Modeste, back in Russia, needed money; when did Modia not need money? And when, from now on, would Peter Ilyich ever refuse to supply it?

To Modeste Ilyich

Clarens, Nov. 6, 1877

"Just when you need money, Modia, I have suddenly become, if not rich, at least comfortably off for quite a long time. The person you know of has sent me three thousand francs, and will send me a thousand and a half every month. It is all arranged with such wonderful delicacy and kindness that I feel very little embarrassment. *Dieu!* how kind that woman is, how generous, how tactful. And at the same time, wonderfully clever, because while she does me great service, she does it in such a way that I cannot for a moment doubt that the service gives her pleasure."

Back in Moscow, the European post must have brought relief to more than Modeste Ilyich. Nadejda read the long,

merciless description of this wife of Peter's and knew that
not the wife but she herself had conquered. Peter had declared himself unequivocally; this was no lover's quarrel;
this husband hated his wife, scorned her and would scorn
her forever. His frankness gave Nadejda the right to declare
herself in turn. Concerning Antonina, she need never again
show the conventional, careful attitude of the outsider toward a marriage. She could say what she chose, and from
now on, she said it.

Nadejda to Peter Ilyich

Moscow, Nov. 12, 1877

"Thank you very much for writing me a portrait of your
wife, Peter Ilyich. I found her just as I expected, and that is
why I never wanted to send my daughters to any Institute.
One very rarely remains oneself there—good natures are apt
to become spoiled, bad ones to grow worse, and the lazy to
become completely idle. I feel very badly, Peter Ilyich, that
you blame and disturb yourself by pitying your wife. You are
not guilty of wronging her in any way, and you may be sure
she will not suffer at all from the separation. She is one of
these fortunates ones, exaggerated by her education, who
never suffer deeply or long because they cannot feel anything deeply. They live an objective, completely material
life—which you have taken care of—the ideal life for such
natures. To eat well, and even better, to sleep—this you have
made possible for your wife and you deserve only gratitude
from her. Such natures cannot be unhappy because they are
satisfied with themselves, and so they always flourish in soul
and body. Even if something irritates them, it is merely
another sensation. They have no feelings; things slip over
the surface without wounding. If someone should tell you
that she weeps, don't be disturbed, Peter Ilyich; be sure it
is only for show. Any woman who is married, especially if
she loves the man—and who does not want to have a child,
has no heart. I must confess that I myself am no dreamer
and have no sympathy for dreamers—I am a realist; my
nature needs the most fervent poetry, but it must be founded
on reality. The joy of having a child is full of that real
poetry, and I feel it passionately."

In justice to Peter Ilyich, let us picture him as blushing slightly when he read those last lines. He had told Nadejda that Antonina did not like children, but he had not meant to convey a scene where he as potential father, had urged the young wife on to duty. Also, letters from Antonina were beginning to come; a man must turn to any philosophy that would permit him to face this pursuit with a measure of confidence and self-respect. Religion? When, the fugitive asked himself, had he thought of God, that God he had accepted in childhood?

To Nadejda Philaretovna

Clarens, Nov. 11, 1877

"Thinking over all that has happened, more than once I have been convinced that Providence has watched over me. When death seemed the only solution, I did not die, and now things are well with me and a new dawn of happiness is rising. As to religion, I confess that my nature is divided and that to date I have found no way to reconcile this difference. On one side, my mind obstinately refuses to be convinced by dogma, either the Orthodox or any other Christian sect. For instance, I never could find any sense in the tenet of punishment and reward, according to whether a man is good or bad. How can one draw a line between the sheep and the goats? Rewards for what, and punishments for what? Also, belief in eternal life is difficult for me to grasp. The Pantheistic view of immortality attracts me strongly.

"On the other hand, my education and the ingrained habits of childhood, combined with the poetry contained in the story of Christ and his teaching—all persuade me, in spite of myself, to turn to Him with prayers when I am sad, with gratitude when I am happy. I should like to know you from that side, my dear friend. You surely have achieved harmony and found the Truth. Could you (if it is not impudent of me to ask) just briefly explain your ideas of religion? Good-bye, my dear and best friend. There are not words to tell you my love and gratitude."

But before he had time to hear from Nadejda concerning her religious philosophy, or from his sister at Kamenka concerning her proposed reformation of Antonina, Peter Ilyich, overtaken by his old digestive complaint, made a hurried trip to Paris in search of medical help. Anatol persuaded him—Anatol was soon to return to Russia and did not like to leave his brother in bad physical condition. The brothers then went down to Florence, and Peter wrote the widow in despair. Imagine, said he, he was going to Rome! Rome would be awful; why, the number of things a tourist must see in Rome was frightening—Peter used the German word, *Sehenswürdigkeiten*. Were all Russians like this, he wondered? If he went to Rome it would be to work, not to run about with a Baedeker in his hand. And yet he would never be able to work in Rome; he knew it! Why had he ever given Rome as a forwarding address to all his Russian correspondents? Now he would have to go there! Why did he leave peaceful Clarens? What will happen to him when Anatol goes home to Russia, as go he must very soon? "Why did I leave Switzerland?" cries Peter Ilyich. "Why did I go to Paris? Why am I here in Florence? Stupid, stupid, horribly stupid!"

And in the midst of it, he received a note from Nadejda spurring him to hardness against Antonina, and suggesting it might be time for the homeward journey.

Peter Ilyich replied that she was quite right; he ought to come home. But where, in Russia, could he go? Not Petersburg, where his old father lived. . . .

"You know that one reason for my marriage was to fulfill an old and ardent wish of his. My flight from Moscow, my illness and departure for abroad all had to be concealed from him; even now he does not really know what happened. He was told only that my nerves were upset, that I had gone abroad with my brother because my wife could not go for business reasons of her own, and that she was to join me at the first opportunity. He did not like it and could be quieted with difficulty. I think he will probably never know the truth. It is hard for me to lie to him and I would eventually be forced to answer his questions about my wife and why I live without her (he liked her very much), and to tell him the truth would be dangerous. Heaven knows how it might affect him. Also, I hate Petersburg; the mere sight of it plunges me in gloom."

And Moscow? Moscow would be even worse.

"I can't tell you, dear Nadejda Philaretovna, the terrible tortures I suffered there in September. I was within a hair's breadth of going under. The wound is still too fresh. I am not yet ready for my old Moscow life—I am still ill—I could not stand it.

"The only place I should really like to go is Kamenka, but even Kamenka is closed to me now and for some time to come. When my sister learned what had happened, she immediately went to my wife in Odessa. I see clearly now that she made a great mistake in inviting my wife to Kamenka instead of confining herself to a meeting. My sister is very kind and very clever, but this time she did the wrong thing. Knowing me and immediately perceiving what my wife was, she began with wonderful enthusiasm to re-educate her, trying to persuade me by letters of my wife's many good qualities, and how in time she would make a splendid life companion. More than once I wrote her that because all guilt is on my side, mine also is all responsibility and that I accept the future consequences of my thoughtless behaviour, but I begged her for God's sake not to mention the possibility of our ever living together again. I don't understand what got into my sister at the time. What she could not see was that my hatred for my wife, even though unwarranted, is an unhealthy state of mind, that I must be left in peace, and that not only should she not describe her, but not even mention this woman whose very name and everything that reminds me of her drives me mad. The result was those letters from my wife of which I have already told you, in which she appeared either servile and insincere, or humble and loving, or accused me of baseness and dishonesty, or out and out implored me to love her. It was terrible.

"My sister, who thought to influence my wife for good, has succeeded only in raising her spirits to such an extent that my wife wrote my brother here that she is very gay and that a colonel has fallen in love with her. It is all very awkward; the very woman who unwittingly has done me so

109

much harm lives now at my sister's, the one place that is home to me, that has always been my refuge from worry and, for me, the warmest place on earth."

Back in Kamenka, the kind Alexandra Davydoff was in truth having far from an easy time. She did not realize, at first, what this girl was; as the happy mother of a household Alexandra's sympathies were all with the abandoned wife. But not for long. Day by day Alexandra, generous though she was, lost patience with this wife of Petia's. What a woman! One thing to cry, another to cry all day, dropping great tears on little Natasha's spelling book, frightening the child and making no explanation. What a misfortune that Petia, himself a bundle of tortured nerves, should have tied himself to a creature even more emotionally unstable than he.

Oh, but far more unstable! Petia, for instance, was often sick with nerves, but in all his relationships he was loyal, or had been, up to now. Of course, he was much too quick to take offense at personal criticisms of his music and cherished such offense for years, ridiculously. But his friends were lifelong friends, his devotion to his brothers and to all his family, unswerving. Whereas Antonina's life, by her own description, seemed submerged in excited quarrelling. Antonina could not keep to one plan or one occupation longer than an hour . . . Now Petia, while flighty emotionally and liable to the wildest excitement over nothing, was a worker, regulating his days like a clock and hideously distressed when this routine was broken. Oh, an impossible combination, these two, and any comparison between them, mere folly . . . Quietly but with determination, Alexandra began to question her guest as to future plans. . . .

But Antonina, it seems, was not interested in plans. She desired to stay where she was, and said so with greatest cheerfulness. She seemed more than sure of her welcome at Kamenka and what was more embarrassing, she had nowhere else to go. With her own brothers and sisters and various friends she was not at present, she said, on good terms. . . . No, no, said Antonina. "I like it here, and here I shall stay."

From grandmother to child, the Davydoffs were kindly

folk, accustomed to deal gently with their little world. Husband and wife held a conference, the result of which was a letter from Leo Davydoff to Anatol Tchaikowsky in Venice, bidding Anatol be sure to stop by at Kamenka on his way from abroad—and take this woman to her mother down in Moscow.

Leo was a mild letter-writer, but "for God's sake" echoed in every line.

II

Onegin *and the Fourth Symphony*

Alexandra Davydoff did not, however, write to her brother. She disliked Peter's wife—but this did not absolve Peter himself from guilt. Her position would need time to define itself. For another month, therefore, uncertainty was to be Peter's portion and his punishment. Afraid to come home and face the criticism, afraid to have Anatol leave him, he began, fortunately, to recover balance in spite of himself, and the measure of his recovery lay in the music written. His work was desultory. Nevertheless, what he did was good, and *Onegin* progressed slowly to the point where the first act would be ready for Anatol to carry back to Russia.

And in Moscow, two persons awaited the Italian post with eagerness; Modeste, to whom his brother's welfare meant as much as anything his life held, and that other person on the Boulevard Rojdestvensky, busy with her children and her affairs, supervising as usual the condition of the fifty begilded, beplushed rooms—but living, now, for news of Peter Ilyich.

Not once, during these dangerous times of Tchaikowsky's unbalance, did the widow cease urging him to write music. She never told him to forget his music for a while if it would not come, and to rest, be gay and talk to people. No— she said a righter thing. "Take care of your health, Peter Ilyich. I await your new music impatiently." She had no one now, to give her news of Tchaikowsky; Modeste was in

Moscow but she did not know him, and Nicholas Rubinstein was energetically touring Russia for the Red Cross — Russia still being in a state of armament; — the latest Turkish War was progressing painfully toward its painful climax, the Congress of Berlin. As soon as the widow received Tchaikowsky's letter asking about her religion, she sat down to answer at enormous length; her letter is so vague as to be almost incomprehensible. She declares herself a "realist," an "idealistic materialist," a believer in man and man's nobility. "My heaven and hell exists on earth only, and I do not regret the joy of heaven because whenever on earth I find the kind, the true, and the good, I enjoy such happiness as I doubt if heaven can give." Even music she looks upon as a physical, earthly thing. "I love music passionately; I don't deny myself this pleasure, but I never dream meaning into it. I feel a purely physical pleasure that is so delicious I regret its passing."

Peter took Nadejda's letter with him from Florence to Vienna and read it on the train. It inspired him, he said, with a great desire to answer at length, but he would not have time until he completed the first act of *Onegin*. The voices and bar-signs must be written in so Anatol could take it home. Peter Ilyich has said little about work since his departure from Russia, but the completed sketch for *Onegin* had been in his pocket when he left home, even the orchestration was definitely planned. What he had done in Switzerland was mostly routine and the composer never said much about his compositions when they reached this final stage. The rest of his letter would seem to show that Tchaikowsky understood the widow's so-called "realism" more clearly than she did herself. Or perhaps his mind, better educated than hers, was more agile at definition.

Tchaikowsky's letter is straightforward and clear and by that same token, remarkably devoid of the *clichés* and catch-words of the time. Realism, it will be remembered, was the *ism* of the day. Zola was already internationally articulate; Tolstoi, Dostoyevsky and the great romantic "realists" were about to burst upon a world prepared for them by such as the widow von Meck. Peter Ilyich writes from Vienna:

"First I must ask how you can imagine that your *profession de foi* could change my feeling toward you or diminish my fervent love and devotion to your candid, intelligent, infinitely kind self? Is it possible that a little discord in views and opinions can change our feeling for one another? Just as I, who have not changed one jot in my unending devotion to you after reading your confession, so you, I hope, won't cease feeling friendly toward me if I allow myself to object to some points in your letter.

"The intelligent man who sincerely believes in God (and there are many such), has a shield against which the blows of fate are absolutely vain. You say that you have discarded established religion, that you have found a substitute. But religion implies reconciliation with life. Have you that? I answer 'no,' because if you had, you could not have written me as you did from Como. Do you remember? That sadness, that dissatisfaction, that undefined aspiration toward an undefined ideal, that alienation from people, that capacity for finding only in music (the most idealistic of arts) the answer to vital problems—all was proof that your own religion does not bring you real spiritual peace. Do you see what I mean? I think you are in accord with my music because I too am filled with yearning for the ideal. Our conflicts are the same. Your doubts are as strong as mine; we swim on the shoreless sea of skepticism, looking for a harbor we never find. Isn't it because of this that my music means so much to you and is so near your heart?

"I think also that you are mistaken in calling yourself a realist. If by realist one means a person who hates all pretense and every insincerity in life and art, then surely you are a realist. But, keeping in mind that the true realist will never look to music for consolation and peace, as you look— I should prefer to call you an idealist. You are a realist only in the sense of not being sentimental, not liking to waste your time on the fruitless and commonplace dreams that are natural to many women. You dislike empty phrases, insincere words, idle sentimentality, but that does not mean you are a realist. And you cannot be one. Realism implies a certain narrowness of mind, an ability to satisfy very easily

113

and cheaply the desire, the quest for truth. Deprived of that thirst for knowledge, for an answer to the riddle of life, the realist denies even the necessity to search for truth, and is skeptical toward those who look for peace in religion, philosophy or art. The realist is not interested in art—music especially—because it serves as answer to a question that in his restricted being, simply does not exist. This is why I think you are mistaken in trying to enlist under the banner of realism. You say that music gives you an agreeable physical sensation, and nothing further. Permit me to protest! You deceive yourself. Is it true that you like music as I like 'Yquem' and salted cucumbers? No, you love music as music should be loved, which means that you give yourself to it with your whole soul, submitting yourself without reserve to its magic influence.

"Perhaps it is odd that I allow myself to question your own self-portrait, but my opinion is: first, that you are a very good person, and have been so from birth. You love truth because you have a deep natural affinity for it, and as deep a hatred of falsehood and evil. You are clever, and so you are a skeptic. A clever person cannot help being a skeptic—at least his life must contain a period of cruel skepticism. When natural skepticism inevitably brought you to the point of denying dogma and tradition, you began to look for a way out of the labyrinth of doubt into which you had fallen. You found some help in your pantheistic ideas of the world and in music, but full peace you did not find. Hating evil and falsehood, you walled yourself within the narrow circle of your family as a defense from the spectacle of human degradation. You do a great deal of good, your passionate love of art and nature makes doing good a necessity for a noble spirit such as yours. You help your neighbor, not as a bribe for future happiness in a heaven which you do not credit—yet do not quite deny—but simply because you are so created that you cannot resist doing good.

"Sweet, dear Nadejda Philaretovna, if it is stupid and naive of me to try to prove that you don't know yourself as well as I do, if my assumption that I can explain your nature is ridiculous and impertinent, forgive me. I can tell you that your letter brought you somehow much closer, made you even dearer to me. Oh, how I love you, and how very, very eager I am for you to know it. Alas! words are never adequate.

"Tomorrow I shall write again and try to tell you my own religious ideas. And I will explain why I can't return to Russia just now."

This is flowery language, but to the point nevertheless. Not only had Nadejda's skepticism never brought peace, but it would some day bring her the very negation of peace. "Hating evil," wrote Peter Ilyich, "you wall yourself within the narrow circle of your family as a defense against the sight of human degradation" Now Tchaikowsky, for all his refusal to assume the ordinary responsibilities of life, for all his fleeing from the consequences of his own acts, had never denied life and the world, and shut himself from it. He loved the world and was by nature extremely friendly, so much so that Moscow in late years had become a very difficult place in which to work. Friends were to Peter a temptation and because they took time and strength from his work—a dissipation. Nadejda's withholding of herself, on the other hand, was done without purpose and for its own sake; it followed rather than denied her inclination; its source lay in fear and therefore it was dangerous.

It is more than possible that Tchaikowsky sensed this, and in his letter to Nadejda, gropingly tried to express it without offense. His next letter, written a day or two after the first one, is directed rather toward himself than his friend; very evidently he had been seeking, in the midst of his trouble, to recapture the fresh unquestioning faith of his childhood—and was finding, instead, his real religion: music.

Peter Ilyich to Nadejda Philaretovna

Vienna. Dec. 5, 1877

"To continue my answer to your letter:

"I feel quite differently from you about the church. For me it has kept much of its poetic appeal. I go to Mass quite often—the liturgy of John of Chrysostom is, I think, one of the greatest of artistic creations. If one follows our Orthodox service attentively, with full understanding of every rite and symbol, one cannot remain spiritually untouched. I love the evening service too. To go on Saturday to some small ancient church, to stand in that half darkness all filled with the smoke of incense, to meditate, searching an answer to the eternal questions—Why, When, Where, and To What End: to be wakened from contemplation by the choir's—'From my youth many passions fight within me' and to abandon oneself to the magic poetry of that psalm, to feel oneself overflowing with quiet ecstasy when the King's doors open and 'Glorify the Lord from Heaven!' resounds—I love it all and it is one of my greatest joys.

"So, a part of me is bound with strong ties to the church, and part has, like you, long ago relinquished all belief in dogma . . .

"You see, my dear friend, that I am made up of contradictions, and though I have lived to a very mature age, have not settled my mind nor appeased my restless spirit either with religion or philosophy. Truly, there would be reason to go mad were it not for *music!* Music is heaven's greatest gift to man—poor wanderer in the dark. Only music can interpret, pacify, and quiet. Music is no straw to be grasped as a last resort, but a faithful friend, patroness, and comforter. For her sake only can one live on earth. In heaven perhaps there will be no music. Let us then live fully on this earth."

Nadejda's reply is spirited; this time she defines her position more coherently. Writing again from Moscow she declares herself pleased that Peter Ilyich did not treat her long letter lightly, but tried rather to comfort her by evoking some remnant of the old childhood beliefs. This, she says, is impossible; many people have tried to convert her but not only can she not agree with them, she cannot even sustain the pretense of agreement which is necessary to maintain social relationships.

"My alienation from people is a result of this difference between my ideas and the world's. . . . Yet I believe so strongly in the existence of right, of goodness and of truth (my own conception of truth) that if, like Galileo, I were tortured for it, I should say as he said when he left the torture chamber 'and yet it turns.' . . . You think, Peter Ilyich, that the rich are never really put to the test; let me remind you that the rich care even more what the public and their friends say about them than the poor do. You must remember that I have not always been wealthy; sometimes I am frightened; but my creed holds me up and I do not bow my head before injustice or even ridicule—which people fear especially."

Her letter affected Peter Ilyich profoundly. In the first place, the very sight of the envelope was reassuring; it was registered, which meant money enclosed—and Peter was down to his last cent. Five days before, Anatol had left him in Vienna and gone home to Moscow with the first act of *Eugene Onegin* in his pocket—and undoubtedly a railroad ticket bought with what remained of Nadejda's last check. Peter had travelled alone to Venice, sunk in gloom and terrified of solitude. At his hotel was waiting a telegram from Nadejda; he tore it open, expecting an order for money, but all he found was a cheerful message concerning the capture of Plevna from the Turks! Peter sent the widow a gloomy letter of thanks for her thoughtfulness in wiring him the good news—and on the same day wrote Anatol that he was reduced to his last ten *lire* and had received from Russia "nothing as yet save news of Plevna." Day after day passed, another Russian mail came without the *lettre chargée*. Kashkin wrote that all their friends had met in Rubinstein's rooms to hear the score of *Onegin,* which Taneyeff * had played on the piano. The music was marvelous, said Kashkin; it had left the hearers breathless. Even Rubinstein was enthusiastic; more than that, he was much relieved. From Clarens not a month ago, Peter had written that he was *homme fini.* . . . "Something is broken in me," he had said; "my wings are clipped and I shall never fly very high again. Now I am working hard at *Eugene Onegin* and my symphony, but I work at the instrumentation of them as though they had been conceived by someone else. . . ."

Certainly, thought Rubinstein and the friends assembled, this music of *Onegin* was not the creation of a broken man! They rushed out and telegraphed Peter Ilyich—but nothing they said could raise him from gloom. He was alone and penniless in a far country. Exactly three *lire,* he wrote Anatol, remained now in his pocket. So he wrote Nadejda

* Taneyeff, Tchaikowsky's most talented pupil, was a strict classicist, an indefatigable counterpoint scholar whose words are now only beginning to be known. Sabaneyev calls him the "Russian Brahms."

and told her how lonely he was—with never a mention of money. He was ashamed to be forever complaining; he simply could not, he declared, keep anything from her. Why, he asked (carefully keeping the only important point from her) was a man of his age so weak and silly as to sit all day in magic Venice weeping and lamenting, instead of going about enjoying himself?

"Meanwhile," the letter went on, "I have put in a second day of steady work on the symphony. Work, I hope, will little by little crowd from my heart this longing for my dear brother. How everything here reminds me of him! How painful it is to look and walk in a town where so recently we wandered side by side. He telegraphed from Kamenka so say that my wife is leaving my poor sister at last. The latter made me very happy yesterday with a long letter in which she admits that at first she could not forgive me because in process of crippling my own life, I hurt an innocent and loving woman. Now she understands there was no love, only a desire to marry. My brother-in-law writes me the same.

"I have also had the very good news that the first act of *Onegin* delighted my *confrères,* beginning with Rubinstein. I was quite fearful of their verdict, and what they say is therefore very, very pleasant. And yet I am sad, terribly sad because my brother is not with me.

> "Good-bye, dear Nadejda Philaretovna,
> "Your
> "P. Tchaikowsky

"I have not yet received your letter."

The postscript was delicate, but unavoidable. Nadejda could have no doubt as to what it referred. Nevertheless it was unnecessary; on the day he mailed it, salvation arrived. Peter Ilyich instantly wrote the good news to Anatol: "My God, what would I do without Mme Meck! Have received a letter from her with an order; she sent me enough for two months in one—an eight-page letter, again on philosophy, but much clearer and better written than the first one. May she be a thousand times blessed!"

Nadejda's long confession affected Peter Ilyich profoundly, and in more ways than the financial. He was genuinely moved by her frank and spirited avowal of religious skepticism—a skepticism which seemed only to strengthen her deep faith in mankind. Immediately he read it, Peter regretted the letter he had sent from Vienna, rebuking his friend for her personal philosophy.

"It was very naive and clumsy of me to write as I did," he apologized under date of December 17. "People are only too disposed to judge their neighbors by themselves. Because I have not the strength to evolve a sound solution of my own, because I vacillate like a weather-cock between traditional religion and the critique of reason, I simply wanted you to swim in that ocean of doubt with me. I forget there are people like Spinoza, Goethe, Kant, who can manage without religion. I can only envy those people. It seems that I am destined all my life to doubt.

"Compared with you, how weak I am, how powerless to fight! I don't say that as a pose, but as frank confession of my spiritual weakness. I am sure that from my confession you must have come to somewhat the same conclusion, and I am ashamed. With you I feel the way a small person feels in talking to a very tall one. I mean it. Since reading your letter my respect and love for you has become if possible, stronger.

"Much of what you write appeals to me. I like your proud attitude toward public opinion. When I was my normal self, before my present breakdown, I assure you that my disdain for the 'qu'en dira-t-on' was every bit as strong as yours. Now, I must confess, I have come down to average in this. Well, I am ill, which means my spirit is ill too. I too have always disliked publicity, have always been uncomfortable when too much notice was taken of me. The story of my marriage, flight, and illness must have sharpened tongues, and the thought irritates me. Unfortunately, my work as an artist necessitates publicity, and the part of an outsider, a disinterested spectator, is impossible for me."

Peter's spirits went rapidly up. Not only were his pockets filled with money and his heart with assurances of Nadejda's love, but other good fortune was on the way: Modeste and his deaf-and-dumb pupil were coming over from Russia to join him, perhaps spend the winter in Italy. Peter himself had engineered it a week ago, before leaving Vienna. The minute Anatol left him, he had sat down and written Conradi, the father of Modeste's pupil, and with the eloquence born of desperation had urged the benefits of Italian sunshine for young boys. The result, a telegram from Modi received in Venice: "You have conquered Conradi; we are coming soon."

Telling Nadejda the good news, Peter expressed himself as "unbelievably happy." And all through this man's life, happiness brought the same result; a great outpouring of music. A few moments peace, a little respite from worry with something pleasant to look forward to, and Peter Ilyich was charged with music, trembling with it, almost suffocated with the desire to get it out of himself and onto paper. Nadejda von Meck knew this; from the very first she recognized it, and posterity blesses her name accordingly. She needed Tchaikowsky's music herself and she desired the world to share it with her, but she laid upon the man no test, no trial of strength, no fabricated spur of uncertainty or fear. "I am your friend," said she, again and again. "I will give you money. You can count on me. Be at peace, Peter Ilyich; it is my privilege to befriend a great man."

Two days after Tchaikowsky had her long, kind letter with the remittance, and also the news from Modeste, he wrote Nadejda of his happiness—adding: "I am working enthusiastically on the symphony" (Tchaikowsky referred to the Fourth, the one he called "our symphony"). "The first movement is nearly ready. I can confidently declare it the best thing I ever wrote."

And the next day:

Venice, Dec. 21, 1877

"I have not only worked steadily at the orchestration of our symphony, but I am engulfed by it. Never before has any orchestral composition cost me such labor, but never before have I loved any work so much. At first I wrote simply for the sake of finishing the symphony, plowing through all difficulties—but little by little I was agreeably surprised to feel enthusiasm take possession of me, and now it is hard to stop working. Dear, sweet, Nadejda Philaretovna, perhaps I am mistaken, but I think this symphony is something out of the ordinary, the best thing I have done up to now. I am very happy that it is yours, and that hearing it, you will know how at every measure I thought of you. If it were not for you, would it ever have been finished? In Moscow, when I thought all was ended for me, I wrote on the first draft the following, which I had forgotten and only found here when I started work: 'In case of my death, I desire this paper to be given to N. Philaretovna von Meck.' I wanted you to have the manuscript of my last work. Now, thanks to you, I am not only alive and safe, but can give myself fully to work, conscious that from my pen comes something that, I think, is destined for remembrance. Yet perhaps I am wholly wrong—enthusiasm for one's latest work is natural to all artists.

"Anyway, at the moment I am in high spirits with such interesting and fascinating work to do."

To crown all this beatitude (no one can say that Peter Ilyich was not easily pleased) came further good news from home:

"Yesterday I had a most reassuring letter from Anatol. I am loved in Kamenka as before, so my mind can be quite at rest on that subject. I kept thinking they all pitied me, and it was a very bitter thought. The last letters I had were very comforting; yet what my brother has lately written gives me definite assurance that all the inhabitants of Kamenka who are so very dear to me, have forgiven and understand everything—that I acted blindly, with no malice of forethought. My wife is still there. She told my brother she wants to become a nurse and he says he will arrange it. I shan't go into detail, but everything I hear about her is balm to my conscience.

"Today I began the last half of the second movement of the symphony. The work becomes easier by the hour. In spite of interruption, I hope to finish everything for our New Year."

Meanwhile Nadejda von Meck, in Moscow, was having her own troubles. The December weather had been too much for her, she wrote; she was down with a cold, and coughed all through the concerts of the Symphony Society. Letters from Italy were slow in coming; they had to go north to Vienna then eastward to Russia. While Tchaikowsky was writing in high spirits from Venice, his Vienna letters, therefore, were only just being delivered to Nadejda in her huge bedroom on the Boulevard Rojdestvensky. After the philosophic letters, others came from Vienna, entirely concerned with music and musical criticism. Tchaikowsky was never at his best as critic; moreover, from the vantage point of posterity, out-dated musical criticism is apt to make amazing reading.

These long letters concerning music and philosophy and the good life were salutary for Peter Ilyich; perhaps the widow knew it and asked her questions with a purpose—that in replying, her correspondent might take momentary leave of his personal troubles. After Vienna, Tchaikowsky did not permit himself to be alone again but sent to Russia for his servant, Alexis Safronov, and to everyone's surprise, that stolid and highly unimaginative person found his way from Moscow without mishap. But two weeks in Venice was more than enough for Peter Ilyich, even with Alexis for companion—the two went everywhere together. His only consolation had been his good health, due in no small part to his symphony. "Working on it cheered me greatly. When I knew Modeste was coming from Russia and when I plunged into work, I was suddenly at peace. Three movements are now ready. I don't know how long this enthusiasm for my latest work will last, but just now I look upon these three movements as the crown of all my musical efforts. Can you read between the lines to whom thanks are due that I could begin it? Must I tell you that those thanks are endlessly, deeply sincere? Better to say nothing when a thing is so obvious."

In Milan, Tchaikowsky heard Marchetti's opera, *Ruis Blas*. The music was agreeable, but the fat, ungraceful performers made him fear for his own newly completed opera, *Eugene Onegin*.

"Where shall I find Tatiana, as Pushkin imagined her and as I tried to portray her in music? Where is the artist that can even approach the ideal Onegin, that cold dandy, socially correct to the marrow of his bones? Where can we find Lensky, an eighteen-year-old youth with thick curls, with the impulsive and original manners of a young poet like Schiller? How Pushkin's charming picture will be vulgarized when transformed to the stage with its routine, its stupid traditions, with veteran players taking the part of sixteen-year-old-girls and beardless youths. The moral is: Writing instrumental music is far more satisfactory, has fewer disappointments. How I agonized over the production of my operas, especially *Vakoula*!"

From Milan, Tchaikowsky wandered down to San Remo to await the coming of Modeste and his boy pupil. He had the usual hideous time trying to settle down; finding himself at first in a big, fashionable hotel, he sent Nadejda a shocking list of prices for room and board. Furthermore, on going down to dinner late, what was Peter's horror to run into at least a hundred elaborately dressed guests coming out of the dining-room. They all seemed to know one another and they looked him over from head to foot with a superciliousness indubitably British.

Peter fled the British and ran about San Remo looking for rooms; Alexis was less than useless in these crises. A Frenchmen urged the two to come—at huge expense—to his house; as inducement he said he was a political refugee, "like Rochefort, condemned to death." All this threw the composer—himself a refugee—into frantic gloom and homesickness.

"Why is it," cried he to Nadejda: "that the simple Russian landscape, a walk in summer through Russian fields and forest or on the steppes at evening, can affect me so that I have lain on the ground numb, overcome by a wave of love for nature, by the indescribably sweet and intoxicating atmosphere that drifted over me from the forest, the steppe, the little river, the faraway village, the modest little church —in short, all that makes the poor Russian natal landscape. Why...?"

Yet home, Peter said, was closed to him. And when at last he found a place to live in San Remo, he laughed at his own misery: "I am like the old woman in Pushkin's story—the more reasons I have to be happy, the more miserable I become! But now that you are my friend, dear Nadejda Philaretovna, may I not tell you all, all that takes place in my poor sick soul?"

There is but one answer to that question, and Peter Ilyich knows it. Never, never can he confess to Nadejda the deep, basic sickness that underlies all his misery.

12

A battle with the Chief. Onegin *completed.*
Nadejda inquires about love

Shortly before he left Russia in the autumn, Tchaikowsky had been appointed musical delegate to represent his country at the Paris Exposition which was to begin on January 1st, 1878. Well aware that he was nervously and temperamentally unequal to such a position, Peter had put off the onus of a definite refusal by saying he could not afford to go. And now, in San Remo, four months later, he received notice that the Minister of Finance had appointed him delegate at a salary of a thousand francs a month, that his country was proud to afford him the honor of such an appointment, and that he was to proceed to Paris immediately and stay there eight months!

Had he been ordered hung at sunrise, Peter Ilyich could not have been more dismayed. Babylon, it would be—he cried to Nadejda, and he would be a madman in Babylon. "The very thought of appearing before the Chief, of meeting all the musicians, dragging myself to dinners and musical soirées, having no time to write (my only weapon against my malady) makes me ill; it is beyond my strength." A huge questionnaire accompanied the official letter from the Russian Government; how many concerts would Tchaikowsky arrange? What quartet societies, what choral societies would appear?

Was *Onegin* to be laid aside for eight months, and the Fourth Symphony? To put them by for eight months, now at the height of creation, would be to kill them forever. What could Rubinstein be thinking of, to urge such a plan—for it must be Rubinstein, pertinent and definite as always, who had suggested the very pertinent and definite thousand francs a month.

Nor was it a help to realize that Russia's political position in Europe was extremely unfavorable. Victimized by England in the person of Disraeli, by Germany in the person of Bismarck, Russia had not yet begun to make friends with France. In Paris they would hiss the Russian bear as they had hissed it before. For this very reason, Peter knew it to be his patriotic duty to advertise Russian music abroad; up to now, only the brothers Rubinstein had advertised it. But he could never do it. He knew he could never do it.

For three days therefore, Peter roamed the bright San Remo streets in a torment of indecision. The fact that he recognized his indecision as part of his nature, did not decrease his discomfort. It was difficult for the world to guess —even difficult for Rubinstein who knew him so well—that this man, so charming at a dinner party, endured tortures of fatigue and self-reproach after every social gathering. To Anatol he wrote now:

"Tolia, I have hidden something from you. Since the day you left me in Vienna, every evening before bed I drink several glasses of brandy, and during the day I drink a lot too. I can't live without it. I am calm only when a bit tipsy. I have come to depend upon this secret drinking, so that the mere sight of the little brandy bottle I keep always by me gives me pleasure. I write my letters better when I have had a drink. It is a proof I am not yet well. In Paris, to keep going I should have to be drinking from morning till night. My hope lies in Modeste. A quiet life with someone I love and work to do is what I need. In brief, for God's sake forgive me, but I cannot go to Paris. I should be worthless there, both to myself and others."

On the same day—but omitting all mention of the bottle, Peter wrote Nadejda:

"Whether I am being cowardly or wise, I see clearly that I

cannot go to Paris. If you or my brother had seen my condition today, you would have said, 'Stay where you are.' Today I shall answer officially, saying I am ill and asking them to name another delegate. Now, until I have your approval and my brothers' and sister's, I shall be in torment. Another thing . . . if I had accepted the position I could have lived entirely or at least partly without your help. And however kind you are, however rich you may be, the sum you send is too large at the present rate of exchange (which will now go lower due to England's mean tricks). It will torment me that I am taking too much from you . . . Everything does; I have become sickly suspicious. Perhaps I shouldn't say that; please forgive it. I swear it has never for a moment occurred to me that you could regret the money. No, absolutely no! Yet I must do all I can to protect such a kind and generous friend from expense. . . ."

Rubinstein himself was touring Russia for the Red Cross and knew nothing of this insubordination; never dreaming of a refusal, he had not even written Peter Ilyich. But as soon as the Moscow Conservatory group had the news they began telegraphing San Remo in remonstrance. Karl Albrecht intimated that the Chief would be furious. So Peter sat down and wrote Rubinstein a friendly enough letter, reminding him that a man who even in health was incurably shy and no organizer, could hardly be a credit to his country in the guise of musical ambassador. Then he wrote Albrecht.

"I shall do nothing whatever to advertise my wares. If they wish to play and sing my music, let them; if they don't, very well. I spit, spit, spit upon it all!!! Must I tell you again that if I were rich I would live in a desert, rarely visiting even Moscow, which I love deeply? In August I shall take up my professorship again (which I might say I loathe with all my heart). I shall live out my life in the White City" (Moscow) "in quiet and seclusion, with a few intimate friends—you among them. And until my last breath I shall spit upon the world, its opinion, its fame and its honors.

"One thing I know from bitter experience: no man can

force his life into a mold contrary to his real nature. And all my nature, each fibre, each cell, protests against the post of delegate."

And now the Chief returned to Moscow from his Red Cross tour, and now the thunder began to roll in earnest. He wasted no time in writing Peter Ilyich, nor did he spare anyone's feelings. Blaming Tchaikowsky bitterly for his refusal to go to Paris, Rubinstein accused him of cowardice, laziness and a willingness to sit in the sun with the widow's bankroll in his pocket.

It can be imagined with what feelings Peter Ilyich read these words. In the first place, the Chief's accusations were far from just; since his departure from Russia, Tchaikowsky had not only worked hard but had accomplished much. The first act of *Onegin* finished, the Fourth Symphony completed and both works delivered to Moscow. And the worst of it was that the Chief was evidently trying to do a little spade work over on the Boulevard Rojdestvensky. Peter, with Rubinstein's letter in one hand, sat down and wrote Anatol with the other:

January 20, 1878, San Remo

"Last evening I had a disturbing letter from Mme Meck, filled more than ever with expressions of affection but complaining of something unpleasant that has happened. Without actually saying who is responsible for her feeling so badly, she writes in a bantering sort of way, bedecking Rubinstein with sarcastic phrases that, combined with other hints, lead me to conclude it was surely Rubinstein who offended her. From what she says I even understand that R. went to see her and talked about me. Comparing what she says with his letter, my guess is that R. tried to persuade her to stop sending me money, telling her I am growing lazy, etc. A nice gentleman! Fooh, what a bounder!"

Raging up and down his room in San Remo, fortifying himself with wine, Peter Ilyich got ready to tell the Chief what he thought of him.

To Nicholas Rubinstein

January 26, 1878

". . . As to Mme Meck, you are cruelly mistaken concerning her character and her relations with me. Secondly, your reproach for my accepting her help, even supposing it was the result of any action of yours—I should find unfitting. It would be useless to tell you the long history of my connection with Mme Meck. I ask only one thing—that no one but you and Karlusha (Albrecht) shall suspect anything. It would be extremely disagreeable to have it come back to her that through me, someone knows of our relationship.

"I must add that your *insinuations* about her, regardless of your friendly intentions, for which I am very grateful, can only harm my relations with her and disturb her very much, as from remarks of yours she has concluded you know of my past association with her, which she wanted to keep the greatest secret. . . . In regard to that lady, I must tell you that never has kindness, delicacy, generosity, and infinite tolerance been united so fully in anyone. I owe her not only life but the ability to continue work, which for me is more precious than life. I am indignant that you understand her as little as you do. Certainly she is not erratic. To me she is simply the eternally kind hand of Providence. One must know her as I know her now, to believe there are people so unbelievably kind and trusting. My role in regard to her is not to be envied. I simply exploit her kindness—an agonizing realization, were it not that she knows how to pacify and stop the pricks of my conscience."

After heaving these letters into the Russian mail system, Peter Ilyich felt better, and said so to his friends. He felt even more cheerful next day when Nadejda's letter came—during all this time he had not heard from her concerning the Exposition.

"My dear, sweet friend," she wrote; "please don't let the fury of the Thunder-hurler distress you. Think only of your health and peace, take care of yourself, because that is your duty to society as a composer and a man who gives delight to others—and to your country as our best representative of ability and talent. It was not worth your while to waste yourself on such a thing as the Exposition; you cannot stand the work of a hunting-dog; you would have excited yourself God knows how much, and that you have no right to do. Thank God you refused. Nor is it worthwhile to quarrel with Rubinstein. How can he understand you? If he becomes unbearable, it is always easy to say farewell to him. He and the poor Conservatory will be the losers; not you, certainly. You will be welcomed anywhere, *à bras ouverts*."

The widow went on to joke a little about Rubinstein, but no amount of ridicule on the part of Nadejda could persuade Peter Ilyich to look lightly upon the Chief's anger. He waited anxiously for Rubinstein's reply to his own furious letter—and was surprised to have his antagonist turn the other cheek. Rubinstein answered with words of peace, even of apology. Said this shrewd scion of a shrewd family, "The trouble is, Peter Ilyich, I haven't the knack of expressing myself properly in writing."

Tchaikowsky replied in kind, and all was seemingly forgiven. But no amount of mutual apology nor effusion of friendliness could hide the fact that the relationship of these two men was altered, now and forever.

And while Rubinstein in Moscow is plotting to turn defeat into victory, while Nadejda in the same cold white city is coughing her way through luxurious rooms, overheated in this January weather—Peter Ilyich in Italy is hurrying northward from San Remo to meet Modeste and his young pupil, due in Milan on the evening train from Russia. "To see my brother and his sweet boy was light and warmth to my soul," he wrote Nadejda. All night the two sat up, talking as only Russians can talk, inexhaustibly, until the pale early sun filtered through the shutters.

Next day they planned festivities in the city, but at three in the afternoon Milan heard the news of Victor Emanuel's death, and the theatres were closed.

"I was very sorry to hear of the King's death," Tchaikowsky's letter continued, "but thanks to that sad event, I was able to finish what was yet undone in the symphony,* which

* The Fourth, which the composer was now orchestrating.

I had brought with me especially to get a metronome in Milan and mark the exact tempi. After working all evening and part of the night I was able next morning to wrap up a completed symphony and send it to Moscow. So our symphony is now flying at full steam to Rubinstein. With the title I put the dedication, 'To my best friend.' What will the story of that symphony be? Will it live long after the author has disappeared from the earth, or will it fall quickly into the abyss of forgotten things? I don't know, but I know that at the moment, with a blindness perhaps natural to parents, I am not capable of seeing the defects of my youngest child. Also I am sure that in structure and form it marks a step in my development, which goes very slowly. In spite of my mature age" (Peter was thirty-eight) "I am far from reaching the limit of my capacity. Perhaps that is why I value life so highly."

Now that he had Modeste, everything pleased Peter Ilyich; even Rubinstein and Moscow lost their terrors. The little party went to Genoa and looked at pictures; there was no use, Peter wrote, in his trying to like pictures. But Modia liked them and Modia, said Peter proudly, *knew* about them, too! For the moment, Peter Ilyich is proud of Modia, of Modia's pupil, of himself. "My sweet and dear friend," he writes Nadejda, "I owe you all my happy moments. . . ."

And in Moscow the widow von Meck is delighted, that "our symphony" is finished, and she hastens to send a money order for the printing. Would Peter Ilyich care to publish the symphony abroad as well as in Russia? "Do as you think best," she finishes. "I should like to promote your works abroad; I should like to show the world what good things we have in Russia."

Fifteen hundred francs fell out of the envelope and the brothers Tchaikowsky sighed with relief. Last quarter's allowance, it seems, had long since disappeared—had "dissipated itself," is the way Peter expressed it in writing. In fact, the four of them were living on what remained of Modeste's monthly salary from Kolia's father.

The conditions under which a man recovers and maintains health are as authentic an indication of his essential character as can be found: for Peter Ilyich, these conditions were quiet days devoted to creative work, as now; and with nature accessible and a brother at hand, this was a life as nearly ideal as the man would ever know. The little party of four returned from Genoa to San Remo and settled down, the time passing so quietly, wrote Peter, that it was hard to tell one day from another.

Up in the hills behind San Remo was the little town of Cola, nearly two hours walk, and Peter Ilyich one afternoon followed the Cola path, meeting not so much as a peasant gathering olives. He went briskly and when he was tired, rested under a tree, gazing down through silvery olives to a glimpse of incredibly blue sea. . . . "It was a magnificent quiet," he wrote; he had felt a sudden uprush of happiness, an ecstasy and a gratitude which immediately craved to communicate itself to Nadejda. So Peter got up and started home to write his friend, and what did he come upon but a whole glade of violets! He was so pleased, he said. He had been buying them on the streets for some time but had not been able to find one growing; he had picked as many as he could carry. . . .

Back on the Boulevard Rojdestvensky, in her boudoir over the city street where sleighs slid silently by on the hard-packed snow, Nadejda von Meck opened a crinkly envelope and six bits of fragrance fell into her lap. "They will remind you," she read in the beloved handwriting — those precise, thin strokes, delicate as the stems in her hand — "of the South, the sun, sea, warmth. . . . There in the woods I was completely happy, and immediately it was very necessary to tell you about it."

As to Peter Ilyich, he was getting well, and to be healthy in exile is to be restless. On the 13th of February, 1878, he mailed a completed opera to Moscow: *Eugene Onegin* was finished. On the same day he wrote Nadejda; ought he to go home now and take up his duties at the Conservatory? Was it possible that Rubinstein had been right in accusing him of laziness? Was he wrong to use Nadejda Philaretovna's money to remain abroad and rest?

"In short, I believe I could again take up my old occupations, but it would be very hard. I want very, very, very much to have more rest and to return in September completely refreshed, having forgotten—as far as one could forget—the unhappy event that darkened my life half a year ago. Truly there is a queer contradiction in my appealing to you thus for advice. I ask you for the truth, begging you not to let other considerations confuse your judgment as to what is my duty—and in the same breath you can feel me saying, 'For God's sake, don't demand my return to Moscow because I should be very unhappy.'

"Yes, I want you, my dear friend to tell me once more that there is nothing harmful in my rest, in my 'idleness,' and that I am not wrong in using your money to live here. Only now do I quite appreciate the tremendous benefit of these four months' isolation—the sojourn in a foreign land, which in the beginning was sometimes hard, making even Rome seem unbearably irksome, but which now quite satisfies my unconquerable desire to live away from everyday contact with people. Anyway, I shall not permit myself to give in to my *far niente* for too long. Believe me, I have an instinctive distaste for idleness in the real sense, and if one can call the way I now live idle (because I work for myself and not for others, to satisfy my own desire to write) it will not last long.

"I shall not hide from you, precious friend, that I feel a great joy today in the knowledge that I have finished two big compositions in which I think I have gone ahead, and very much ahead. The rehearsals of the symphony will start soon after you receive this letter. N. Ph., if you are quite well then, won't you find time to go to one of the rehearsals?

"As to the opera" (*Onegin*), "I am actually glad the Conservatory has postponed its performance. Next year they can give it in full, and in the meantime they can learn it.

"I am in a most rosy mood, happy to have finished the opera, happy that spring is coming, happy to be well, free and safe from people and social life, and most of all, happy that I have such strong supports in life as your friendship, my brothers' love, and the knowledge that I have the chance to perfect myself in my career. If conditions are favorable—and today I want to believe they will be—I can leave a sound memory behind me. I hope this is not an illusion, but an honest estimate of my powers.

"Give Milochka a tender kiss on the forehead, my friend. Thank you for everything, everything.

"Your
"P. Tch."

One senses in the words of Peter Ilyich more than health —as though his pen were borne along by that extra life, that upsurge of unreasonable joy which is the privilege and the birthright of genius.

13

The Fourth Symphony is performed. Peter gives it a program

Reading in the guidebook that full-blooded, excitable people should not live in a place where the colors were bright and the air stimulating, the Tchaikowsky brothers looked at each other, nodded simultaneously and ordered Alexis to pack their bags. Florence, no doubt, would have a more tranquil shadiness. . . .

Peter was resting now, for a week or two. *Onegin* and the Fourth Symphony were gone from under his hand and he was not ready for another big work. On the 22nd of February, he went alone to his room, and sitting down, watch in hand, awaited the moment when, hundreds of miles away, the trumpet notes of his symphony would sound the motif that the composer himself had characterized as the relentless voice of fate.

On that day, under Nicholas Rubinstein's baton, the orchestra of the Moscow Conservatory gave the symphony its first performance, and on that day Nadejda braved snow and ice and cold and illness to make her way alone to the balcony of the concert hall, where she might sit unseen and unmolested by friends. *To my best friend* was written on the symphony, but only one person in the audience knew who the best friend was—although that suave gentleman with the baton could have ventured a guess.

It was two days before the composer received any slightest news of the reception accorded his favorite child:

To Nadejda Philaretovna

Florence, Feb. 24, 1878

"I received your telegram yesterday morning, my dear friend, and it gave me unspeakable pleasure. I was uneasy, first, that your health might interfere with your being at the concert, second, that you might not like the symphony. Even if you had not liked it much, it was very possible you would have sent me congratulations just out of kindness, but from the tone and wording of the telegram, I see clearly that you are satisfied with what was written for you. In my deepest heart I am convinced it is the best thing I have written. It seems a little queer to me that I have not had any word of the symphony from my Moscow friends. The score was sent more than a month and a half ago. With your telegram I had another, signed by Rubinstein and all the rest, and saying that the symphony was perfectly performed — not a word as to its quality. Perhaps that is to be understood. Thank you for the news of my beloved child's success, and for the cordial words of the telegram. In imagination I was present at the concert. I calculated the exact minute when the introductory phrase would resound, and all the details followed as I tried to imagine what impression the music would make. The first part (the most complicated and the best) probably seemed long to many, and not quite easy to understand the first time."

Tchaikowsky waited a week, two weeks, and still no word —after the telegram—from his Moscow friends. He walked the streets of Florence, alone or with Modeste, trying to conceal his chagrin from his brother and from himself.

At last came a letter from Nadejda, a huge, fat roll of paper that answered eagerly all the questions Peter Ilyich, writing a month ago from San Remo, had asked concerning his future. Page after page, assuring him of her undying friendship, begging him not even to think of returning to the Conservatory for a long, long time, beseeching him to accept from her the money to live.

"In my long life I have come to the conclusion that if a genius is to develop and gain inspiration, he must have security from material want. Without it he will deteriorate, stagnate, grow weak, whining, helpless. And you know, my wonderful friend, how precious your talent is to me, how I long to take care of it. In your music I hear myself, my moods, the echo of my feelings, my thoughts, my grief. So how could I *not* take care of you? We are far apart only in distance; but for that we should be nearly one person; we feel the same about everything, usually even at the same time."

Friendly words, and reassuring—but was Nadejda not going to so much as mention the symphony? Surely she had heard the performance; why then did not her letter begin with news of it? Why was not her first word concerned with this thing that meant more to Peter than life itself?

"The public received your symphony very well," he read at last, "especially the *Scherzo*." (This was the *pizzicato* movement for which the composer had said he had great hopes.) "Applause was great and at the end they called for you. It must have been Rubinstin who came out; I didn't see because I had started to go out. But I believe the composition was somewhat marred by a poor performance; the orchestra was worse than I ever heard it. Usually they give a good enough performance, but this time surely they did not rehearse enough."

Faint praise this, from a lady whose natural style was furiously extravagant. But if Tchaikowsky was disappointed over her first response he did not show it, but replied eagerly. With Nadejda's help he could, he wrote, return to the Conservatory next autumn and to his teaching—not as a hateful chain to drag but as something he had himself chosen.

"Once and forever, N. Ph., I tell you that I will accept from you without false shame anything you want to offer me. I know that you are wealthy, but wealth is relative. A large ship needs large waters. You have great means, but because of that, great regular expenses.

"Your letter today gave me such joy, my priceless Nadejda Philaretovna! How immeasurably happy I am that the symphony pleased you, that my music entered your heart and you experienced the feelings that filled me in writing it!

"You ask if the symphony has a definite program. Ordinarily, when asked that question concerning a symphonic work, I answer, 'No, none whatever.' And in truth it is not an easy question. How can one express those vague feelings which pass through one during the writing of an instrumental work which in itself has no definite subject? It is a purely lyrical process, a musical confession of the soul that, filled with the experiences of a life-time, pours itself out through sound, just as the lyric poet pours himself out in verse. The difference is that music is an incomparably more delicate and powerful language in which to express the thousand vari-colored moments of the spiritual life. Usually the seed of a future musical creation germinates instantaneously and most unexpectedly. If the soil is eager, if there is a disposition to work, that seed takes root with amazing power and speed, appears above ground as a little stalk which puts forth leaves and branches and finally, flowers. This simile is as near as I can come to a description of the creative process. If the seed appears at a favorable moment, the main difficulty is past. The rest grows of itself.

"Words are vain to tell you the boundless joy that comes over me when a new idea is conceived and begins to take definite shape. One forgets everything; one is a madman, trembling and quivering in every organ, with scarcely time to outline the sketches, so rapidly does one idea pursue another. One thing however is indispensable: the main idea of the piece, together with a general outline of the separate parts, must not be found through searching but must simply appear—a result of that supernatural, incomprehensible and never-analysed power called inspiration.

'But I digress from your question. Our symphony has a program definite enough to be expressed in words; to you alone I want to tell—and can tell—the meaning of the work as a whole and in part. You will understand I attempt to do so only along general lines. The Introduction is the germ of the entire symphony, the idea upon which all else depends:

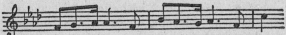

"This is 'Fatum,' the inexorable force that prevents our hopes of happiness from being realized, that watches jealously lest our felicity should become full and unclouded — it is Damocles' sword, hanging over the head in constant, unremitting spiritual torment. It is unconquerable, inescapable. Nothing remains but to submit to what seems useless unhappiness:

"Despair and discontent grow stronger, sharper. Would it not be wiser to turn from reality and sink into dreams?

"Oh, joy, at last the sweet and tender dream appears! Some bright human image passes, beckoning me on:

"How delicious and how remote, now, the distressing first theme of the Allegro. Little by little, dream possesses the soul. Forgotten is sadness and despair. Happiness is here! But no, this was only a dream, and 'Fatum' awakes us:

"So life itself is a persistent alternation of hard reality with evanescent dreams and clutchings at happiness. There is no haven. Sail on that sea until it encompass you and drown you in its depths. This, approximately, is the program of the First Movement.

"The Second Movement expresses another phase of suffering. It is the melancholy that comes in the evening when we sit alone, and weary of work, we try to read, but the book falls from our hand. Memories crowd upon us. How sweet these recollections of youth, yet how sad to realize they are gone forever. One regrets the past, yet one would not begin life anew, one is too weary. It is easier to be passive and to look back. One remembers many things—happy moments when the young blood ran hot and life fulfilled all our desire. There were hard times too, irreparable losses, but they are very far away. It is sad and somehow sweet to sink thus into the past.

"The Third Movement expresses no definite feelings, rather it is a succession of capricious arabesques, those intangible images that pass through the mind when one has drunk wine and feels the first touch of intoxication. The soul is neither gay nor sad. The mind is empty, the imagination has free rein and has begun, one knows not why, to draw strange designs. Suddenly comes to mind the picture of a drunken peasant, a brief street song is heard. Far off, a military procession passes. The pictures are disconnected, like those which float through the mind when one is falling asleep. They are out of touch with reality; they are wild and strange.

"The Fourth Movement: If you truly find no joy within yourself, look for it in others. Go to the people. See—they know how to make the best of their time, how to give themselves up to pleasure! A peasant festival is depicted. No sooner do you forget yourself in this spectacle of others' joy, than the merciless Fatum reappears to remind you of yourself. But the others are indifferent to you; they do not so much as turn their heads toward your loneliness and sadness. Oh, how gay they are! And how fortunate to be ruled by such simple, immediate feelings! Here one sees the existence of simple, deep joys; enter into them and life will be bearable.

"This, dear friend, is all I can tell you about the symphony. Of course what I have said is neither clear nor complete. This follows from the very nature of instrumental music, which does not submit to detailed analysis. 'Where words cease, there music begins,' as Heine said."

A day or two later Tchaikowsky sent Nadejda another letter from Florence, writing at night, with only a bare post-scriptum mention of the symphony—a sad little letter, breathing homesickness and nostalgia.

"How terribly far we are from each other! You in winter, I in a country where the trees are already green and where I can write this letter at an open window at eleven in the evening. And yet I think of that winter not with aversion but with delight. I love our winter, long and steady. One waits and waits for Lent to come, and with it the first signs of spring. What a miracle is our spring, with its suddenness, its rich power! I love it when the streets run torrents of melted snow and the air is vital and vigorous. With what affection one greets the first green grass! How one rejoices at the coming of the rook, and after, the larks and the others, foreign summer visitors! Here the spring comes on slow feet, little by little—one cannot say exactly when she has arrived. And I cannot be moved by the sight of green grass when I have had it before my eyes in December and January.

"Do you remember I wrote you from Florence about the boy I heard one evening on the street, whose beautiful voice so affected me? Three days ago, to my great joy I found the boy again, he sang for me again *Perchè tradir mi, perchè lasciar mi*, and I was in ecstasy. I don't remember when a simple popular song has had such effect on me. This time he introduced me to a new Florentine song, so charming that I want to find him again and make him sing it several times, so that I can write down the words and music. (It is about one Pimpinella; what does it mean? I don't know, but will surely find out.)

"One must visit Italy to see its absolute pre-eminence in the vocal art. At every step one hears beautiful voices in the streets—this very minute a very pretty voice in the distance is singing, with open throat, a song in a high chest tenor. Even if the voice is not lovely, every Italian is a naturally good singer. They have the right *émission de voix* and the art of singing from the chest, not through the throat and nose, as with us.

"Imagine, I haven't had one word from my Moscow friends about my symphony! It is very strange."

In Florence, that year of 1878, after shipping the Fourth Symphony and *Onegin* to Moscow, Tchaikowsky wrote many short piano pieces, dedicating them to Modeste, his companion at the time. One of them, Number 12, was a Venetian melody that had been sung under his window during that lonely week in Venice just after Anatol had left him to return to Russia. To Anatol he dedicated five songs published with *Pimpinella*, among them the still popular *Don Juan's Serenade*.

Florence in March was beautiful and brilliant, but it was no place, Peter wrote Nadejda, for a composer who wanted to work. The street songs were lovely and so were the bells, but other sounds were not. He had tried to write systematically, working on short pianoforte pieces, but English ladies in the hotel "played eternally on the piano, across the streets someone boomed exercises on the trombone and in the streets they screamed as well as sang." Restful in a musician's memory loomed the high still mountains of Switzerland; would not little Kolia also—Peter asked his brother— profit by a change to Clarens?

Modeste was never difficult to persuade; a day or so later —March 7th—the four of them took the night train for Geneva and after an anxious trip with a tired small boy, arrived at Clarens, Tchaikowsky's old retreat. Here they found winter; snow was underfoot and in the air, but from the moment they stepped from the train, the stillness delighted Peter Ilyich. At the hotel, mail was waiting from Russia; Peter glanced eagerly through it for the handwriting of his Moscow musical colleagues—and did not find it. He waited a few days longer and then wrote Nadejda:

To Nadejda Philaretovna

Mar. 12th, 1878

"This is going to be a confession. I am deeply chagrined, offended, and amazed by the incomprehensible silence of all my friends concerning the symphony. I have had no news except from you, and indirectly, through Kotek, who told me that his friend Porubinofsky, a pupil of the Conservatory, was very much pleased with it. I expected this symphony would at least interest my musical friends, even if it did not stir and move them. I expected them to understand how impatiently and greedily I awaited sympathetic criticism, and that each would describe in detail his impressions, as you have, my dear friend. I needed it very much. And, imagine, not one word except a telegram to say the symphony was performed perfectly—an assurance, as I see from your last letter, that was not true!

"Again you appear as my consoler. If it were not for your friendship, which repays me a hundred times for the neglect of my colleagues, I should be disappointed beyond words—desperate. You understand me, dearly loved friend. You understand that, having written a big composition into which I put my whole soul, I knew that of the crowd which heard the composition there would be only a few who would be able to appreciate it even in part. One consoles oneself with the thought that friends will understand, cheer one, appreciate. And then, not a word, not one word of congratulation from them. It is painful and very mortifying.

"I wrote you about the boy singer whose wonderful voice in Florence touched me so. I heard him once more on the eve of my departure and wrote down the words and music of a little song, which I send you, with my accompaniment. Is it not a sweet little song? And what queer words!"

Nadejda's reply makes one glad that Peter Ilyich had such a friend, and glad also that he had confided in her. At last she seemed to understand his real grief at Moscow's silence concerning the symphony.

Nadejda to Peter Ilyich

Moscow, March 18, 1878

"I had just sat down to write you, my sweet, beloved friend, when your letter came enclosing the song, *Pimpinella*. Thank you, my dear, for that lovely thing. . . . I quite sympathize with your distress at the neglect of your friends, my sweet, my dear, because I know that the greatest sorrow can come not from enemies, but from those we count as friends. I understand how painful it is, but to tell the truth I did not expect anything better from any of them, and if what the lower hierarchy thinks can give you pleasure, I can tell you the opinion of one of the cleverest, most mature and ardent lovers of music, your pupil Pahulsky" (The same Pahulsky who afterward married Nadejda's daughter, Julia), "whom I see very often and of whose sincerity and depth of feeling I can judge absolutely. He is mad about your symphony. For several days he could speak of nothing else, think of nothing else, every five minutes he would sit at the piano and play it. He has a very good musical memory, and I owe to him my close acquaintance with our symphony because he plays it constantly to me now. He has a real passion for music and was an admirer of Wagner before hearing your symphony, but after the first rehearsal he came to me in such a state of excitement that I thought something had happened to him. 'That is music!' he said, 'What is Wagner now, and why do *we* all exist on earth?'

"From what he says I see that you are mistaken, dear friend, in thinking that you have not known how to inspire your pupils with love for their work, because I see with what respect and gratitude Pahulsky remembers your course. He says that a word of yours even in rebuke, meant ten times more than the orations he hears now. With what enthusiasm he tells how you would come into the class and before starting, sit down at the piano and strike several chords. 'But, my God, what chords they were!' he says. And I hear from him that the greater number of pupils miss you very much. You see, my dear, those that envy you are the only ones that do not love you; so be indifferent to the neglect of the Moscow friends. They are friends as far as their natures permit them—one cannot expect more. Your symphony certainly pleased them, it could not be otherwise, but envy prevents their expressing it.

"As to the public, certainly it is hard for it to understand such a composition immediately. Pahulsky tells me that in the intermission, before the symphony was played, a gentleman, unknown to him, not of the Conservatory, explained to a gathering around him that it was doubtful if the public would like this composition because they could not understand it. If it was clear to me on hearing it the first time, it is because I know by heart the character of your creations. I am not disturbed or confused by the suspensions and tied notes, and organ points because I have grown accustomed to them, and the daring sequences, the wonderful harmonies, thrill me before others have got accustomed to these new sounds. Yet they too, will someday appreciate it."

No sooner had she mailed this than Nadejda received Tchaikowsky's letter from Florence, explaining the emotional program of the Fourth Symphony. She was delighted. What Peter said was proof that in writing this music he had been moved by true inward inspiration, the quality for which above all other qualities she revered him as a composer. Only the other day, some musicians had tried to convince her there was no connection between the notes of a symphony and the inner feelings of the man who wrote it. The whole thing, said they, was a matter of mechanics, of technique.

Tchaikowsky's answer to Nadejda is in his best vein. How well he himself knew that he was at his best only when his "specialty," as he called it, was concerned.

To Nadejda Philaretovna

Clarens, Mar. 17, 1878

"I have your letter, my beloved friend, and read it with the greatest pleasure. Let me answer your questions in order. It is very pleasant to talk with you about my method of creation. I have never before revealed these mysterious manifestations of the spirit—partly because not many have requested it, partly because those that asked did not inspire me with the desire to answer. But it is very good to describe the process of composition to you because you are unusually sensitive to my music. Never has anyone, except perhaps my brothers, made me as happy as you with your sympathy. If you only knew how precious that sympathy is to me, and how little I am spoiled by it!

"Do not believe those who tried to persuade you that musical creation is a cold, purely mental exercise. Only the music that pours from the depths of an artistic soul, moved by inspiration, can touch and take possession of the hearer. There is no doubt that even the greatest musical genius has sometimes worked unwarmed by inspiration. It is a guest that does not come on first invitation. In the meantime one must work, and an honest artist cannot sit with his hands crossed because he is not inclined to compose. If one waits for inclination instead of advancing to meet it, one easily drifts into laziness and apathy. One must hold fast and have faith, and inspiration will come.

"You ask how I work in regard to orchestration. I never compose in the abstract—never does the musical idea come to me except with suitable exterior form. So I find the musical thought simultaneously with the orchestration. When I wrote the *Scherzo* of our symphony, I imagined it just as you heard it. It is impossible if not performed *pizzicato*. If played with the bow it would lose everything. It would be a soul without a body and all its charm would disappear.

"As to the Russian element in my compositions, it is true that I often begin to write with the intention of using one or another popular song. Sometimes (as in the *Finale* of our symphony) this happens of itself, quite unexpectedly. As to the Russian element in general in my music—the relation to the popular songs in melody and harmony—I grew up in a peaceful spot, saturated from earliest childhood with the miraculous beauty of Russian popular song, so that I love to the point of passion every expression of the Russian spirit. In short, I am a Russian through and through.

I feel perfectly well today and very happy; my work was very satisfactory. Beside the small pieces I am writing a sonata for the piano and a violin concerto, and hope to go home well-provided with sketches. Be assured that I shall be very careful in my choice of words for the Romances," (songs) "and I hope you will be pleased.

"I love you without end,

"Your

"P. Tch."

14

The Violin Concerto. Peter defends his Symphony

And now a Russian visitor arrived in Clarens—a welcome one this time. Kotek, the young violinist who had once been go-between for Nadejda and Peter Ilyich, and who had lost his position in Nadejda's household by gossiping about the messages entrusted to him. Peter had pled his cause with the widow in vain; now the brothers welcomed the young man joyfully, and the mountain-top resounded to much sonata-playing—nor is it unlikely that Kotek's violin was help and inspiration in the first sketching of the Violin Concerto.

"Thanks to my work and the agreeable company," Peter wrote Nadejda, "I don't know where the time goes, or whether it is winter and snowing outside. The sonata and concerto interest me immensely. It is the first time in my life that I have begun anything without finishing what preceded it. I have always kept firmly to this rule. But I could not control the desire to write sketches for a concerto, and then I became so interested I put the sonata aside, but from time to time I still return to it.

"I have no news of the symphony from Moscow. Not one word of sympathy or a compliment. Jurgenson writes that Rubinstein will play my concerto." (The B Flat Minor Concerto Rubinstein had criticized so severely in 1874.) "Do you know the concerto? If not, I should very, very much like you to hear it. It is one of my favorite children. Why does Rubinstein consent to play a concerto he thought so impractical before? Anyway I am grateful. He will certainly play it perfectly. . . .

"Being a little superstitious and remembering that not very long ago, good fortune seemed a quite impossible occurrence, I am frightened sometimes and the consciousness that luck is fickle darts through my head quickly, like lightning. But then I remember you, and joy and peace return. The first movement of the Violin Concerto is ready; tomorrow I begin the second. From the day I began to write it, this favorable mood has not left me. In such a spiritual state, composition loses all aspect of work—it is a continuous delight. One does not notice the passing of time, and if nobody came along one would sit writing the whole day. But I do not renounce my settled routine, and the last two days, thanks to the beautiful weather, our after-dinner walks would have been very long and delighful."

The sonata Tchaikowsky mentions at the beginning of this letter was the G major Piano Sonata. It was not important and, like the rest of his solo piano compositions, is seldom heard today. But the Violin Concerto was another matter and proved more than worthy of Tchaikowsky's optimism concerning it.

To Nadejda

Clarens, March 22, 1878

". . . As I write, Rubinstein is giving his concert in Moscow. Were you there? I imagined you sitting in a corner of the balcony. It would be very good to know that you were there and heard my concerto! And isn't it better to hear music from the balcony than in the orchestra with all the elegant people who are less interested in music?"

Nadejda had indeed been at the concert. "What a joy your concerto is," she wrote, "and how that man Rubinstein can play! Superhumanly!

"He will play your concerto again in Petersburg for the benefit of the Red Cross. I am very glad; I should like so much to have your compositions promoted more abroad—here my Russian pride speaks. It is maddening that they know (Anton) Rubinstein well, that cosmopolitan composer, and have no opportunity to know our Russian 'pur sang,' national composer, our pride—you, my sweet friend!"

Tchaikowsky replied that his friend need not disturb herself about his fame abroad. It would come of its own accord, or not at all.

One night while the composer was still in Switzerland, Nadejda fared forth to a concert and spent a delirious hour; coming home late, she committed the reckless extravagance, the usually-to-be-regretted-indiscretion, of writing at two in the morning to the man she adored:

Nadejda to Peter Ilyich

Moscow, March 14, 1878
2 o'clock A.M.

". . . I have been to the concert, where I heard your *Marche slav*" (composed the previous year). "I cannot express my feelings as I listened; sheer delight brought tears to my eyes. I was unspeakably happy at the thought that its author is in a certain sense mine, that he belongs to me—that no one can take him from me. For the first time since I have known you, I heard a composition of yours in unusual surroundings. In the Hall of the Nobility I somehow sense many rivals, sense that you prefer many friends to me. But here, in a new setting, surrounded by strangers, I felt that you could not belong to anyone as fully as to me, and that no one could rival me. 'Here I possess and love.'

"Forgive this delirium—do not fear my jealousy; it binds you to nothing—it is my own, and ends with me. From you I need nothing more than I receive now except perhaps a little change of formality. I should like to have you treat me as one ordinarily treats friends—use 'thou.' In a correspondence it should not be difficult, but if you find it awkward, I shall let it pass because I am happy just as we are; may you be blessed for that happiness. A moment ago I wanted to say that I embrace you with all my heart, but perhaps you would find it strange; so I will say as usual—good-bye, my sweet friend.

"Yours with all my heart,
"N.v.M.

"If this seems improper, take it as the delirium of an abnormal imagination, excited by music. Never be astonished at such paroxysms in me—truly my mind is unwell."

Tchaikowsky's treatment of her outburst was both honest

and kind, but at the sound of that small intimate syllable *thou*, he retreated.

Peter Ilyich to Nadejda

Clarens, March 24, 1878

"I had mailed you a letter, dear friend, just before receiving yours, which touched me deeply. The happiest moments of my life come when I see that my music enters deeply into the hearts of those I love, and whose sympathy is dearer to me than fame. Is it necessary to tell you that I love you with all my heart? Never before have I met a soul so closely related to mine or one that so sensitively responded to my every thought, every heart beat. Your friendship has become as necessary as air. Whatever my thought, it always includes the image of my far-away friend, whose love and sympathy has become the corner-stone of my existence. When I compose, one idea is ever in mind—you will hear and feel what I am writing, and this compensates in advance for all the misunderstanding, all the unjust and sometimes hostile opinions that I am fated to hear from the crowd—not only from the crowd but from my so-called friends. In vain do you imagine I can possibly find anything strange in the endearments you express in your letter. In accepting them from you I have only one fear—that I am not worthy of them. I say this, not as empty words or because of modesty, but simply because at such moments all my imperfections, all my weaknesses, appear in higher relief.

"As for the change to 'thou,' I simply have not the courage for it. I could not bear any falsity or pretense in my relationship with you, and feel it would be awkward to address you with the familiar pronoun. We imbibe conventions with our mother's milk, and however we should like to rise above them, the smallest infraction produces uneasiness and the uneasiness, falsity. I want to be myself with you always, above all else I prize absolute frankness. So, my friend, I leave it to you to decide. The uneasiness of which I speak will certainly pass as I become used to the change, but I think I should tell you that in the beginning I should have to force myself. Whether I use you or thou, the substance of my deep love and affection will never change. It is hard not

148

to fulfill immediately your smallest wish, yet on the other hand, I cannot use a new form without your taking the initiative. Tell me what to do. Until you answer, I write you as before.

> "Loving you greatly,
> "P. Tch."

One feels in this letter no constriction of falsity; it flows easily and directly, the way words should flow between intimate friends. And how well Peter understood the widow, with her ecstasies and her black glooms and her two-in-the-morning deliriums. Next day she would regret her indiscretion—who should know this better than he?

Nadejda did regret it; on the last day of March she wrote again:

To Peter Ilyich

Moscow, March 31, 1878

"I have just had your letter, and thank you with all my heart, my dear, incomparable friend, for your sincerity and frankness. Those very qualities are what I love so much in you. I prize them highly, they inspire me with infinite confidence in you, and the most precious thing in our relationship is that I believe in them. And you understand that I, less than anyone, am spoiled by sincerity.

"Now let me explain why I desired the change in form. While writing, I was in such an abnormal, exalted state that I had even forgotten what planet I was on—I was aware only of your music and its creator! In that state, it was distasteful to use 'you,' the refined creation of decorum and convention, which often covers hatred and hypocrisy. At that moment, I hated saying 'you'—but the next day, when I returned to normal, I regretted what I had written because I realized it put you in an awkward position, and I feared greatly that you might consent against your will for the sake of indulging me. I thank you the more, my precious friend, that you freed me from the guilty knowledge that I had abused another's kindness, and I thank you too for thinking so well of me and expressing it so frankly. And so, let the matter be buried in fact and in memory."

And now at last, onto Peter's Swiss mountain-top came news of the symphony. Taneyeff wrote it, Taneyeff the faithful, the conscientious. Once a pupil of Tchaikowsky's, now a teacher and composer in his own right, Taneyeff's musical scholarship commanded Tchaikowsky's respect fully as much as did the Rubinstein's pianistic virtuosity. And Taneyeff deserved respect. Amid the notoriously convivial, easy life of Moscow artistic circles, Taneyeff, in his house on the outskirts of Moscow with his old nurse, lived like a monk, like a saint, devoted to music as to a religion.

Here is what Taneyeff found to say about Tchaikowsky's "favorite child," his Fourth Symphony:

From S. I. Taneyeff to Tchaikowsky

March 31, 1878

"The first movement is too long in proportion to the others; it gives the effect of a symphonic poem to which the composer has slapped on three more movements and called it a symphony. The trumpet fanfares that make up the Introduction, and that afterward appear from time to time, the changes of tempo in the secondary theme—all give an effect of program music. Anyway, I don't much like the first movement. The rhythm ♫♩ is repeated too often and becomes tedious.

"The *Andante* is lovely although I don't care much for the middle part. The *Scherzo* is wonderfully, absolutely successful. But the *Trio* sounds like a ballet dance and I don't like it at all.

"N.G." (Rubinstein) "prefers the *Finale*, with which I disagree. Knowing what you can do with a folktune when you want to, the variations here on *In the field there stood a birch tree*, don't strike me as important or interesting.

"There is one defect in this symphony to which I shall never become reconciled: every moment contains places that remind one of ballet music—the middle section of the *Andante*, the *Trio* in the *Scherzo*, and the suggestion of a march in the *Finale*. Listening, involuntarily I see Mme Sobeshansky pirouetting, or Hillert II, and this annoys me so I cannot appreciate the true beauty of the music.

"This is my honest opinion. Perhaps I have expressed it too frankly, please don't be angry with me. It's not surprising that the symphony does not wholly please me. If you had not sent *Onegin* at the same time, I should probably have been entranced with the symphony. It is your own fault! You composed an opera that puts even quite meritorious music in the shade. *Onegin* gave me so much pleasure, I spent such delicious moments with the score that I cannot find one thing wrong in the whole of it. A wonderful opera. And yet you announce that it's time for you to stop writing music! You never wrote so well. You have achieved perfection; profit by it and take heart."

Tchaikowsky wrote back immediately, and with a touching humility. Nevertheless he defended the "ballet music" charge with spirit. In truth, this tendency to burst suddenly into waltzes is very typical; Tchaikowsky does it in nearly every big composition, sometimes in highly inappropriate places, as in the elegiac piano trio written some years later in memory of Rubinstein, and in his opera *Pique Dame*, just when the story is blackest. But the waltzes are so rhythmic, so melodious—in fact, so irresistible—that one welcomes them, appropriate or not, with a smile of pleasure.

Tchaikowsky to Taneyeff

Clarens, April 8, 1878

"Dear Serge,

"I read your letter with the greatest pleasure and interest. As answer I ought to send you a detailed criticism of your own score, but this I shall have to postpone. . . . Don't be afraid you were too severe in your criticism of my Fourth Symphony. It was your honest opinion and I am grateful for it. What I need is criticism, not dithyramb. Yet much that you said surprised me. I don't in the least understand about the 'ballet music', nor why you don't like it. Is ballet music, to you, any gay melody in dance rhythm? If so, you must have little sympathy with most of Beethoven's symphonies, in which one finds such melodies at every step. Are you trying to say that my *Trio* is written after the style of Gerbes and Pugni? I don't think it deserves that!

"Speaking generally, I can't read anything censorious into the expression 'ballet music.' Ballet music is not always bad, it can be good, as in Delibes' *Sylvia*. And when good, isn't it good whether Sobeshansky dances it or no? I can only conclude that you dislike my ballet places because they are ballet, not because they are bad. Perhaps you are right, yet I can't see why a symphony should not contain occasional dance tunes, even with an intentional whiff of the street—*rude comiseni*. Beethoven used this effect more than once. Again, I rack my brains to find any ballet music in the *Allegro*. It is a complete puzzle to me.

"As to your remark about my symphony being programmatic, I quite agree but don't see why you consider this a defect. To the contrary, I should be sorry if symphonies that mean nothing should flow from my pen, consisting solely of a progression of harmonies, rhythms and modulations. Most assuredly my symphony has a program, but a program that cannot be expressed in words; the very attempt would be ludicrous. But is this not proper to a symphony, that most purely lyrical of musical forms? Should not a symphony reveal those wordless urges that hide in the heart, asking earnestly for expression? Furthermore, I must make a confession: in my naïveté I imagined that the idea behind my symphony was obvious, that everyone would comprehend without any definite program. Please don't think I am trying to parade myself as a person with deep feelings too great for utterance. I did not try to express any new idea; as a matter of fact the work is patterned after Beethoven's Fifth Symphony—not as to musical content but as to the basic idea. Don't you see a program in the Fifth? Not only does such a program exist but there is no question as to what it means. My symphony has much the same basic idea, and if it does not appear clearly, it only means that I am not a Beethoven—which is no news to me.

"Let me add that there is not a line of my symphony that was not deeply felt, an echo of the sincerest part of my nature. Perhaps this does not apply to the middle of the first movement. Here, seams can be discerned, gluings and forced passages that have a labored artificiality. I know you will laugh when you read this, skeptic and mocker that you are! In spite of your love for music, you never seem to believe that a man can compose solely from inner compulsion. But just wait—your time will come! And when it does you will begin to write, not because others claim it from you but because you yourself feel the need to write. Then and only then onto the fertile field of your talent (if I sound florid I am only saying what I feel) will fall the seed of glorious fruit. Meanwhile your field awaits the sower. I will write more about this another day; your score has some beautiful details. . . .

"Since I wrote you I had given up hope of composing, many things have changed in my life. The devil of authorship suddenly and quite unexpectedly returned to take possession of me. Please, Serge, don't read any sign of annoyance in my defense of my symphony; naturally, I should like to please you with everything I write, but I am quite satisfied with your unfailing interest. You can't believe how happy I am that *Onegin* pleases you. I value your opinion greatly, and the franker you are, the more it really means. So, thanks from my heart, and don't ever fear to see me wince; from you I need just that edged knife—the truth—whether favorable or no."

Nadejda wrote gloomily from Moscow; she was ill again, and complained of "heart cramps," which Peter assured her were due to nervous tension; he himself often suffered from them. Don't lie down, he advised Nadejda. Walk about your room with the windows open; even a cold in the head is a thousand times preferable to one such cramp. Secondly, put compresses of cold faucet water on the heart, and thirdly (Peter liked to classify both advice and confession with these hortatorial firstlies, secondlies and thirdlies), thirdly, drink a large glass of *good* wine—Sherry, Madeira, Malaga or even Port. This, of course, not as cure but as palliation: "Even the strictest hygiene," concluded Peter Ilyich from the depth of hard experience, "is helpless against nerves, because no health measure can defend us from the anxieties which Fate devises and springs upon us suddenly."

This was written from Clarens on April 11th, and this morning, said Peter, he had finished the Violin Concerto entirely, orchestration, corrections and everything. Only a few days remained before they would start home; Kotek was already gone. He would use the few intervening days to rest, not beginning any new music. . . .

During these rest periods from composition, Tchaikowsky, if he had a piano available, spent much time reading music, old and new, and always, in the evening, wrote Nadejda about it. And now he went back to his adored one, his god, Mozart. "This sunny genius, whose music even in remembrance moves me to tears." Only a week ago he had written those words to Nadejda, and she had replied indignantly, as she always did to eulogies of Mozart:

"I am astounded, Peter Ilyich, that the man who wrote such an amazingly beautiful thing as the first movement of the Fourth Symphony, could admire that epicurean, Mozart. Tell me, would the soul of a criminal shudder in listening to Mozart's music? Not a bit; on the contrary, in it he would find himself justified. But hearing yours, he would break down. Do you realize what that means? My God, it is not something to be explained in words. Indeed, how can one compare you with Mozart? I must stop or I shall talk on for three days."

Nadejda was not bored by Mozart's music, she was shocked by it, and this was a natural reaction for a romanticist—especially a Victorian romanticist like Nadejda, to whom art, if it was to justify itself, must be the vehicle either of emotion or morality. Mozart's pure classicism, the sheer abstraction of it, the lucid perfection of its form was to her a dangerous sophistication and she bridled against it, perceiving here a whisk of the devil's tail.

Tchaikowsky replied that hereafter he would refrain from trying to convert his friend to Mozart, yet such a silence would be very difficult! To him, Mozart's classic clarity conveyed the very opposite of what it conveyed to Nadejda von Meck:

"You say," he wrote, "that my worship for Mozart is quite contrary to my musical nature. But perhaps it is just because —being a child of my day—I feel broken and spiritually out of joint, that I find consolation and rest in Mozart's music, wherein he gives expression to that joy of life which was part of his sane and wholesome temperament, not yet undermined by reflection. It seems to me that an artist's creative power is something quite apart from his sympathy with this or that great master. At any rate, dissimilarity of temperament between two artists is no hindrance to their mutual sympathy."

Now, on the eve of departure for Moscow and all the emotional turmoil that Moscow would contain, Peter seemed more than ever to need the deep, healthy simplicity of classicism. He sealed his letter, convinced that he really would stop bothering Nadejda Philaretovna about Mozart (in a month he was at it again) and wrote a note to his publisher, Jurgenson. Whenever Tchaikowsky had been long away from home, he sat down and wrote someone a meticulous report of his musical accomplishment during the vacation. This time he had been away six months and had completed two big works, he told Jurgenson, and a violin concerto. "In fact you will have to face quite a few new compositions of mine. Seven short pieces are ready, two songs and a pianoforte sonata" (G major) "on which I have begun work. By the end of summer I shall have to engage a whole railway truck to send it to you. I can hear you tell me, with your usual energy, to go to the devil."

15

Home again. Tchaikowsky tells his methods of composition

Peter Ilyich to Nadejda Philaretovna

Kamenka, Wednesday,
April 24, 1878

"We arrived at last, yesterday evening. All day I had been very nervous, wondering how I would be received at Kamenka. My sister, Anatol and the rest of the family met us. They all expressed so much love and sympathy that I calmed down very quickly and began to feel I was in a cordial and friendly atmosphere. As my sister's house is crowded, she has prepared a quite separate house for me—very pleasant. It is a clean, cozy little cabin, rather far from the settlement and the Jews, with a view of the village and the winding river in the distance. The garden is full of sweet peas and reseda which will bloom in two months and spread its wonderful aroma. . . . My cabin is arranged very conveniently and comfortably. Even a piano has been procured and put in the small room next to the bedroom. Work will be a pleasure."

Though Peter vowed he was so calm, Anatol dared not stay more than a day or two in Kamenka before hurrying up to town to put the divorce wheels in motion. And now began weeks of struggle: attacks, counter attacks and all the bitter recrimination of a divorce suit. The difficulty was to persuade Antonina to file suit; briefly but passionately, Nadejda had written Tchaikowsky to pay the woman off, and to be quick about it. Antonina was told that Leo Davydoff, Tchaikowsky's brother-in-law, was shouldering the bill; Leo Davydoff believed it was the Moscow Musical Society.

Nadejda urged Peter to ask Rubinstein's help. Why not write frankly, asking Rubinstein to use his persuasion with the girl, and at the same time, telling him why a life with Antonina was impossible—that the two were utterly unsuited. "I don't like," said Nadejda, "the way people are talking; why should the girl acquire this undeserved aura of martyrdom? If any one is a martyr, Peter Ilyich, it is you."

Nadejda's letters were a wonderful comfort to Peter just now. In his little cabin below the big house at Kamenka, he tried to work on the G major Piano Sonata he had begun in Clarens, but he was too anxious and nervous for any real accomplishment. Fever and nightmares pursued him. "Come away from there, my beloved friend!" cried Nadejda, from Moscow. "They tell me you are growing thin, and that you have done no work. My estate at Brailov is empty; will you not be my guest there, quite alone, until it is time for me to go south? Now that the weather is warm one longs to go far away, back to nature, to the forest and the nightingales over the river. Only music can surpass nature. . . . I press your hand. Do not forget her who loves you with all her heart . . ."

Tchaikowsky asked his sister what to do, and Alexandra said they would miss him dreadfully, but of course to go down to Brailov. It was the middle of May when Peter made the journey—and the instant he attained the country, care fell from him. Brailov was a gorgeous estate of twelve thousand acres, situated in the Ukraine among the foothills of the Carpathians. On it were farms and forests and beet-sugar factories and much coming and going of superintendents. There were huge, beautiful gardens and a river for boating. Horses to ride and drive; in short, all the extravagant fairyland of an old-fashioned Russian estate. Even without wealth, the Ukraine in May was paradise; lilacs bloomed, nightingales sang in the wood, shepherds played their pipes, leading their flocks over fields all pink with clover.

Tchaikowsky stayed two blissful weeks, writing daily to his hostess in Moscow; it is to be doubted which of them enjoyed his visit the more. His life fell into a delightful routine of garden walks, forest walks, tea by the river, coffee on the terrace, long evenings alone in the moonlight. At mealtime in the huge dining-room he was a bit timid, he confessed to Nadejda, feasting before so many servants, but he could feel their good will and knew they were trying to make him comfortable. He liked to play Nadejda's harmonium, especially he enjoyed experimenting with the overtones. He had amused himself composing some short pieces, romances and violin pieces; would his hostess permit him to leave them here as a small testimony of his love for Brailov and Brailov's hostess?

Of these three pieces, one was the original *Andante* of the Violin Concerto. Together the three make a melodious but unimportant package; musically they correspond to those books placed in the guest-room by the bed-lamp. Tchaikowsky called them *Souvenir d'un lieu cher*. Separately they are, *Mélodie, Méditation*, and *Scherzo*.

Rubinstein had been right; Peter Ilyich always paid his debts. Soon, very soon now, he would have to face the Chief and those hungry rows of students waiting to devour his strength. But here, for the moment, was heaven, solitude; Peter feared but one thing and that was the mail. And even that, when it came, proved favorable: Antonina wrote that she would divorce him! Peter was beside himself with joy; he ran round the garden for an hour and a half, he told

Nadejda, capering, leaping, singing—anything to "stifle by sheer physical weariness the pain of my happy excitement."

"Thank God!" wrote his hostess immediately, from Moscow. "Hurry, Peter Ilyich, hurry! Shape the iron while it is hot; the person may change her mind! Telegraph me what money you will need for this so I can send it without delay. I shall be very happy when you are free. God grant it may be soon."

Moscow was awful. By some especially designed malignancy of fate, the Chief had a birthday that week, and Tchaikowsky could not avoid going to the party. Everybody was there. *Everybody*—Tchaikowsky's letter fairly groans. They shouted, they drank healths, they exclaimed over Peter Ilyich, resurrected after eight months; they embraced him —and they asked questions.

As to the Chief: "I read in his eyes that he has little sympathy with me, and that only expediency makes him bear the sign of friendship. He cannot forgive me for refusing to be a delegate to Paris, which from his point of view, I ought to have accepted as a great kindness. He does not like people who do not consider themselves under obligation to him; he would prefer everyone around to call themselves his creations. In short, I am not *persona grata* to him, and he could not hide it."

And immediately Peter Ilyich made his escape from the birthday party, he fell into a hotter fire. At five o'clock the Clerk of the Consistory was waiting to tell him what a man must do to get a divorce. Anatol had arranged this meeting the day before, and all during Rubinstein's party it had been hanging over Peter's head. Anatol went along; like a prisoner led to execution Peter walked to the appointed spot. It was terrible, he wrote Nadejda. This clerk was a horrible man, cynical and sordid, who recited the instructions with a face either leering or indifferent. Lies would have to be told, false witnesses procured to enact a scene the details of which he simply could not—Peter wrote—repeat to Nadejda.

As to the Certain Person herself, she was nowhere to be found—something between a blessing and a curse. It would have been horrible to see her, but on the other hand, a man cannot divorce a ghost. She was undoubtedly hiding—to what purpose only heaven knew—and Jurgenson had undertaken to find her and with Anatol, manage everything. Tchaikowsky waited and fumed and despaired, and when nothing happened and Antonina did not appear, he fled. Let the case rest until autumn—he cried, and went down to Leo Davydoff's private estate at Verbovka, just south of Kamenka.

Jurgenson found the Certain Person and concentrated all his tact, all his business ability and experience to persuade her to the divorce she had at first agreed to and then repudiated. He failed in some bewilderment; the conversation turned, he wrote Peter, like a squirrel in a cage. In all his life he had never met a more ignorant and difficult person. She insisted that Jurgenson was one of the divorce lawyers and said she would talk with no one but her husband. All the Tchaikowskys and all the Davydoffs—including Peter's sister Alexandra—were villains who had schemed against Antonina since the beginning. Indeed, she was convinced the whole divorce had been planned before the marriage ever took place. "Plotted," said Antonina, "by Anatol Ilyich, Rubinstein and Alexandra Davydoff." If these wicked people would remove themselves, Peter Ilyich would fall at her feet. . . .

All this Jurgenson reported to Tchaikowsky and Tchaikowsky reported to Nadejda von Meck who had by now gone down to Brailov for the summer. Here she found the violin pieces, *Souvenir d'un lieu cher*, and professed herself charmed with them—although one senses a reservation of her usual unconditional praise. She wrote that she knew she would like them better when she could hear them played on the violin; Pahulsky was with her, but he was so near-sighted he could not read over her shoulder on the piano rack and had not yet made his own copy of the violin part.

Peter wrote from Verbovka that he would not need the ten thousand roubles Nadejda had offered, because in the end the Certain Person had refused Jurgenson the divorce, declaring that if witnesses came forward to swear to her husband's infidelity, she would shout his innocence to the court. This was dangerous ground for Peter Ilyich, although he did not say so to Nadejda. If Antonina began explaining to the court about her husband's innocence of adultery, to what lengths might she not elaborate his inabilities! A third of the original sum — say three thousand roubles — would be enough, Peter told Nadejda, to persuade Antonina to leave Moscow forever. At least, so Antonina herself said, and the matter of a regular annuity could be arranged later.

Nadejda replied sympathetically as always. But for the present she saw there was no more to be done. It was becoming plain that Peter Ilyich simply was not of a calibre to deal with this creature.

For the moment, Antonina had won, and everybody knew it. Even Nadejda dared not press the matter further. Naturally, all this told upon Tchaikowsky's health, and tedious though health symptoms may be in the telling, they are inescapably significant in the analysis of a personality like Tchaikowsky's, where every occurrence of daily life registered physical reaction. Was he victorious — then the man did not know the word fatigue; he could write music for twenty hours at a stretch. Did he suffer defeat — symptoms appeared — and always the symptoms were symbolic of desire to escape.

Peter Ilyich to Nadejda Philaretovna

Verbovka, July 16, 1878

"I quite enjoy all the health one can wish, except for a new and very strange thing that occurs every evening. At nine o'clock, unbearable sleepiness with complete loss of strength comes over me, so that I can neither talk nor listen. I want to run and hide myself — to disappear, cease to exist. Yet I know from experience that I must fight this sleepiness if I don't want to have heart cramps all night, with nightmares and painful dreams. The struggle continues all evening. Of course, it is only a question of nerves to which one must pay no attention. Strength of will and a glass of wine save me from it.

"The work progresses rather slowly, and not as successfully as I could wish. The sonata has been ready now for a long time and today I began to copy several romances, some of which were written partly abroad, partly at Kamenka in April. One of the romances I copied today is composed to Lermontoff's 'The love of the dead man.' I wrote it because in one of your letters you used that poem as proof of your contention that poetry and music are related."

But defeat at the hands of Antonina had its compensation. At least, Tchaikowsky did not have to sit all summer in the heat and dust of Moscow, waiting upon the pleasure of the Consistory. Verbovka was pleasant, prettier in its surroundings than Kamenka. Uncle Petia plunged into family activities. A play was in preparation in honor of Anatol who was visiting them and everyone was to take part—all the nephews and nieces and cousins. The peasantry was to be invited as public. Uncle Petia was musician and prompter.

"In the meanwhile," he wrote Nadejda, "the rather tedious work of copying my music progresses slowly. Four things are ready, including Brailov's violin piece. Now to begin the series of children's pieces, then copy the Mass, and after that I shall take your advice, and rest. Then I shall be thinking of something new and big to write. I don't know why, but I have grown cold to 'Undine'. I want to find an operatic subject that will be deeper and more exciting. What would you say to Shakespeare's *Romeo and Juliet*? True, it has been used many times both as operatic and symphonic canvas, but the richness of that tragedy is fathomless. Rereading it, I became enthusiastic about the idea of an opera in which I would preserve Shakespeare's plot and action throughout with no changes or additions, as in Berlioz' *Juno*."

Nadejda herself was not sorry to forget Antonina for a while, and return to a correspondence about music. She always wrote cheerfully from Brailov; the country was a happy place, with one's children running in and out. She wrote inquiring as to Tchaikowsky's methods of composition; did the melody come first to him, or the harmony? Did the proper orchestration occur with the musical idea or afterward? And in opera, which was primary inspiration, the literary subject or the musical theme?

Tchaikowsky loved these questions and answered not with one letter, but three:

To Nadejda Philaretovna

Kamenka, July 6, 1878

"I have your letter, dear N. Ph., and hasten to answer. You want to know my methods of composing? My friend, that is a rather difficult question, because the circumstances under which new compositions are born vary extremely. Yet I shall try to tell you in a general way how I work, and in order to explain the process of composition, I must first divide my compositions into two categories:

(1) The ones I write on my own initiative because of sudden inclination and urgent inner need.

(2) Compositions inspired from outside, such as the request of a friend or publisher, or commissions, like my *Cantata* written for the Polytechnic Exhibition or the *Marche Slav*, written for the Red Cross concert.

"I hasten to explain here that experience proves the value of a work does not depend upon which of these categories it belongs to. Very often a piece that was artificially engendered turns out quite successfully, while pieces invented wholly on my own inspiration are sometimes less successful for various incidental reasons. The circumstances surrounding the composer at the time of writing, upon which his state of mind depends, are very important. When he is creating, the artist must have calm. In this sense, creative activity is always objective, even musical creation, and those are mistaken who believe the artist can use his talent to relieve himself of specific feelings of the moment. The sad or happy emotions which he expresses are always and invariably retrospective. With no especial reason for rejoicing, I can experience a happy creative mood, and conversely among the happiest surroundings I may write music suffused with darkness and despair. In brief, the artist lives a double life, an everyday human one and an artistic one, and these two lives do not always coincide. Anyway I repeat that for composition, the important thing is to rid oneself temporarily of the troubles of everyday existence, and give oneself unconditionally to the artistic life.

"For compositions belonging to the first, or inspired-from-within category, not even the least effort of will is necessary. It is enough to submit to one's inner voice, and if the everyday life does not rise up to crush the artistic life, then work proceeds with the strangest ease. Whatever emerges from the pen at such times, or simply remains in the head, is always of value, and if not interrupted from outside, will be the artist's best work.

"For commissioned work one must sometimes create one's own inspiration. Very often one must first conquer laziness and lack of inclination. Then different impediments arise. Sometimes victory comes easily, sometimes inspiration evades entirely. But I believe it the duty of an artist never to submit, because laziness is a strong human trait, and nothing is more harmful to an artist than to let laziness get the better of him. One cannot afford to sit waiting for inspiration; she is a guest that does not visit the lazy, but comes to those who call her.

"I hope, my friend, you will not suspect me of self-praise when I tell you that my appeal to inspiration is never vain. I can only say that this power, which I have called a capricious guest, has long ago become so accustomed to me that we live inseparable, and she leaves me only when she feels herself superfluous because my everyday human life has temporarily intruded.

"But always the cloud dissolves and she reappears. So I may say that in my normal state of mind I compose music always, anywhere, at every moment of the day. Sometimes I watch with curiosity this busy flow of creation which, quite by itself, apart from any converse I may be having at the moment, apart from the people I am with at the time, goes on in that section of my brain that is given over to music. Sometimes it is the elaboration, the melodious detail of some little work planned beforehand, another time a quite fresh, original musical idea appears and I try to retain it in my memory. From whence it comes is a mystery.

"Now I will sketch for you the actual process of composition—but let me postpone it till after dinner. *Au revoir.* If you only knew how difficult it is to write you thus, yet how agreeable!

"I write my sketches on the first piece of paper that comes to hand, sometimes a scrap of notepaper, and I write in very abbreviated form. The melody never appears in my head without its attendant harmony. In general, these two musical elements, together with the rhythm, cannot be conceived separately; every melodic idea carries its own inevitable harmony and rhythm. If the harmonies are very complicated, one must indicate the voice parts in the sketch. If the harmony is very simple, I often jot down the bass, or write out a figured bass; at other times I don't need even that. It stays in my mind. Concerning instrumentation, if one is composing for orchestra, the musical idea carries with it the proper instrument for its expression. Yet one often changes the instrumentation later. Words must never be written after the music, because it is the text that calls out the suitable musical expression. Nor can one write a symphony and then find a program for it, because here again, each episode of a chosen program evokes its own musical illustration. The preliminary sketch of a work is extremely agreeable to do; sometimes it affords a quite inexpressible delight, but it also means anxiety and nervous excitement. One sleeps badly and often quite forgets to eat. But the actual execution of the project is done very calmly and quietly. To instrument a composition that is already ripe, having been worked out in one's head to the last detail, is a very jolly business. One cannot however, say as much for the composition of piano pieces or songs or little pieces in general. These are annoying to work on; just now I am busy with such work.

"You ask if I stick to established forms. Yes and no. In certain compositions, such as a symphony, the form is taken for granted and I keep to it—but only as to the large outline and proper sequence of movements. The details can be manipulated as freely as one chooses, according to the natural development of the musical idea. In vocal music, where everything depends upon the text, and in fantasies (like *The Tempest* and *Francesca*), one can create one's own form. You ask about melodies built upon the common chord. I can prove to you absolutely, and can give you examples to show how by means of rhythm and the shifting of notes, one can build a whole million of new and pleasing combinations. This concerns of course, only homophonic music, in polyphonic music such a melodic structure would destroy the independence of voice parts.

"The melodies of Beethoven, Weber, Mendelssohn, Schumann and especially Wagner, are frequently built on the notes of the triad, and any talented musician can always thus invent a new and pretty fanfare melody."

To Nadejda

Kamenka, July 7, 1878

"This is a continuation of yesterday's letter.

"Talking with you yesterday about the process of composing, I did not express myself clearly concerning the work that follows the first sketch. This phase is especially important: what has been written with passion must now be looked upon critically, corrected, extended, and most important of all, condensed to fit the requirements of the form. One must sometimes go against the grain in this, be merciless, and destroy things that were written with love and inspiration. Although I cannot complain of poor inventive powers or imagination, I have always suffered from lack of skill in the management of form. Only persistent labor has at last permitted me to achieve a form that in some degree corresponds to the content. In the past I was careless, I did not realize the extreme importance of this critical examination of the preliminary sketch. For this reason, the succeeding episodes were loosely held together and seams were always visible. That was a serious defect, and it was years before I began to correct it, yet my compositions will never be good examples of form because I can only *correct* what is wrong with my musical nature—I cannot change it intrinsically. I know also that I am very far from achieving the full maturity of my talent. But I see with joy that I am progressing slowly, and I ardently desire to take myself as far along this road to perfection as I can go. Therefore, I was inaccurate yesterday when I said I wrote out my compositions unhesitatingly from the first sketches. It is more than a copy, it is a detailed, critical examination of the first plan, corrected, rarely added to, and very often cut.

"I have something to propose. You say you would like to see my sketches. Will you accept from me the manuscripts of *Eugene Onegin*? In the autumn the pianoforte arrangement will be published, and perhaps you would be interested to compare my sketches with the published work. If so, I shall send you the manuscripts on your return to Moscow. I suggest *Onegin* merely because I never wrote anything else so easily; the manuscript has so few corrections that it is not hard to read."

To the suggestion at the end, that Nadejda accept the manuscript of *Onegin*, the widow made her own terms: "My dear, wonderful one," she began, with a barrage of her marvelous and wholly naive Russian superlatives, "if you consent to let me have the manuscript for five hundred roubles, I shall be most happy to take it, but I beg you to tell me without reservation whether that sum is equal to its worth."

"The manuscript has no price!" vowed the composer in return. And anyway, was he not a hundred times in Nadejda's debt? "For the first time in my life, I find a person who is interested in my unfinished work. And I am far from being so famous that my handwriting has a price."

Nadejda accepted the manuscript—but her conscience, she said, would always reproach her.

She was somewhat alarmed by Tchaikowsky's account of how he composed; was not all this frightfully fatiguing? Should he not rest more? "Reserve your powers, Peter Ilyich; give yourself a chance to reach the apex of your talent and to remain there as long as possible for the glory of your art and the joy of mankind. If my anxiety has any effect on you, and if you will restrain yourself even a little for me, I shall be very happy."

"My dear," replied the composer, "nothing could be more reasonable than your advice as to resting more and using one's inventive powers less. But how can I? Once the sketch is outlined, I cannot rest until I finish it, and then the moment the composition is done, I feel an irresistible desire to begin a new one. For me, work (*that* work) is as necessary

as air. I have only to give myself up to idleness to be possessed by unhappiness, doubt that life will give me the
chance to bring my talents to whatever perfection they are
capable of reaching, dissatisfaction with myself, even self-
hatred. The thought that I am good-for-nothing, that only
my musical work redeems my defects and raises me to
manhood in its truest sense, begins to overwhelm and torture me. The only means of escaping these tormenting
doubts and self-flagellations is to start a new task. So I turn
like a squirrel in a wheel. Sometimes a quite unconquerable laziness comes over me, apathy, disappointment in
myself—it is a very deplorable condition, and I fight it as
hard as I can. I am much inclined to hypochondria, and
know that I must control my inclination toward idleness.
Only work saves me. And I work. Still, thank you for your
friendly advice. I shall try to follow it as far as possible."

Peter Ilyich was becoming daily more dependent upon
Nadejda. Let her neglect him for a week, and he fell into
panic. It happened now; he waited for a letter as long as he
could, and then wrote suggesting they mail their letters on
stated days, every so often. Nadejda was pleased, but she
said her headaches might cause her to fail him; every
month she had one—a ferocious, blinding pain that lasted
three days. Today she had only just recovered in time for
great festivities at Brailov. They were celebrating, as they
did every summer, the combined name-days of Nadejda's
brother, her eldest son Vladimir and his small new son,*
Volichka, "a charming little creature. The garden has been
illuminated, fireworks and Bengal fires have been prepared.
It is effective—the pavilion on the pond is all lighted, the
pond itself is bordered with lights, and a little boat in the
middle is hung with colored lanterns. We always open the
gardens to the public and people swarm in. . . . Keep well,
and don't forget her who loves you with all her heart.

"N.v.M."

"P.S. I think *Romeo and Juliet* much better as an operatic
subject than *Undine*."

Tchaikowsky replied in much embarrassment; how could

* Vladimir II, afterward husband of Barbara von Meck.

167

he have been so naive as to ask a busy woman of affairs to have a writing pact with him! She had urged him again to Brailov; she herself was going abroad and the entire estate would be vacant; he accepted with pleasure. But before he left Verbovka he wished to report on the work he had done:

To Nadejda Philaretovna

Aug. 5, 1878

"I write you, my dear sweet friend, with a light heart, happy in the knowledge of work more or less successfully accomplished. Today I wrote the last page of the *Liturgy*, and so all the lengthy and annoying work of copying is done. Now I shall rest and recover new strength. Do you know what I think? People who work feverishly and hurriedly are really the laziest people in the world. They hurry to gain the right to be idle. Now my secret weakness for doing nothing at all will have full freedom. It is more than time, because I broke down a week and a half ago and have not yet returned to normal. I feel myself quite well only to feel ill again immediately after."

Kamenka in late August was flat and hot and dusty. In Leo Davydoff's fields, smoke rose menacingly from the stacks of burning beetles. Peter Ilyich was glad to give Alexis the order to pack the boxes for Brailov. And if Brailov had been enchanting in spring when last they saw it, how gorgeous it was now in the full panoply of summer! To sit on the terrace above the garden was to be drunk with color—dahlias, chrysanthemum and the flaming "fire-bush."

Peter stayed about ten days at Brailov and returned to Verbovka, in his pocket the sketch for five movements of a brand new orchestral suite. This was to be the first of three suites for full orchestra. At his brother-in-law's Tchaikowsky worked on this music with furious delight; only a few days remained before he must return to Moscow; the Conservatory would soon open for the autumn term.

"I cannot tear myself from work," he wrote Nadejda. "Yes, beloved, best of friends, who advised and prescribed rest for me, I have broken my promise to devote some time to rest. I am not at all tired, which is always true when I have worked with no pressure other than the heart's urge. I think I have no right to fight my nature when it lights with inspiration, and so I beg you not to be cross because I did not keep my promise. As I worked, my thoughts were always with you; again and again I asked myself if these passages would please you, or these melodies move you. So it can be dedicated to no one but you. *To my best friend*; either I shall put it in the heading, as with the symphony, or if you prefer, put nothing on it at all, that the dedication may be known to none but ourselves.

"From now on, my friend, address me in Moscow. At least I shall return there a normal and quite healthy man, which I owe to you, and never for a second shall I forget it."

16

Autumnal Petersburg

In September, 1878, Tchaikowsky, Nadejda von Meck and Rubinstein were geographically far apart. Nadejda was in Switzerland, at Interlaken, driving out twice a day to look at the view. As to Nicholas Rubinstein, with a spring in his spine worthy of ten Cossacks — he was in Paris, waving his country's flag at the Exhibition; whether or no he was to draw shouts from a hostile populace, Nadejda herself would soon bear witness.

And Peter Ilyich, with a cold in his head, was on the train from Verbovka to Kiev, the first lap of a northward journey — and he was miserable. At a way station he picked up a newspaper, and turning to the music page, read the most horrible attack upon the Moscow Conservatory. Not upon its music but upon its morals and professional intrigues. In fascinated horror he read and reread, searching breathlessly for his own name. M. Tchaikowsky, said the paper, was too busy with his music to take part in intrigue. . . Heaven and a kind reporter had been with Peter this time, but in truth any attack on the Conservatory was an attack on himself; he was too much part of the institution to escape. Nicholas Rubinstein was torn to pieces; the entire Conservatory, it seems, was no more than a sink-hole to be fumigated.

"It was like a blow on the head!" Tchaikowsky wrote Nadejda. At Kiev he changed trains. Settling down in a compartment occupied by three strangers, he threw away the newspaper and told himself he was a fool to be so sensitive. In the old days he had been able to pass over such scurrilous attacks as if they were nothing; vacation, he told himself, must have softened his hide. Most certainly he would have to harden himself, and rapidly, if he were to live in Moscow. . . .

In the compartment Tchaikowsky's fellow travellers were talking; their voices droned on. . . . What were they saying, what were those names they repeated? Napravnik, Davidov. . . . These were Petersburg names, Petersburg musical names. Davidov (no relation to Tchaikowsky's aristocratic brother-in-law) was Director of the Conservatory there. Obviously, the travellers were Petersburgers. . . . And concerning the musical world they were all too well informed. Their voices rose, they laughed, they were having a good time and Peter Ilyich, every nerve taut, listened for his name. It came.

Followed a nightmare. . . . The gentlemen did not leave a stone unturned; the only thing about Tchaikowsky they did not see fit to mention was his music. All about his marriage, all about his madness, just what kind of madness, how it came on and why. . . . It wasn't actual insanity that had seized Tchaikowsky, said one of the gentlemen, eagerly. . . . The composer was still entirely capable for daily life and for music. There was no violence about what ailed him, but on the other hand, it was incurable. . . .

The train stopped at a station. Peter got out quickly and moved his things to another compartment—but no sooner had the train started than the people in the seat opposite recognized him and although he had never laid eyes on them before, began to question him intimately.

"I was seized with an indescribable, unconquerable desire to run away and hide, to leave it all." (How Nadejda, reading this, must have trembled in sympathy for this hunted creature whom she loved!) "There came over me an inexpressible fear and horror of my future life in Moscow. Naturally, I began immediately to plan for a definite break with society. At moments I was seized with a longing and thirst for absolute rest—death. Then it passed and there reappeared the old desire to live, to do my work and to say to the end all I have not yet said. But how to reconcile one with the other— how to save myself from contact with people, live apart from people and yet to work, forge ahead—?"

In the darkness, lights flashed by; there was a roar; pungent cindery smoke filled the compartment as the train slowed down to enter the Warsaw Station. Peter Ilyich picked up his bag and walked out and down the train steps. . . . Just a year ago, Anatol had met him at another Petersburg station, had dragged from the platform a babbling, weeping stranger they said was his brother. . . .

And now, a year later, down the platform a man came running—"Tolia!"—"Petia." "Oh, my dear brother . . ."

This time it was Anatol who broke down. Peter put his arm about the younger man's shoulder and spoke quietly. "Don't cry, Tolia. Don't feel so. I am home again, and I am well. . . ."

He and Anatol installed themselves in their eldest brother Nicholas' apartment. Nicholas was in the country. After four days Peter wrote Nadejda a letter so long that it must have consumed all night in the writing. In part he said:

"My dear, do you know what I fear? I fear that the Moscow life, the feeling I tasted on the train to Petersburg, the Conservatory with its uncongenial surroundings and the deadly, irritating class work, will unavoidably bring on an attack of misanthropy as soon as I take up my contracted profession and outside relations with people—that it all will possess me so completely I shall be helpless to fight it. It cannot yet harm my health—that is still strong enough to withstand much. What I fear is apathy, disgust for work, and if that should happen I would be no more than a worthless melancholic. I give you my word not to let myself go. I shall fight. But you can do me a great service by your advice and guidance. When I plan my life, I continually revert to the thought of you! What will N. Ph. say, what would she advise?

"Answer one question, my dear friend! What would you say if after a short time, I should quietly leave the Conservatory forever? What if, in a year, two years. I should make my home far away from the former scene of my active life? Up to now I have always considered it somehow my duty to remain at the Conservatory because of the dearth of people qualified to teach my specialty; that, however uncongenial the work, I ought to sacrifice myself. Lately, I have had my doubts about this. First, I was and always shall be a bad teacher because in every pupil, man or woman, I see a sworn enemy, created to torment me.

"Secondly, is it not my duty to give all my time and strength to the work I love, which for me embraces all the meaning and significance of life? You will ask perhaps, where and how I should settle down if I decided to leave my teaching. At present, while my ties to those about me are unsettled, I cannot answer this question definitely. Nothing would induce me to live in Petersburg or Moscow. I could never endure Petersburg; Moscow I love, but with some pain and bitterness. I like it as a place, as a city—even its climate —but you know why Moscow, more than any other place, is difficult for me. I should like to live the greater part of the year in the country, at my sister's and at Brailov, if you would allow me to come there in spring and autumn. It would be pleasant also to spend some time in Clarens or Florence. In short, I should like the same nomad life I have lived for the last year. My God, what freedom to work, how happy I should be; how much and how well I would write, what a calm spirit I could have, far from the sordid gossip of my former life!

"A final reason—only in the country, only abroad and when free to change residence at will, am I protected from meeting the person whose nearness will always disturb and burden me tragically. I am speaking of the person you know of, the living monument of my madness, whose aim is to poison every minute of my life if I do not go far away. So my friend, what would you say if I left the Conservatory? I have by no means decided. I shall go to Moscow and try to become used to it. But I must know how you feel about it all.

Not for anything in the world would I do anything contrary to your advice and opinion. Please answer my question."

And while Peter Ilyich sat imploring his friend through the black Petersburg night, Nadejda, in Paris, was writing to him. She had gone there for the Exposition which was still in full swing. She wanted to tell Peter Ilyich all about it and about Rubinstein's part in it. But Peter would wait a long time for a reply to his letter, and during those three weeks of waiting he would again and again beseech his friend's advice; until he knew whether Nadejda approved his decision to resign at the Conservatory, Peter could not leave for Moscow and Kamenka.

If he could bury his head in music, wrote Peter to Nadejda, he might forget his troubles, but unfortunately, Petersburg afforded no hiding place.

"Because of the Russian concerts in Paris just now, the newspapers are full of my name and the more publicity pursues me, the more I dread it. I cannot meet even strangers without real distress, and as my acquaintance in Petersburg is wide, I have to hide all day to avoid chance meetings. In the evening I dare not go to public places. My life is like that of a fugitive from the law! I have become quite a misanthrope, my friend, and seem to have lost the ability to live with other people. Ah, well, you understand this better than anyone."

Moreover it was September, and the dark days were approaching. All through the winter, lamps would flare except for a brief sun at noon.

"Petersburg," wrote Tchaikowsky, "has the most mournful, oppressive effect on the spirit just now. The weather is terrible—foggy, endless rain, dampness. One meets Cossack patrols at every step, as though we were in a state of siege. And the return of our army" (from Turkey) "after paying a shameful price—all of this is depressing. These are terrible times, fearful times. On the one hand an absolutely terrified government, so abandoned to fear that Aksakoff is exiled for a brave, truthful word. On the other hand, unhappy, mad youth, exiled in thousands without a trial—exiled where even the crow brings no bones. And between these two extremes, a public indifferent to everything, sunk in egotism, looking on without protest."

No wonder Peter Ilyich was lost in this life, and no wonder he implored Nadejda von Meck's support in his decision to leave it—and Moscow—for freedom and work. He was not even sure of Nadejda's whereabouts; he knew she had intended to go to Paris, but he had not heard if she had really arrived. Meanwhile the newspapers continued to report the Exposition, each according to its particular reportorial bias, and Tchaikowsky, aware that Rubinstein as delegate could make or unmake his reputation in Europe, was naturally anxious as to which way the Chief might jump.

"I cannot get at the truth," he wrote Nadejda. "Some newspapers say my compositions had great success in Paris. Others say they failed. From all that appears here in the papers about these concerts, I see without astonishment—but not without bitterness—how many enemies I have. I have never been interested in intrigue and always tried to keep out of it. I can truly say I have never intentionally harmed anyone in my life; yet I have enemies who rejoice at my failures and who minimize and poison every success. There are moments when I not only wish to live far away, off the beaten track, but when I want to stop writing even—to cease having any part in the social scheme. Of course, this feeling is temporary. If I can only get into surroundings that protect me from contact with strangers, I can work."

And the very day before Peter Ilyich thus voiced his misgivings as to the Russian concerts at the Exposition, Nadejda had been to one of them. Rubinstein was having a spectacular success in Paris. Europe may have despised Russia, but Europe "yielded submissive," as one newspaper phrased it, "to the compelling power of a Rubinstein." The Chief, wily old fox who knew what he wanted and why, had played Tchaikowsky's B Flat Minor Piano Concerto, the very piece he had once condemned so flatly as unplayable. Wildest enthusiasm had greeted it. Nadejda missed that concert, but she did not miss the next. This is what happened to her:

"When we entered the hall," she wrote, "I was in a state of great nervous excitement and agitation. I wanted so much to have our Russian music, particularly your music, known and appreciated in Europe! I feared the opinion of Paris. First came Rubinstein's overture to *Ivan the Terrible*. The orchestra and the volume of sound drove me to despair, and with horror I thought of what they would do to your *Tempest*, that *Tempest* that made such an impression on me first, which charmed me so, and which is so dear to me in every way. But when the opening notes sounded, I forgot everybody and everything. Dead quiet reigned in the hall, no one breathed. When the chord with the suspension sounded, I trembled through all my nerves, and Paris, the stupid public, patriotic pride — the whole world — faded further and further away — only *The Tempest* existed, love, and its invisible author, pouring forth great, luxurious sound, capable of filling the world, giving happiness, blessing and delight. O, my God! I can never tell you what I feel when I listen to your music! I am ready to surrender my soul, you become a god: everything from the depths of my spirit, responds. What I love especially are the times when you speak from your heart, so eloquently, so charmingly, that one could listen forever. There is such a place in *The Tempest* — according to the program, in *Ile Enchantée*. It is the part in which you have all the violins go full blast — what richness, what delight, and how hard to have it end! When *The Tempest* ceased, I had left my body . . . I wanted them to play the Fourth Symphony, I wanted the *Marche Slav*, I wanted your compositions only. The audience was satisfied."

She broke off to thank Peter Ilyich for dedicating his latest orchestral suite to her; would he please print the dedication right out on the page, as he had on the symphony, so that she might have the pleasure of seeing the sweet words, and realizing they were for her? And again about the concert, a scandal had occurred! The trumpeter had tuned his instrument a tone and a half too low, or so she had been told. "Whether it was true or not," she added, "the chord delighted me."

Unfortunately, this letter was three weeks finding its way home. A pity Peter Ilyich could not have received it sooner, he was in deep need of just such fervent, uncritical devotion. In Petersburg he called on Davidov, Director of the Conservatory founded by Anton Rubinstein. During the evening, gossip raged concerning Nicholas Rubinstein, and Tchaikowsky was glad to get away. He might criticize the Chief privately, but in his heart he still felt grave discomfort at such public disparagement.

Peter Ilyich took the train for Moscow, and the bad taste of last evening's talk remained with him. Anatol saw him off at the station and behaved well; the boy was evidently in better control of himself than a fortnight ago. "Take care of yourself," the brothers told each other simultaneously at the train-steps. "Be calm, be always calm"—and laughed at the coincidence of their warning. Settling himself alone in the compartment, Peter smiled again; what a relief to be leaving Petersburg and the fog and the Cossacks and the interminable Tchaikowsky cousins!

17

Moscow once more. The Chief prepares a surprise party

The Moscow bells rang, the Moscow dogs barked, every street corner called a welcome. Tchaikowsky's hotel was near the Conservatory and all his old friends came to see him, tramping up the broad stairs and down the carpeted corridor to his door. Peter tried to make them welcome. But his smile was strained, his fingers uneasy in the palm of a friend; the visitors sensed it and took offense. This meagre smile, this sudden darkening of the blue eyes that in the old days had been so gay, so candid—how could anyone know that not ingratitude cast this shadow, but fear?

176

Moscow, Sept. 24, 1878
2 A.M.

"I cannot sleep, and so talk to you, precious, beloved friend. People have just left me (Laroche and Kashkin) whose society was once pleasant to me. Why was I so annoyed with them that I couldn't hide it, and both remarked on it several times? Why do the three days spent here seem three endless years? My whole spirit is centred now on one idea, one aim—to leave here somehow; a gulf has opened between my past and future, and I must cross it or fall into depths of misery, anger, and disgust for life.

"I wanted to tell you about my conversation with Davidov" (Director of the Petersburg Conservatory). "The situation is this: Here in Moscow I have to work not less than twenty-six hours a week; it has never occurred to the head of our Conservatory to consider my work as a composer, to save me from exhaustion and give me a chance to devote more time to the beloved work. He has never made any distinction between me and the crowd of other teachers. Davidov, with tears in his eyes, told me that if I would change to Petersburg I should have only four hours to work, and would receive twice as much pay. He would arrange a class in advanced theory—free composition—and would not insist that those four hours be given within the walls of the Conservatory. He could not believe that for twelve years I have been teaching harmony and have been obliged to give the Conservatory twenty-six to twenty-seven hours. Several times previously, indirect propositions to leave Moscow for Petersburg have been made to me, but this is the first direct offer.

"The conversation made a great impression on me, although the change of service attracts me very little. However advantageous Davidov's offer may be in comparison, it would still not give me freedom. Not for anything would I let myself be tempted by bigger pay for less work, hurt Rubinstein's feelings and make him an enemy for life. On the other hand, the conversation with Davidov opened my eyes to many things and helped fortify my resolve to drop

177

this work that I find so uncongenial, in a city where life has become unbearable.

"I could tell you much about all this, but it would only take time and irritate me. Let me say one thing: even if in my secret heart I have always suffered because the Moscow directors refused to single me out from the general run of teachers, only now do I understand how little they cared to encourage my composing. I shall not say a word of this to Rubinstein. First, it would only bring about a misunderstanding between him and Davidov. Second, it would spoil his picture of himself as everyone's benefactor. Third, already having decided to leave here, it would be foolish to inject more poison into our already poisoned relationship. Fourth, poor Rubinstein has been so venomously and incomprehensibly set upon by the newspapers that I feel sorry for him (he is very sensitive to newspaper criticism). Fifth, I owe him much as an energetic exponent of my work, and should like to part with him as friends.

"In short, it is equally impossible for me to stay here or go to Petersburg. One thing remains—to resign the position of professor without publicity or fuss and become free as a bird, if not forever, then for two or three years at least. My God! Is such happiness possible? I shall await your opinion with great impatience and a trembling heart. I should like so much to convince you concerning my decision to leave Moscow—I am so afraid you will not approve; still, I feel that persuasion and fear are unnecessary. You can read my heart from half a word, from a hint. I think you will approve."

Poor Peter Ilyich, for whom a decision was always as painful as though the operation were done with knives upon his own flesh! At last he received Nadejda's letter about the Paris concert and *The Tempest*.

"You cannot imagine," he replied, "what an effect your praise has upon me; if you only knew how rarely I hear praise! I am so happy that my music moves and touches you. No one has ever said what you often say of my music. Always, now, when I write anything I have you in mind, wondering what will stir you, what will leave you untouched.

A famous actor said that he always selected one sympathetic person from the audience and played for him. I write music for you."

To Nadejda Philaretovna

Moscow, Oct. 2, 1878

"Beloved friend!

"A week has passed since I came here, and it seems an eternity. My way of living is absolutely a nightmare. At the designated hour I appear at the Conservatory, go straight to the class-room, sit through my time, and then like an arrow hurl myself into a cab and go somewhere out of town: either to the Neskuchny Garden, or to Kunzevo, or Sokolniki. Only there do I find peace. I am very grateful to the Muscovites for not caring for nature. I found complete solitude in all those places, especially in Kunzevo, where I once stayed from ten in the morning until six in the evening without meeting one living soul in the beautiful alleys of the park. In the evenings I lock myself at home or wander in a far corner of the Zamoskorechie and give myself up to the saddest thoughts. The worst of it is that I cannot work at all, and must therefore kill time. And how to kill it! It is awful to see the hours pass one after the other without accomplishment, without significance.

"I feel myself a guest at the Conservatory—everything there is strange to me. I have ceased boiling and raging, and look with blunt indifference upon everything that once irritated me so painfully. I feel things cannot go on this way, cannot last, and that I shall leave Moscow. I tell you frankly that if it were not for that thought, for the assurance that somehow I shall soon be free, only one thing would be left —to take strong drink often and without restraint.

"Ah, my friend, if you knew how hard it is for me and how ashamed I am to distress you by my complaints and my dissatisfaction with life! You do so much for my happiness and yet I always complain, I never find lasting happiness or tranquillity so that I can work steadily. And why did I have to return? Why did I have to arrange everything here without being sure in advance that I would be able to breathe the atmosphere of Moscow? Alas! It seems I cannot.

"I have been wanting to go to your home on the Rojdestvensky Boulevard, but, believe it or not, I have not had the energy. I fear you will not believe it when I tell you that I haven't once been in that part of the city, beyond the Conservatory. I have limited myself to my own street and the Zamorskorechie. Fear of meeting someone has become a mania. And truly, I am a maniac."

In the midst of Peter's distress came a telegram from Nadejda in Paris, saying she was writing, and he would soon have a letter. Immediately his tone changed: "A great light shines in my soul," he said. "Every word from you gives me energy, strength and hope . . . Rubinstein will be here in a few days, and as soon as I have your letter I shall form some plan of action and begin to carry it through."

But before Nadejda's letter was received, Nicholas Rubinstein returned from the Paris Exposition — a conquering hero. Moscow loved nothing better than to welcome home such a one and to crown him with bay. A great dinner was given in his honor at The Hermitage; toasts were drunk, everybody embraced everybody. Rubinstein himself was in fine fettle — and he knew exactly what he was doing. The banquet was long, the food abundant and extravagant. As the first toast was proposed — "To Nicholas Grigorievitch, who has done our country a great patriotic service, etc. etc.," — Rubinstein got to his feet and instead of bowing his thanks, turned directly to Tchaikowsky, waved a hand, and smiled. . . .

Peter Ilyich, his empty glass in his fingers, knew every eye in the room was suddenly open him; his smile froze on his face. He heard the Chief's voice, silky, insinuating; "*there* is the man to whom your praise is owing. Not to me . . ."Not Rubinstein's playing but Tchaikowsky's music had captured Paris; the Piano Concerto, *The Tempest*, the *Serenade* and *Valse*, the *Chanson sans Paroles* — Ah, but the Conservatory had reason to be proud of its son, its premier professor, its pre-eminent artist whose compositions had carried the name of Moscow thus to Europe! Where would Russian music be without Peter Ilyich Tchaikowsky? *Where would the Mos-*

cow Conservatory be? Was not Tchaikowsky's the name that made the world aware of our Conservatory, and would it not be so for many years to come?

For years to come — so this was it. This was the Chief's scheme; every word was a stone in Peter's prison wall. After weeks of struggle he had made up his mind to resign forever from the Conservatory and had only awaited the Chief's return so to inform him. Their last meeting had been far from cordial; Tchaikowsky had persuaded himself that Rubinstein would not care much whether he left the Conservatory or no. . . . And now here was the Chief on his feet, purring praises. . . .

Rubinstein sat down; The Hermitage roared applause and called for Peter Ilyich. . . . Peter got to his feet, looked once at Rubinstein and began to speak his thanks . . . "I came home absolutely desperate," he wrote Nadejda. "After the services Rubinstein had rendered mé in Paris, after this ovation arranged by him at the dinner, it would be blatant ingratitude on my part to cause any difficulty for him by leaving the Conservatory."

Not only was Tchaikowsky's carefully nursed indignation against the Chief completely undermined by this stratagem, but he carried now a genuine burden of gratitude; there was no doubt that Rubinstein had played his concerto magnificently in Paris — and if Tchaikowsky remained in his service, it would be played again as gloriously.

Peter spent a bad night — what there remained of night. Next afternoon he went to see Rubinstein, and the Chief's first question disarmed him further. "What is the matter, Peter Ilyich? You seem gloomy. Are you ill? Karlusha (Albrecht) says no one ever sees you. Why do you hide yourself? Will you not talk frankly with me?"

"I could not lie to him," Tchaikowsky wrote Nadejda. "I told him nearly everything. I became terribly excited, confessed that my life here was unbearable, that a mania of misanthropy had seized me and I could never conquer it. I said right out that I could not stay here long."

Rubinstein's reply was surprising in the extreme. Tchaikowsky expected expostulation, persuasion, expected to be told it was all imaginary, this misanthropy, and with courage it would disappear. Nothing of the kind took place, Rubinstein laughed, shrugged his shoulders, remarked that the withdrawal of the Tchaikowsky name would mean a loss of prestige for the Conservatory — and was silent.

Peter left the house chagrined but relieved. Evidently he was not valued at all as a teacher, only as a composer. Well, he would be a composer, and nothing else. Nevertheless in his heart, Tchaikowsky knew he was a good teacher. What then, was in Rubinstein's mind, what game was he playing? Next day Peter wrote Nadejda:

"I saw Rubinstein again today; he was friendly and seems as gay and serene as on the day of his arrival. Last year he said I was mad, and that the madness would pass. Does he still think it will pass? Alas, he is badly mistaken! Every hour, every minute I am convinced this madness will never leave me. The worst is that I cannot work here, and without work, life loses all meaning for me.

"Oh, God, to be away from all this! If only your letter would come! I can do nothing until I know what you think."

At last Nadejda's letter came; she had taken her household down from Paris to San Remo; there she found Tchaikowsky's frantic letters forwarded from Paris. Instantly she replied — and without equivocation:

"Of course, Peter Ilyich, leave the Conservatory! For a long time I have thought it absurd that a person of your brains, training, education and talent should be at the mercy of a man inferior to you in every way" (Rubinstein). "A man despotic and unscrupulous. I purposely gave you no advice before, but all the time I sincerely hoped you would yourself decide to drop a position that involved continual submission to our mutual friend.

"As to the usefulness of your teaching to future generations, I believe you will give them much more by your compositions than by combining fifths and octaves in the classroom. Many exist who can do nothing but that — whereas you can leave monuments in art that will be the best guide and example for studious youth. In a word, to abandon a position that is not in keeping with a man's dignity or talent, seems to me quite right and accords with all my principles.

"What you have done has my blessing, dear friend," wrote Nadejda. "As to your plans for spending half your time in Russia, half abroad, it is what I have desired for you. I too shall spend the winter abroad. If you could come somewhere near me, beloved friend, how happy it would make me! Why could we not both settle in Como and live on the shore of the Lake, a mile or two apart? How good it would be!"

Nadejda regretted that Peter Ilyich had not accepted her invitation to live in her Moscow home while he was in the city. But if Peter Ilyich would not live in her vacant house, would he do her the favor of stopping in for a few moments some afternoon? No one would see or speak to him; the order had been given. If he would just go in, play her pianos, smoke, look at the pictures, it would please her greatly. Again she reassures him about his plans for leaving the Conservatory:

To Peter Ilyich

San Remo, Sept. 20, 1878

"I had only just finished my letter to you when yours of September 12th was brought to me. Davidov's offer" (of a position in the Petersburg Conservatory) "delights me beyond words, my dear Peter Ilyich, because it proves there are people who appreciate you. But I agree that you must not accept, especially as there is no risk of forfeiting such favorable terms. I am quite sure you will always be able to get them all over Europe, but full freedom and plenty of time for rest are necessary to you as a composer with such rich imagination. You say quite rightly, beloved friend, that I can understand what you feel from half a word. More than that—I understood your present state and the necessity for a change before you yourself felt it. For a long time I have wanted you to be *quite free*."

183

How gay, how relieved was Peter Ilyich when he read these words!

"Your letter has come at last, my best, my ever kind, beloved friend," he wrote. "This is just a line to thank you for giving me, as my good genius, the chance to free myself from hateful slavery. How I shall work, how I shall try to prove to myself that I am really worthy of all you do for me! Very, very often, I am troubled because you give me too much happiness. Then if I don't write, don't work, I begin to despise myself and fall into great despair because of my nothingness and unworthiness, and because of the discrepancy between your idea of me and the real 'I.' When I work, when what I do has satisfied me, then the abyss fills and I reach the measure of all the kindness and affection you have given me. And I shall work! My God, what happiness, freedom! I will go to your house today. Good-bye, my beloved friend."

To Nadejda Philaretovna

Moscow, Oct. 12, 1878

"Yesterday—at last—I was in your wonderful house, my dear. Ivan Vasilievitch" (Nadejda's steward) "met me with great cordiality and let me wander freely through the rooms. I stayed two hours and looked over everything very carefully. Needless to say I am absolutely delighted with the beautiful hall and other formal rooms, but your private apartments pleased my heart most—also the rooms in which you suggested that I live. I found them quite ready to receive a guest. What a wonderful little place! With what pleasure I could live in those rooms, as cozy as they are luxurious. Unfortunately, it is impossible. Being a professor at the Conservatory, under obligation to others, I cannot hide myself in your sweet little retreat. My address must be known, and what would they say if I began living at your house! And yet I can't imagine anything more convenient than that little corner in your home, inaccessible to everyone.

"I played on your instruments: the Bechstein and Steinway are beautiful. The Deben organ is very good both as an instrument and a piece of furniture. I ended my first visit to your house by asking Ivan Vasilievitch to show me everything down to the smallest detail. I went in every room, even your beautiful bathroom. An upholsterer is working in the house just now. Iv. Vas. begged me to come again when everything is in shape. Of course I shall; it was all so pleasant and inviting! Why is it being put into complete order when you are spending the winter in Italy?"

He went home to his hotel and enjoyed the visit again in his letter to Nadejda, going on to tell his plans about leaving the Conservatory. To avoid publicity, he and Rubinstein had hatched an elaborate plan. (This time, the Chief knew he was really beaten. Having plotted to keep Peter Ilyich in the Conservatory he now turned and plotted quite as energetically to get him out with the least possible disturbance.)

The plan was for Tchaikowsky to disappear quietly to Petersburg. From there in due time he would write the Chief saying that ill-health prevented his return. In the meantime Rubinstein could himself take over some of the harmony classes, and Taneyeff could take the rest. Only a month of prison, then, remained, yet what an eternity a month would seem!"

Nadejda replied enthusiastically. Thank God her friend had escaped! She regretted only that he must now endure the official farewells, the "dinners, speeches, tears."

Tchaikowsky regretted it also; in fact, he decided he simply could not endure it.

To Nadejda

Moscow, October 14, 1878

"My dear!

"Here is what occurred to me last night. Why should I remain here a whole month for no good reason? My life now is so senseless that even a month of it is hard to bear. I wanted to stay for two reasons: first, to give Taneyeff time to prepare himself to take my place; second, the first concert of the Russian Musical Society is scheduled for the third of

November, and Rubinstein is going to play my piano concerto. As to the first, it so happens that the advanced classes in harmony will be taken not by Taneyeff but by Hubert, who needs no preparation. Taneyeff is quite prepared for the first course in harmony. As to the concert, I would not go to it for anything in the world, so shall not hear Rubinstein play anyway.

"Other reasons kept me here, mostly a feeling of embarrassment toward the Conservatory. I didn't want a hurried departure to advertise how little I care for my *soi disant* friends here. After all, I have reasons for disregarding questions of delicacy, and secondly, all argument falls before the fact that my life is now so blatantly nonsensical, so unbearable, so stupid that I cannot stand even a month of it. I shan't conceal the fact that I have had to fortify myself with wine. Well, in a word, *j'ai precipité les évènements.* Today I told Rubinstein that I would leave at the end of the week.

"So my friend, in less than a week I shall be *free!* My plan is to stay in Petersburg during October and go abroad to Clarens in the beginning of November."

The week passed; time moves apparently, even when wine fails to rally the heart.

"I held my last class yesterday," wrote Peter on October 19th. "I go to Petersburg today, a free man! The sensation of freedom is indescribably joyful. And it is good that no disagreeable feeling is mixed with it. My conscience is quite clear; I go with full assurance that the Conservatory will not suffer from my absence. The thought that I am not being ungrateful makes me happy, though I don't doubt there are some who accuse me of ingratitude. Thinking over all my years of work in the Conservatory, I cannot but realize that nothing was ever done to relieve me or encourage the only part of my work that gives point or value to my life. On the other hand, I go at peace with Moscow. I shall remember with gratitude that here my artistic strength developed, here fate ordained that I should meet the person who was destined to become my good angel."

That same afternoon, Tchaikowsky made his farewells; not the least of them was a last visit to Nadejda's house. Ivan, the steward, received him like an old friend and let him wander at will through the big silent rooms, but Ivan could not know that this smiling, friendly gentleman was here to pay his respects, and take quaint *congé* of Ivan's absent mistress.

That same evening Peter dined with his old friends! Rubinstein—whom he now could afford to call friend—Albrecht, Jurgenson his publisher, Kashkin and Taneyeff. Their genuine regret at the parting touched him, he wrote Nadejda, and he himself felt sad at the breaking of ties which had endured twelve years.

Nadejda was in Florence when she received Peter's Moscow letters. Only one thing worried her—what he had said about "fortifying himself with wine." She replied seriously and with directness. She well understood, said she, the state of nerves in which wine becomes a necessity, but she knew also the frightful and irreparable harm that wine can do. "My dear, my kind one," pleaded the widow, "if you really want to do something for me, don't use that dangerous remedy. Control yourself, have a care for your talent—if not for your own sake, for the sake of others. Your destiny is high, and worthy the sacrifice of a moment's relief from depression and unhappiness—especially as the best treatment for that unhappiness lies in the very occupation with which you will attain your destiny! Believe what I say, my priceless one."

Tchaikowsky did believe what she said, and knew also that there was real foundation for her fears. He was always making resolutions not to drink; his diary records many such. . . . "From now on," he replied to Nadejda's admonitions, "I give you my absolute promise to think of you when I am tempted, and in your friendship I shall find strength to hold out. But now that I have attained freedom—that greatest blessing—I do not believe I shall ever again reach the point where I have to look to wine for oblivion."

Tchaikowsky wrote this letter from Petersburg. His old opera, *Vakoula*, was to be produced at the Imperial Theatre and rehearsals were in progress—much impeded by a temperamental tenor who refused to sing.

As for writing music, he was getting nothing done at all, complained Tchaikowsky, and he would not stay in Petersburg another minute, *Vakoula* or no *Vakoula*, were it not that Anatol was so nervous and queer he was afraid to leave him. Petersburg was filled with cousins; one ran into them at every step. "They talk about music!" moaned the composer. "They try to find out when I shall be promoted to the position of Director of the" (Petersburg) "Conservatory! They ask me to play for them! They are all State clerks and look upon me as a musical clerk, professing themselves astonished at the injustice of the powers in not making me a director."

And now once more the kind sister Alexandra Davydoff came to the rescue with a warm invitation to Kamenka. She offered her brother a brand new cottage, sunny and quiet. Peter replied that he would come right away, and he came. How quiet the autumnal countryside, the thin snow lying white against his cabin door in the early morning, the farmhands singing on their way to the barn. After the long, arid period of Petersburg and Moscow, inspiration returned, and Tchaikowsky found himself working again on the orchestral suite (Suite Number One) that he had sketched upon his last visit to Brailov. He liked the suite, he said. "Our symphony is being printed," he reported to Nadejda, who was now in Florence. "Taneyeff spent a long time on the piano arrangement. The Sonata" (G major Piano Sonata) "is also being printed, and the *Liturgy* and children's pieces" (twenty-four easy pieces for piano). "Also twelve other things (these were also piano pieces) and the Romances" (six songs dedicated to Anatol). "All will be ready shortly."

This list, with the important exception of *Onegin* and the Violin Concerto, nearly comprised the sum of Tchaikowsky's work since he had begun to know Nadejda von Meck, eleven months before. He did not mention here the three violin pieces composed at Brailov and dedicated as *Souvenir d'un lieu cher*, nor the *Skobeliev March*, composed at Kamenka on commission for Jurgenson and signed—because Tchaikowsky considered it worthless—by a pen name.

Without Nadejda, Tchaikowsky would have written nothing at all that dreadful year. He would have gone mad, he would have killed himself—and likely enough, would have killed Antonina too. Nadejda saved him. Her money gave him freedom from Antonina and from fear. It gave him back his full strength that heretofore had been sapped by the gruelling routine of teaching. Nadejda herself did not aspire to wield a personal influence over Tchaikowsky. That she saved him rather by her money than, say, her personal magnetism, she knew well.

For her — and for us — it is enough that she saved him.

18

Florentine Idyll

And while Tchaikowsky sat in Kamenka enumerating his year's work, Nadejda von Meck in far-away Florence was hatching a daring plan. Here she was, queen of the Villa Oppenheim out on the magnificent Viale dei Colli. Gardens and terraces surrounded the villa, and the gardens were peopled by ancient, weather-beaten statues. The Archangel Michael himself stood guard over her silent fountain! Beyond and below Michael, below the silvery olives and the groves still flaunting their November scarlet — lay Florence, and on beyond Florence rose the dark Apennine Hills.

It brought tears to the eyes, said Nadejda! It was heaven, but for one great omission, that want of one incomparable friend. Peter Ilyich could repair that omission — nobody else. Why, therefore, should he not come to Florence now, right away? She would prepare an apartment for him, either in town or somewhere out here among the hills. He would have no care in the world but one — the only real care either of them had anyway — his music!

Tchaikowsky read these words in Kamenka not long after he had posted a letter to Florence asking Nadejda not to send a *lettre chargée* this month because living cost him nothing at his sister's. When he had read the invitation, he did not hesitate a second. He telegraphed a joyful acceptance, and then he sat down and wrote what came close to being a love letter. "What greater delight than to think of living where you can be with me?" (Well Tchaikowsky knew she would not be "with" him!) "To make you happy, to be of service to you, I would come not only to Florence, but to the most distant ends of the earth."

Peter Ilyich made his travelling arrangements and then retired as always before a journey—for a day's nervous dysentery. (This rather violent and frequent disorder played too large a part in Tchaikowsky's life—and death—to be left politely un-mentioned.) He was to leave Kamenka on Tuesday, November 26th. All day Friday and Saturday he wandered about his rooms, hoping the "symptoms" would disappear before train-time. On Saturday night he was feeling a bit less pallid when Leo Davydoff, vigorous, handsome and hearty, came in. Peter, it seemed, was to have a treat tomorrow. A big hunt had been arranged; everything was ready—keepers, dogs, beaters. . . .

"Splendid!" says Peter weakly, who can not endure the sight of blood or suffering.

"I remained with the hunt," he wrote Nadejda next day, "until five in the afternoon, in spite of increasing pain and weakness. Finally I got home, with a pain in my head so awful I can't describe it, and nausea and weakness. I threw myself on the bed and there came on the most dreadful nervous attack I have ever experienced."

Peter cancelled his plans for leaving Tuesday, but sick or well, he was determined to be gone by Wednesday. So on Wednesday Uncle Petia was put on the train, and with a sigh of relief said good-bye to the snow and the cold and the kind relatives who planned treats and wolfish send-offs.

And as he sped southward, a faint uneasiness troubled Peter Ilyich; deepening as he drew ever nearer to Florence. He had been more than a little reckless, engaging to spend three weeks not half a mile from Nadejda Philaretovna, and on the self-same boulevard. If she invited him to call, he would simply have to comply, and even if she did not require an actual visit, it would be more than likely they would meet accidentally, out walking. And then an end to this safe and comforting relationship, an end to all his security. What a fool he had been to come here and jeopardize everything! He might have known that no woman on earth, not even a saint like Nadejda Philaretovna, would be able to keep her distance forever. These misgivings he voiced afterward in a letter to Modeste.

When the train at last drew into Florence, Pahulsky was waiting eagerly on the platform. They drove straight to Tchaikowsky's apartment and Pahulsky left him there. Peter Ilyich flung off his coat and explored his new home. It was almost magnificent. A dining-room, two bedrooms and a dressing-room furnished for his comfort to the minutest detail—and a drawing-room with a splendid grand piano. Flowers were everywhere to greet him; there was a big table where he could write music, with every kind of stationery, pencils and pens, and propped against the inkstand, a note from his hostess. Peter Ilyich tore it open: "Welcome, my dear, beloved, wonderful friend!" he read.

"How glad I am, *mon Dieu*, how glad that you are here! To feel your presence near me, to know the room you are in, to admire the same scenery, to feel the same temperature as you, is a joy that cannot be expressed! I hope you will like the place I selected—*soyez-y le bien venu, mon délicieux ami*. You are now my guest, beloved and dear to my heart. But if anything should be in the least inconvenient for you, please let me know immediately. I am not bound by any lease and you could move at any moment.

"In regard to walks, let me recommend, as nearest you and most charming, the walk to the monastery of Campo Santo and the Piazza San Miniato. This is a delightful place. You go there by way of our Viale. We walk every day, no matter what the weather; we always go out at eleven and walk a little beyond Bonciani, where you live, my dear friend. There we return the same way exactly, at noon, for luncheon.

"I have put newspapers and periodicals in your apartment. In two of them you will find accounts of yourself. Besides these, all our newspapers and periodicals are at your service.

"*Au revoir*, my dear friend beyond compare! Peter Ilyich, take a good rest. It worries me the way you are so often a little ill. Heaven grant that your sojourn here will benefit your health.

"Devotedly,
"N. v. M."

Now what a woman!—thought Peter Ilyich; was ever man so blessed as he? She had thought of everything; that bit of information about the walks, giving the exact time and place where she was to be found every morning, was the very height of consideration; she had given it so he would not be afraid to go out.

Peter Ilyich to Nadejda Philaretovna

Florence, Dec. 3, 1878

"Truly, dear friend, I cannot find words for my complete delight in everything that surrounds me here. I could not imagine more ideal conditions of living. Last night I was a long time getting to sleep, and roamed through my charming apartment enjoying the wonderful stillness, aware that below my feet was the lovely town of Florence, and that at last I was near you. When I opened the shutters this morning, the charm grew. The quaintness of the outskirts of Florence attracts me greatly. As to the apartment, its only fault is that it is too comfortable and spacious! I am afraid of growing spoiled. One invaluable asset of the apartment is that I have a large verandah where I can walk and enjoy the fresh air. This means a lot to such an ardent lover of fresh air as I. Yesterday I enjoyed this for a long time, and I can't describe my delight at the complete stillness of the evening, in which one hears only the roaring of the waters of the Arno, falling and tumbling somewhere in the distance. The weather was beautiful, but today to my regret, it is rainy; I have brought you bad weather.

"I intend to have a good rest from the journey today, and to look round and arrange a scheme of life. I shall begin work tomorrow. Pahulsky can come at two o'clock for a lesson. While you are here I want to acquaint you, at least partly, with my new suite, or better, *ours* (like the symphony). To this end I am arranging some of it for four hands—I shall show Pahulsky the tempo and will send it to you. But first the manuscript must reach me from Petersburg."

Alexis took the letter down to the Villa Oppenheim next morning—and thus was inaugurated one of the strangest fortnights ever spent by intimates. That afternoon, Peter Ilyich and Alexis decided to walk to town for the mail, fog or no fog. They passed Nadejda's villa, where from the garden they heard children's voices.

At home a note was waiting from the Villa Oppenheim:

"I cannot express, my dearest Peter Ilyich, how happy I am that you like the apartment and that we are so near each other. Since last night my rooms appear even pleasanter and my walk more agreeable. Today I passed your house, looked at all the windows and wondered what you were doing. I am awfully sorry the weather is so bad, but you did not bring it, my dear, it is so nearly all the time.

"I don't know how to thank you for the pleasure you offer me with *our* suite. How much charm the word 'our' contains. *Mon Dieu*, what happiness, to have something in common with you—and at present we have much in common— How good it is! When you are out walking, beloved friend, go by our villa sometime and see where I live. At present my house is full of people. Write me, my dear friend, your daily schedule. Just now I played the *Canzonet* of your Violin Concerto, and was delighted beyond description. Today I received the printed piano arrangements of *Onegin* and *Vakoula*.

"Is your apartment warm, my beloved friend? What temperature do you like? I was afraid it would be cold and ordered a fire in the fireplace. I am exceedingly grateful to you, my dear Peter Ilyich, for your willingness to help my protégé Pahulsky; I see in it a proof of your friendship that is beyond price. *Au* revoir, dear neighbor. Now I shall often write you short letters. I will send the newspapers tomorrow, they did not come today.

                    "Loving you with all my soul,
                         "N. v. M."

Daily, now, the two grew into closer intimacy, and ever nearer to the danger line of meeting. The surroundings alone were enough to soften anybody's heart. To walk among these hills with their glorious towers and lichened, sprawling walls, to enter Florence and hear the noises of the street echoed so strangely at every turn—the horses' hooves, the cries of street venders. To see flowers everywhere, hung even upon the walls for sale, and then to walk again into the hills at dusk, watching those three great stars—what were their names?—come softly into view over the cypresses. . . .

Frequently, Nadejda von Meck drove by Tchaikowsky's house. She loved to pass at night, when the light in his windows told her exactly where her friend was, whether he had finished his dinner and gone back to the study, or if he was out somewhere.

Peter Ilyich, it will be remembered, loved all the world of make-believe. Indeed, a man who could write the *Nutcracker Suite* and the waterfall music in *Manfred* must have been more at home in cloudland than in the marketplace. And so it proved now. The boulevard that ran by his house and Nadejda's was new and wide, paved on both sides for pedestrians. One afternoon when Peter Ilyich was out walking, swinging along with his quick, easy stride, an open victoria approached, drawn by two spanking roans. A lackey sat beside the driver on the box, and in the back sat two ladies, one in white with a flash of color, the other all in black.

Sure enough, it is Nadejda Philaretovna! And the lady with her must be her married daughter, Lydia Karlovna. Peter Ilyich bows; for one instant his heart ceases to beat. Will they stop? The ladies bow vaguely in return, the driver and lackey touch their hats and the carriage is gone, rolling down to Florence.

Nadejda, apparently, had not recognized him; she was near-sighted. Peter went home and wrote her, and his words are the words of a child that has just seen an angel. To have this spirit, whom until now he has seen only—and how often!—with his inner eye, appear thus for an instant and then in an instant be gone from sight—how strange and how exciting! "Like some enchantment," wrote Peter Ilyich.

A few nights later he saw Nadejda again, at the opera, and this time they both enjoyed it. "Hopeless for me to try and say how happy this made me," wrote Peter, "especially as I knew you had been sick the day before and this meant you were recovered. I sat just where you thought you saw me" (Nadejda had not been sure it was he) "right near the trumpets and trombones which are always so extremely active in an opera! Like you, I left after the second act."

As for Nadejda—"How I love you!" she wrote, "and how happy I am to have seen you at the opera! Rising in the morning, my first thought is of you, and all day I am conscious that you are near; your presence seems to inhabit all the air about me! No matter how cold it is, this is where I want to be; your nearness is a never-ending delight. Dear one, you won't leave Florence before I do?"

Happiness has no story, and these two were, for this brief fortnight, happy. Again and again they saw each other at the theatre; sometimes Nadejda took her little daughter Milochka, and Peter Ilyich would put up his glasses and watch the two converse.

The two became quite used to seeing each other, as time went on. Peter Ilyich, perfectly secure, certain now that Nadejda would never force a meeting, used to watch for her to pass his window. Every morning at twelve o'clock the little procession went by, while upstairs Peter stood behind his shutters. First came Milochka's black poodle, frisking gayly along the pavement, nose to every crack. Then Milochka herself, with her older sister Sonia and the two small cousins, then sometimes, the German governess whom Nadejda found so congenial because she could play piano duets, and lastly, Nadejda herself, tall and distinguished in rich black silk, fashioned as always a little behind the mode.

December came and with it a cold, continuous rain, but nobody's spirits seemed affected. Good news arrived from home, too. In Petersburg the Fourth Symphony had been performed with brilliant success. Tchaikowsky sent Modeste's telegram immediately over to the Villa Oppenheim, and with it a letter. "All day," he wrote, "I have been possessed by our symphony, humming it, remembering where and under what circumstances this or that was written. It carries me back two years—how glad I am that now is now! How much has happened since I wrote this symphony; when I began it, I knew you but slightly, but I remember well that every note was written for you. By some intuition I knew that no one would respond to my music so warmly as you, that our souls were kindred, and that many things expressed in this symphony are more comprehensible to you than to anyone in the world. This symphony is my child and I love it greatly, nor am I afraid of its ever disappointing me."

Only a week remained, now, of this strange intimacy that

was so careful to keep without the bounds of reality. As though in fear of parting, the two redoubled their protestations: "I love you with all my heart," wrote Tchaikowsky, throwing caution to the winds; "with all my soul and with all my strength." Again and again he speaks of his dependence upon her: "During the last ten years, it seems to me that I have not made much progress. I don't say this to tempt you to encourage me; what I mean is that I am no more satisfied with myself now than I was a decade ago. I have not written one thing, no matter how short, of which I may say, 'This is perfect.' Not one measures up to what I *could* do. Perhaps this is salutary, a stimulus to work; if I were pleased with myself, maybe I should never work again! Please make no reply to all this; I know well that I shall never lose your support in what I do. And the knowledge of your sympathy has become a habit with me, so that while I write, you are always in my mind. When I write well, it is pleasant to think you will like and respond to what I have written. In short, I do not believe I could ever write another line of music, if I did not know that no matter what the world thinks, my friend will hear and understand."

On December 17th, at half-past four in the afternoon, Tchaikowsky wrote: "I have spent every moment today until this one, at a new composition. With fear and trembling I have begun, beloved friend, the opera" (*Jeanne d'Arc*).

And now Christmas draws near, and Nadejda must go up to Vienna to meet her boys. Her brother Alexander is bringing them over from Russia for the holidays. From now on it will always be the widow who makes the first move. Tchaikowsky has no responsibilities and must fit his plans to hers. Let no reader, therefore, think of Nadejda as a lonely lady following a man about Europe; on the contrary her hours "with" Peter Ilyich are snatched, a result of much plotting, from the manifold duties of her daily life.

"Good-bye, my beloved, incomparable friend!" writes Nadejda. "I write you for the last time from Villa Oppenheim and from your dear neighborhood. I should be very happy if I could think that sometime, somewhere, this happiness might be repeated. My dear, thank you for everything, for all your goodness and kindness to me here. All my life I shall remember with delight this time spent so near you, in constant communion with you."

Two hundred lire were enclosed in the letter, to settle Tchaikowsky's expenses at the Villa Bonciani, and two thousand French francs to have in readiness should he care to publish the new orchestral suite in Paris. Tchaikowsky accepted the Italian money and paid his bill, but the two thousand francs he returned to Nadejda with the fervent plea that she be not angry with him for so doing.

He goes on to thank his friend for the wonderful days here in Florence. She is the source of all the good in his life, and how can he make her realize it? "I was happy here, and at peace; it was light and bright in my soul, and the nearness of my best friend gave a special charm to all my surroundings. Although, due to the manuscript of my suite arriving so late from Petersburg, I did not accomplish my ambition of leaving Florence with a completely finished suite, nevertheless I began an opera and wrote one of the principal scenes. Therefore I did not spend my whole time in idleness and can take away with me, not only wonderful memories, but a quiet conscience."

Thus they parted, Nadejda for Vienna, where no less than a crowd of Petersburg friends and relatives awaited her. Peter Ilyich, alone in the Villa Bonciani with the stolid Alexis, gazed upon the empty hills and mourned, half in nostalgia for happier days, half in panic because his best friend was gone.

19

Colonne plays The Tempest. *First Orchestral Suite.*
Antonina again

Peter Ilyich languished in Florence, too gloomy to so much as walk by the Villa Oppenheim, let alone think of going through it. Weeks ago, he had told Anatol to mail the first three acts of his orchestral suite from Petersburg. He dared not leave Florence until the manuscript arrived, and he could not work further on *Jeanne d'Arc* without seeing the French libretto. It rained and rained, and Peter Ilyich, for want of occupation, wrote a poem! A wild business, he told Nadejda, for him to be writing poerty; it came very hard but he would finish and send it to her. Finally, even the poem ceased to console him and Peter fled northward to Paris, sure that the suite was lost.

In Paris, Tchaikowsky did the necessary research for *Jeanne d'Arc* convincing himself that Schiller's tragedy, while not historically accurate, was in point of psychologic truth far superior to all other accounts of Jeanne. Early in January, with Schiller's book in his pocket, the composer left Paris for his old retreat, Clarens, in Switzerland. Here, fortunately, the manuscript of his suite arrived from Petersburg after long delay, but Tchaikowsky was too absorbed in the opera to work on anything else.

Tchaikowsky wrote, in all, eight operas, and of these only two are known today: *Onegin* and *Pique Dame*. Himself the most subjective of composers, totally incapable of identifying himself with characters unlike himself, Tchaikowsky had a fatal propensity for plunging into operatic subjects that were quite foreign to his natural talent.

From Vienna, Nadejda wrote a little cautiously about the verses, but she threw caution to the winds in describing Brahms' new violin concerto, which she had just heard Joachim play for the Vienna Musical Society. It was awful! —said she. Even Joachim's marvelous playing could not redeem it; why, it was not a violin piece at all, it was a symphony, with the first themes warring and entangled, then a *cadenza*, then a long, dreamy theme, *pianissimo*, during which everybody went to sleep including the orchestra.

And the more Nadejda disliked German compositions, the more anxious she was to have Europe become acquainted with Tchaikowsky. Why does he not advertise himself a little, she asks?

Tchaikowsky to Nadejda Philaretovna

Clarens, Feb. 7, 1878
"I will follow your advice and send Bülow" (the famous German orchestral conductor) "a copy of *Onegin*. Usually I hate to push myself with musical celebrities, but Bülow is different because he is really interested in Russian music

and in me. Indeed, he is almost the only German musician who admits any musical competition from Russia. You remember what happened to my *Francesca Overture* in Berlin last winter. Bilze played it twice, really an act of civic courage, seeing the unfortunate fantasia had been severely criticized by all the newspapers after its first performance. The audience did not hiss, they just sat in silent hostility; all modesty aside, I know this was merely prejudice. It is admittedly improper for a Russian name to adorn a German musical program. However, this does not disconcert me; I believe that my time will come, although perhaps long after I am dead."

And now Tchaikowsky, having made sure that Nadejda was going to Paris, told her from Clarens that he had only been waiting to know her plans before making his own. He would come to Paris too, and finish the opera there, where he could be near her.

What a victory for the widow! To know that of his own accord Peter Ilyich was seeking her out, to prepare as in Florence, an apartment for him, to direct the landlord as to his comfort and finally, to send Pahulsky to the station to meet Peter's train! No longer need she fear that she could not make him happy; the Florentine adventure was proved, now: Peter Ilyich was hers forever.

As to Peter himself, he said a dramatic farewell to Clarens. The landlady wept, the landlord embraced him, the chamber-maid wept (so Peter wrote Jurgenson) and finally Peter broke down and wept with them. In Paris he was quite stunned with the magnificent apartment Nadejda had chosen, but learning the rent, he soon fled horrified to more modest quarters, assuring Nadejda by letter that he did not require the surroundings of a prince.

Nadejda watched over him like an alert invisible hen. Are his rooms warm enough?—she asks. Why does he lacerate his nerves by reading such books as *The Brothers Karamazov*. Dickens' *Little Dorrit*, that Peter mentioned, is suitable enough, but Dostoyevsky is not for people like herself and Peter Ilyich. . . . Why doesn't he divert himself with pleasanter things? Has he been to call on Turgeniev, here in Paris?

Tchaikowsky's answer is one of the sincerest things he ever wrote:

To Nadejda Philaretovna

Paris, March 3, 1879
Monday

"My friend, you ask why I don't visit Turgeniev; it is a question that calls for a careful and detailed reply. But because you know me so well and because you will understand, I shall answer in a few words.

"All my life I have suffered from social contacts. Perhaps this suffering is due to a shyness severe enough to be called mania, perhaps I do not need social intercourse, perhaps I lack facility in the minor falsehoods necessary to conversing with a new acquaintance. In short, I cannot define what it is that causes me such pain, but I do know that for years I went about in society and pretended to like it, thereby tormenting myself incredibly. It was not all tragedy; I could tell you many funny things that happened. But God alone knows how I suffered, and if at present I am so happy and feel so much at peace, it is solely because I can live, whether here or in the country, alone, and need see only those persons before whom I can be myself. Never in my life have I gone one step to meet an 'interesting' person, and whenever by chance it has occurred, I have met only with disappointment, sadness and fatigue. Two years ago, Count L. N. Tolstoi, the writer, expressed a desire to make my acquaintance, as he was much interested in music. I made a feeble attempt to hide, but he went to the Conservatory and told Rubinstein he would not leave Moscow until I came down to meet him.

"Now, Tolstoi is a highly talented man, and what he has written is congenial to me; there was no way to avoid a meeting that the world in general would term both flattering and agreeable for me. We met, and I certainly played my part: i.e.: I told him how flattered, pleased and thankful I was to know him — oh, a whole series of the usual inevitable falsehoods. 'I want to know you better,' he said. 'I want to talk to you about music.' And he had barely shaken hands before he stated his own musical views. Beethoven was bereft of talent — this was the start. A great writer, a divinely-gifted searcher of hearts, began by giving utterance, in a tone filled with confidence, to nonsense that would have insulted any musician.

"What could I do? Argue back? Well, I did. I started a dispute. To tell the truth, he deserved a lecture, but how could I stand up and give him one, then and there? Maybe another man would have, but I only played my part, pretending to be serious and amiable. Later he called on me several times, and though I am convinced that Tolstoi is a sincere character, kindly and even to a certain extent sensitive to music (I saw him sob outright when I played at his request the *Andante* from my first quartet), still his acquaintance afforded me nothing but pain and trouble, exactly as any other acquaintance would have done. In sum, one can enjoy a man's company only when, due to years of acquaintance and to mutual interests (especially family interest) one may remain oneself. Otherwise, any company is a burden, insufferable to a nature like mine.

"On the other hand, dear friend, when I tell you I am happier now than I have ever been, the words come from my very heart. Yes, now that I may hide in my hole and always be myself, since books and musical notation have become my only society, I am very happy. And as for meeting famous people, let me add that experience has taught me that their books and their music are invariably more interesting than they themselves. But how foolish to write you all this, who know it without my telling!"

A day or two later, Tchaikowsky wrote Modeste that, "quite unexpectedly," he had finished the opera.

"When you write the last word of your novel you will appreciate the profound joy of feeling that burden slip from one's shoulders. For ten weeks to sit down every day at fixed hours and squeeze music out of one's brain—sometimes with ease, sometimes with difficulty—is no simple matter. But how I shall luxuriate in my earned rest!"

Tchaikowsky wrote Nadejda that he would rest for a day or two, and then return to Russia. He did not want to go, but he must. So for a few days he strutted idly about Paris.

How bright and charming these streets, and how he loved this city! Especially fascinating was this new electric illumination installed since his last visit to Paris; he must write Nadejda Philaretovna about it and see if she liked it as well as he. Sauntering along the Rue de Rivoli, past the boulevards, the composer saw his name blazoned on the billboards; Colonne was to conduct a full orchestral performance of his *Tempest Overture* next Sunday at the Chatelet. Although Tchaikowsky had been notified of the performance, a warm glow stole over him; why, these billboards were like home! But the concert itself would not be like home; Moscow roared applause whether or no his music pleased, simply out of kindness for himself. But Paris would offer no wreaths and curtain calls; the music would be badly played and would be hissed as all his compositions had been hissed abroad.

Well, thought Peter, he would go to the concert anyway, incognito, not letting even Colonne know he was there. If the performance was a failure he could leave town; that was one comfort.

As to Nadejda, she was much excited over the approaching concert, even though Peter Ilyich informed her that the Parisian public would show scant support to a "barbarian Muscovite." But on Sunday she was ill and could not go. Peter sat alone in the hall as he had planned, telling himself before the music began, that he really did not care what happened. But the composer was due for a surprise, and not a pleasurable one.

To Nadejda Philaretovna

Paris, March 8, 1879

"I cannot resist writing you my impressions about *The Tempest*. The performance itself was neither very good nor very bad. My music was greeted with meagre applause and a few hisses, none of which surprised me because I had expected it. The thing that did surprise me though, was my own reaction; I was hurt. I had thought myself capable of more courage, namely, of complete indifference to public failure. I was terribly excited—a thing I had not anticipated at all!

"But do you know, dear friend, I don't blame the Parisian public for this. I did not like *The Tempest* myself, today. It is too long, its form is episodic and unbalanced, the episodes themselves are ruined because of lack of continuity. This is why I felt badly. I cannot attribute the failure to bad performance or to lack of understanding on the part of the audience. It would seem that *The Tempest* was a poor way of introducing myself to Paris. I cannot complain of Colonne's part in the performance; he must have worked hard and enthusiastically, but it was obvious that the players themselves lacked confidence in my music.

"Immediately after *The Tempest* I left the hall and had to take a long walk before I could compose myself. Now I feel a little sad, but know that by tomorrow my grief will have passed.

"Anyway I feel very grateful to Colonne and shall write to him immediately. I shall have to trump up a reason for not thanking him in person. I can tell him I am only passing through Paris and that I am not feeling well."

Tchaikowsky did write Colonne in much the same words he had used to Nadejda, and the letter was published in the *Gazette Musicale*, with editorial comment concerning the "noble and sincere modesty of this composer."

"As to the feeble applause and somewhat energetic hisses with which the public greeted my unlucky *Tempest*"—said Tchaikowsky's letter to Colonne—"they affected me deeply, but did not surprise me. If a certain degree of prejudice against our Muscovite barbarity had something to do with this, intrinsic defects of the work itself are also to blame. The form is diffuse and lacking in proportion. In any case the performance was excellent, and had nothing to do with the failure of the work."

The contrast between these two letters and Tchaikowsky's next, written from Berlin, is a perfect illustration of that moral childishness and artistic maturity that was Peter Ilyich. After the usual farewells, the composer had begun the long homeward trek to Russia. Nadejda remained in Paris. He reached Berlin in brisk style with none of the accidents that usually beset him en route—no falling down—

stairs, no nervous seizures occasioned by farewell wolf hunts. But in Berlin he halted; he had to halt.

To Nadejda Philaretovna

March 16, 1879

"You will be surprised, dear friend, to learn that I am still in Berlin. Something has happened to place me in a very ludicrous light. Nevertheless I shall tell you, because I always tell you everything. In Paris I managed my funds so cleverly that after paying the hotel bill I had not quite enough left to take me to Petersburg, and when I got to Berlin I could not go any further! So I wired Jurgenson to telegraph some money he owes me. I can't imagine why he hasn't answered; I just wired him again. No doubt I shall have the money tonight or tomorrow morning.

"The whole trouble is that during my last days in Paris I was beset by a mania for elegance such as never before visited me, and I foolishly bought all kinds of clothes and linen. The fact that you know very well what a lot of money I had, makes me the more ashamed to confess this childish extravagance.

"But in spite of this incident I must tell you that my finances are in the most brilliant condition; Jurgenson owes me quite a large sum from the sale of my works."

Brilliant though his finances may have appeared, Peter could not leave his Berlin hotel without paying the bill; he waited two days.

Finally he wired Nadejda in Paris. Instant relief! Back came her answering telegram, and following it like magic, a man from the banking house of Mendelssohn, calling upon the composer personally. In a frenzy of haste to be out of this hateful city—what city is not hateful to a man with empty pockets?—Tchaikowsky hurried to the bank. Where his friend the Mendelssohn banker disappeared to is unknown, but anyway Peter Ilyich could not get his money because he forgot his passport, his visiting card and all means of identification. He had to stay over another day.

With all accounts reckoned, Peter Ilyich abandoned Berlin and hurried home to Petersburg. But the consciousness of his shortcomings continued to trouble him. "Whenever I am in need of money," he confessed to Nadejda, "it means that I am spending lavishly and without sense. The funds you give me are *enormous*; I never before dreamed of such richness, and the fact that I, at my age, cannot keep within my budget speaks badly for me. I hope it will never happen again. Thank you, thank you and thank you, my dear, gracious, kind benefactor."

In the middle of March (1879) Tchaikowsky and his brothers went down to Moscow to hear the Conservatory students give a first performance of *Eugene Onegin*. From a darkened theatre the composer watched the dress rehearsal; between acts, his former colleagues rushed to congratulate him. Even Nicholas Rubinstein, usually so sparing of praise, admitted he had fallen in love with the music. As to Taneyeff, Tchaikowsky's faithful admirer and severest critic, who had taken over Tchaikowsky's counterpoint classes at the Conservatory, he could not speak his praise but burst into most unscholarly sobs which touched Peter Ilyich to the heart. Anton Rubinstein and other Petersburg people came down to Moscow for the performance—after all, a Tchaikowsky first night was an event.

Before the curtain went up, Nicholas Rubinstein asked Peter to come round behind the scenes, and there, to Peter's horror, stood the whole Conservatory, pupils and teachers. Rubinstein produced a large wreath of flowers, and coming forward, formally presented it, amid shouts and calls for "Speech." . . . "God knows." Tchaikowsky told Nadejda, "how hard this was for me." Between the acts he was called again and again before the curtain, but he knew it was himself they were applauding and not the music. Modeste attributed this coldness on the part of the public to an inadequate, semi-amateur performance, and musical history bears him out: *Onegin* is a favorite opera the world over; its touching lyricism, its waltzes, the gay simplicity of its sentimentality, have a peculiarly intimate appeal.

After the performance there was, of course, a supper for the composer at the Hermitage. Anton Rubinstein came along with his brother, but never a word would he vouchsafe as to whether or no he had liked the opera. Speeches and toasts and more speeches, until, Peter records, "everyone grew merry and I went home at four o'clock with a splitting headache."

He took his headache back to Petersburg, where he was living with Anatol—and a day or two later something happened to give him worse than a headache. While Tchaikowsky was out, the porter had received calls from a lady who would not give her name; also, he told Peter, he had seen a woman waiting near the house. Therefore when Peter, that afternoon, came in from a walk and went to his brother's study, he was more chagrined than surprised to find Antonina. She rushed at him, flung her arms around him, and for two hours told him not only how much she loved him, but how much he loved her. All the time, Anatol in the next room had an ear to the keyhole. Anatol, it will be remembered, had been through the School of Laws and knew the value of a reliable witness. At last Tchaikowsky, in despair of ending the scene, handed the girl a hundred roubles, "for a trip to Moscow." Instantly all her tears were dried and she became very sprightly, reciting stories of men who had loved her since last she had seen Tchaikowsky. Modeste and Anatol came in, she greeted them affectionately, whom half an hour earlier she had called her worst enemies.

"Nothing in the world," Peter wrote Nadejda, "can banish her delusion that I am in love with her and that sooner or later we shall be reconciled. She will not even hear the word divorce, and the man whom last year she commissioned to offer me—through my brother—a divorce, she now calls a mean schemer who did it because he was in love with her.

"Modeste says she is not a human being, but belongs to a peculiar species which begins and ends with herself."

And now this girl, who from the calm distances of Switzerland and Italy had faded to a merely disagreeable shadow, began once more to assume immediate and terrifying proportions. Tchaikowsky told himself he no longer feared her: "She can bother me now only when she is actually within a few paces of me," he wrote Nadejda. Also, Anatol was ever at his side. But the trouble with Anatol was, he was not firm enough; Anatol was too much like his brother Peter, he would run rather than step on a fly. Anatol was too apt to assume the character of distressed witness rather than protector. Furthermore, Antonina apparently had no intention of remaining even a few paces distant. She had promised to go immediately to Moscow on the money Peter had given her at the last interview and Peter, guileless soul, thought that she had gone and breathed freely.

Anatol's little apartment was on the first floor. A week after he had given Antonina the money, Peter was at home one morning, trying to work; he had taken the manuscript of the orchestral suite — (Number One, in six movements) — out of his trunk and really felt now that he might be able to do something further with it. He played over a few bars, but the house seemed noisy; there was a bumping on the stairs as though boxes were being carried up; somebody new must be moving into the apartment above. . . . Peter put away his work and went out for a walk; he was somehow uneasy. . . .

He had reason to be uneasy. Those boxes were Antonina's; there was a note under his door when he came in, to tell him so. "In imagination I kiss you innumerable times," read Peter, his face stiff with horror. "I know you don't like it very well when done in fact. It was an accident, my moving into your house. Don't be afraid that I am running after you."

An accident! Either this girl was crazy, or she was a cruelly implacable woman. Peter sat down, the letter in his hand, and waited for Anatol. Light steps sounded overhead; Peter got up and crossing the room swiftly, made sure the hall door was fastened. A few more "accidents" of this kind, and he would be reduced to the old slavery of terror. Petersburg had become impossible; hurriedly he wrote Modeste in Moscow arranging that they meet there and go to Kamenka for a visit, taking the deaf and dumb boy with them.

Down went Peter to Moscow — and down went Antonina a day or so later. The night before he left Moscow for Kamenka, she "broke in" upon him — as he phrased it in a letter, and stayed an hour. In the end Peter promised her more money and she went away. Peter went out to dinner with a friend; on his return he found a note from Antonina asking for immediate funds. . . .

Writing an account of this to Anatol from Kamenka a few days later, Tchaikowsky's pen abandoned all dignity and let fly. He referred to Antonina neither by name, nor as "my wife" nor as the "certain person." What he called her—not once but twice, and in capital letters was: The Reptile.

This was written on the 21st of April. April in Kamenka was by no means spring; it was cold and rainy, but it was a place of comparative safety; Antonina could follow him there only by letter. Tchaikowsy worked hard at the orchestral suite, that same suite which had followed him around Italy by mail until it found him in Clarens, and which he planned to dedicate to Nadejda von Meck. Technically, he was satisfied with this, his first orchestral suite, as it progressed. (He was to write five suites in all, including the *Nutcracker*.) It was a free medium for virtuosity in orchestration, and Tchaikowsky knew how to use an orchestra. The work was in D major, a key the composer seemed to favor; he called it a bold, bright key, and he succeeded sometimes in doing very dark and sentimental things with it. But the First Suite, while it satisfied him technically, did not possess, somehow, that other quality Peter so frankly ascribed to his best compositions; it did not come "from the heart."

Meanwhile, letters from Antonina kept pouring in. . . . "Last night," Tchaikowsky wrote Nadejda, "I could not sleep, and today I am a raging fire—all because I saw that person's handwriting. I am ashamed of my weakness in all this."

"Does the Person *never* leave you in peace?" cried Nadejda in return. "Peter Ilyich, I will gladly send you ten or fifteen thousand roubles, if only it will buy you peace. . . . Energy, utmost energy, should be employed in the prosecution of this matter . . ."

But that particular kind of energy was a quality Tchaikowsky never possessed. He had indeed, but one energy: artistic energy—and it was never-failing. Here in Kamenka he turned furiously to music, covering sheet after sheet with his delicate, precise penstrokes, as though by sheer force of musical creation he could exorcise the demon of this particular pit. He was wildly anxious to finish the suite so he could begin orchestrating *Jeanne d'Arc*, and he did finish it, and mailed it to Moscow. Finally, at Nadejda's insistence, he went down to Brailov for a brief visit; it was May now and the widow had returned from Paris to Moscow to settle her affairs before moving her family to Brailov for the summer. Peter had no thought of waiting for her there, the Davydoffs needed him at Kamenka; there was no doubt he was both a help and pleasure to all of them. To Anatol he wrote that even Brailov was ruined this time by thoughts of the Reptile.

But to the widow he wrote happy letters, enclosing lilies-of-the-valley picked on his rambles. He wrote, he told her, with the very pen she had provided for him in Florence at Bonciani. All the little objects Nadejda had put on the Bonciani desk for his convenience, he had brought home to Russia: penknife, eraser, inkstand and the little bell. He expressed himself as very pleased to find Brailov unaltered; except for a big new portrait of Nadejda in the entrance hall, nothing was changed. "This," he wrote, "has great charm for me. Returning to a place where one has been happy, one wishes everything as it was before, and the slightest displacement of objects is a grief. I liked so much being met by the same Marcel, driven by the same Ethim and if I am not mistaken, by the same horses, and to see the familiar face of the watchman. Entering the house I saw the same furniture and flowers, even smelled the same smells, characteristic of each mouse!"

At Brailov, Tchaikowsky had planned to rest and had not brought the new opera with him, thinking he would do a better job on the big task of orchestration if he waited until he was back in Kamenka. So he walked and picnicked and talked to the peasants and villagers—but always, whether at church or in the forest or day-dreaming pleasantly on the river bank, music was in his mind.

Tchaikowsky stayed at Brailov for three weeks; this time he had written no music to leave as a gesture of thanks to his hostess. So he wrote a diary every day, and left that. Just before he started for Kamenka, something happened to please him. June was nearly here, yet Peter had been able to find no lilies-of-the-valley, although he had searched Brailov from end to end. And on this last morning came a knock at the door, and there was Marcel, the estate super-intendent, smiling, his arms filled with crisp green and white fragrance. Peter shouted aloud, from surprise and pleasure. "Where did you ever find them?" he asked at once, and Marcel answered, "Two miles from here, in the garden of the abandoned farm-house we call Simaki."

He had thought Brailov the summit of earthly happiness, wrote Peter Ilyich to his hostess. What then was Simaki, but heaven?

He did not know that this particular heaven was for him but two months distant.

20

Brailov à deux. The Maid completed, also the First Suite

It was nearly June; Brailov was ready to bloom with brighter flowers than the shy white bells Tchaikowsky loved. All the riot of a Ukrainian summer quivered beneath the wild bright green of the wheat—high time for Nadejda to bring her family south from Moscow. And if Peter had been so happy there in the manor, how much happier he would be at Simaki by the river, alone in his own little house! Heaven then, would be open to them both. . . . Nadejda wrote him so, begging him to occupy Simaki for the summer. "Night-ingales will sing in your garden," said she. "You will have six rooms at your disposal, low-ceilinged, shaded by huge old trees. No one lives within sight, and although I shall not be able to walk near your apartment every day, as I did in Florence, still I can feel that you are near, and then I shall be gay and calm and fearless! Peter Ilyich, come, and I promise that you will never be disturbed; I will send you a light, pretty boat and your Alexis can take you rowing! Ten paces from your house the forest begins, and by moon light you can walk between the forest and the river. . . . Oh, my dear, kind friend, if you would consent to spend the summer there, just two miles from me?"

Nadejda sent this letter, and then set forth for Kiev at the same moment Peter Ilyich was boarding the train from Brailov to Kamenka. In the night, at Kazatino, the trains crossed, and for twenty minutes stood side by side at the station. Tchaikowsky was out roaming around the platform in the rain; he instantly recognized Nadejda's palatial private car. It was enormous, nearly twice as long as the ordinary car, and it was marked with the name of her own Kazan Railroad. All the curtains were drawn and Nadejda was sleeping.

And when in a few days Tchaikowsky replied that he would love nothing better than to come to Simaki, Nadejda was willing to wait another month until he could leave his family at Kamenka. She agreed that he ought not to disappoint his sister and all the young Davydoffs by cutting short his visit.

As to Peter himself, he had swung bodily into that state of half-ecstasy, half-frenzy, which was his when working.

To Nadejda Philaretovna

Kamenka, June 4,
Ten P.M.

"I have begun working very hard. The orchestration of an opera is pleasant and should not call for much strain. It is the kind of work that would give me much pleasure if my nature did not require me forever to hurry, forever to feel a despairing consciousness of the lack of time and my own inadequacy. I want to be done all in a moment, whereas to write a big orchestral score like *The Maid of Orleans* requires months of tenacious work. But in about ten days the first act will be ready.

"P. Tchaikowsky

"With your permission, I shall write you only once a week for a while. Until the opera is finished, I must plan all my days and my correspondence with the strictest regularity. I shall write you every Wednesday."

This sense of hurry was not, with Tchaikowsky, merely a nervous restlessness. It lay far deeper; it was a consciousness of the value of time, a deep conviction which was near to divination—that every moment is God-given, more precious than any single gift man has from heaven. It is a quality not found in little men, and Peter had it at its most intense—a double awareness of the glory of life and the imminence of death. *Death looks over man's shoulder and says, Live! I am coming. . . .*

Three days earlier than his prophecy, on June 10th, 1879, Tchaikowsky finished the first act of the *Maid of Orleans*.

"It is a bulky score," he wrote Nadejda. "And what a pleasure to see it completed! For a musician, an orchestral score is more than a collection of notes and rests; it is a whole picture, in which the main figure and the secondary ones and then the foundation—the scene itself, is realized. Any orchestral score is for me not only prophetic of future pleasure to the ear, but direct and instant delight to the eye. I therefore observe meticulous neatness in my scores and suffer no erasure, corrections or inkstains. Some day I want to display my musical penmanship to you; very soon I hope to show you one of my scores. If, as I hope, I come to Brailov while you are there, I shall send the opera score to you at the big house."

Tchaikowsky had reason to be proud of his orchestral scores, and not merely on behalf of penmanship. He had a real mastery of instrumentation; even today, composers study his scores to see if perchance they may profit by his methods.

Two weeks later, on June 12th, Tchaikowsky reported further advance. He could not sleep, he said, but it was only his accustomed summer wakefulness, which did not interfere with the quality of his work.

"My work advances fairly rapidly. It tires me a bit, especially at this time of year because of the heat and the annoyance of flies. On the other hand, it gives me great pleasure. It is hard to express the delight I feel when an abstract musical thought assumes real form, transmitted to an instrument or group of instruments. This is perhaps the happiest moment in the process of creation. And when I can realize as now, that the music I am instrumenting is my own, there is a double pleasure. Besides, *Jeanne d'Arc* has another charm for me—every note reminds me of that last journey abroad which was so very pleasant. In about two days, I shall be transported thus to Florence and the Villa Bonciani, because I shall then set to work on the scene from which I began the opera in Florence."

Next day, Wednesday, 6 A.M.
"Twenty years ago today my mother died. This was the first real grief I suffered. Her death had tremendous influence upon the course of my life, and that of my family. In the full bloom of maturity, she died quite suddenly of cholera. Every minute of that awful day remains in my memory as if it were yesterday."

Tchaikowsky's letters from Kamenka do not often speak at length or in detail of his work at hand. News is set down at hazard and includes everything from the worm scourge which has attacked Leo Davydoff's beets to an enthusiastic account of his sister Alexandra's healing power over the sick. After two weeks of abstinence the composer again began writing to Nadejda every day, in the form of a diary or bulletin. . . . *Onegin* was to have a second performance in Moscow, ordered by the Grand Duke Constantine . . . Good news had arrived from abroad concerning his compositions; in Wiesbaden and London he had had great successes. And Colonne—that same Colonne whose orchestra had given Peter Ilyich chills and fever, playing *The Tempest* to an unresponsive Paris audience—Colonne had written that he wanted more Tchaikowsky music to play, hisses or no hisses! But the best news of all, said Tchaikowsky, was the fact that his arrangement of the *Liturgy of Saint Chrysostom*—for mixed chorus—had been sung several times in the University Church at Kiev; long ago he had thought the work doomed to oblivion.

Meanwhile Antonina was again in pursuit. She had hunted up Anatol in Moscow to demand an increase in pension. Peter sat down instantly and wrote Anatol, attempting the firmness Nadejda had advised, and succeeding only in being nervous and blustering. "One must be as flint," he wrote, "so as not to let the Reptile imagine she scares me. Believe me, in everything she does lurks a vague but undoubted desire to blackmail. And I haven't the money, not a kopek, and God knows whether it will come soon."

Nadejda, it seems, had offered to send the June allowance some time ago, to which Tchaikowsky had replied that he was in no hurry at all, and this somewhat grandiose gesture was now causing him the utmost concern. Peter Ilyich complaining about money is an unusual and somewhat disconcerting sight; it had never happened until Antonina appeared. Fortunately, his fear was momentary and Peter was soon restored to his gentle, hard-working self.

Meanwhile Nadejda von Meck down in Brailov, all unconscious of these alarums, was joyfully preparing for Peter's visit. He would come, he had said, as soon as he finished orchestrating the second act of his opera. So the widow drove to Simaki farm with her little daughter Milochka, and the two busied themselves over the cottage, hanging curtains, arranging lamps. Milochka became so excited that she went to bed that night and dreamed about Peter Ilyich. Next morning she told her mother she was determined to pay him a visit as soon as he came.

On the 22nd of August, Tchaikowsky and Alexis left Kamenka and arrived at Brailov in the evening. Vladislav Pahulsky met them with his best Warsaw bow, handed Peter Ilyich the keys to his house and garden and expressed himself enraptured to welcome Russia's greatest musician. It was a beautiful summer night and Tchaikowsky was enchanted with all he found. On his writing-table lay a note of welcome from his hostess, just as it had lain the night he arrived in Florence—and just as reassuring. "My dearest friend," he read. "If you need anything, I beg you to ask your servants; your usual staff will be at hand. I hope you will drive and walk in the forest and have tea served anywhere you please. There are so many of these forests that we shall not disturb each other; moreover, we can arrange beforehand who will go to which place. But because I know how particular you are about this, I shall inform you every morning where we intend to go on the day following.

"I greet you, my dear, with both my hands. . . . Loving you with all my heart.

"N. v. Meck

"P.S. On your desk you will find everything necessary for writing."

Instantly and with enthusiasm Peter Ilyich took the post-scriptum hint. It was all perfect—he wrote gayly, and far surpassed his happiest imaginings. Tomorrow he would set to work orchestrating the last act of *Jeanne d'Arc*, and when it was finished he could breathe freely and enjoy the consciousness of having accomplished a difficult task. "A delight," said the composer to his hostess, "that is second to none."

And now began three of the happiest weeks of Tchaikowsky's life. It is a pleasure to read these Simaki letters, because when Peter was happy he was so very happy. The garden was all delicious shade, deep green under boughs of ancient oak and lime trees; from his verandah the land sloped downward to a stream, and through the trees beyond one caught a glimpse of sunny fields and the village. Nadejda had placed at her guest's disposal an old man-servant named Leon, a cook and a coachman with a phaeton and four horses. Completest solitude was his. Pahulsky ran in with frequent messages, but the messages were welcome and the Polish bows were brief. Besides, Pahulsky adored music and Tchaikowsky liked to teach him and here in Simaki, gave him many lessons in musical theory.

Peter Ilyich to Nadejda Philaretovna

Simaki
August 24, 1879
at 7 P.M.

"I am sitting on the verandah enjoying the wonderful night and mentally addressing thanks to the author of my welfare. I slept wonderfully last night, and directly after morning coffee started work and didn't notice the time until they called me to lunch. After going through that indispensable ceremony with the greatest pleasure, I set to work again and kept at it until four, when I decided to take a long walk, seeing the weather had cleared. I went down through the kitchen gardens to a small birch grove, crossed a ditch and after following various paths and pushing through many hedges, found myself in a forest. I don't know what forest it was. I know only that, standing at the edge of it, I could see Mariengay and the spire of the monastery church in the distance, and to the right, the roof of the mills, the barracks and the green alley leading to Simaki.

"I did not meet *one single soul*, which for me is the greatest charm of walking, and after two hours and a half of brisk exercise I was back at my peerless dwelling! I wrote four letters and then brought my desk out to the porch to write you these lines in the wonderful fresh country air, which is something we have to do without in Kamenka.

"I have no words to tell you how well I feel here, how easy and brave. Thank you, my friend. Until tomorrow...."

On that same day, Peter Ilyich wrote Modeste of his happiness, adding, however, that he was a little troubled by the proximity of Nadejda Philaretovna: "I know," he wrote, "that this is foolish and that solitude will not be broken into, but I am so used to thinking of Nadejda Ph. as a kind of far-away, invisible angel that the consciousness of her near and mortal presence is disturbing."

Peter Ilyich was on his guard, therefore, when Pahulsky announced that another visitor was coming:

To Nadejda Philaretovna

August 23
at 8 P.M.

"Mr. Pahulsky has told me that next time he comes he intends to bring Milochka. Now, I am fond of Milochka, I enjoy her charming face in photographs; I know she is a wonderful child, very dear and sweet. Also, I like children very much, and naturally such an offer should receive the answer, 'Yes, I shall be very glad, etc.' This is how I answered Mr. Pahulsky, but it is not what I shall say to you....

"Forgive me, dear friend and laugh if you will at my queerness, but I shall not invite Milochka to visit me, and this is why: My relationship with you, exactly as it now stands, is my greatest happiness and the rock on which all my welfare rests. I do not want it to change even a little. I have become used to thinking of you as my good and invisible angel. All the charm, all the poesy of my friendship with you is based on the fact that you are so close to me, so infinitely dear to my heart, and yet in the ordinary sense of the word, we are not acquainted. And this same condition of not meeting, must extend to those most nearly related to you.

"I want to love Milochka as I have loved her until now. Should she appear in the flesh, the charm would be broken. Every member of your family is close to my heart, Milochka especially—but for God's sake, let it remain as it is. What could I reply if Milochka asked me why I do not call on her mother? I should be compelled to open our acquaintance with a *lie*—a very innocent one, but still, a lie, and I should find this hard. Forgive me, my own dear wonderful friend, for my frankness."

Nàdejda's answer was reassuring: "I understand our relationship, my dearest Peter Ilyich," she wrote, "quite as you do. And like you, I don't wish to change it in any way. I laughed to myself at Pahulsky's naïveté. He really thought Milochka might go to you; she is forever plaguing him to take her. I told her however, that it would be quite out of the question for you to be disturbed at your work. You guessed rightly that the child's curiosity has been roused and she is filled with questions. One day she asked me, 'Is it true you have not even met Peter Ilyich?' I don't remember just when I must have told her we were not acquainted. I replied that on the contrary I knew you very well and loved you very much. She was quite satisfied with this for an answer. So you see, my dear friend, in this matter our feelings are the same, and we understand one another."

But if hostess and guest were content with this strange ghostly friendship, others were not so satisfied. The widow's children were consumed with curiosity concerning Peter Ilyich. Milochka in particular, a child of seven with her mother's black hair and her mother's brilliant black eyes and big, generous mouth—could not bear to let romance rest in the clouds; she must needs bring it to earth, where the young know that romance belongs. So she plotted and schemed, and one day—it was the last day of August—she managed to delay dinner until very late. Dinner in the Russia of 1879 was eaten at four in the afternoon, so at four Peter Ilyich thinking his hostess two miles away in her big dining-room, surrounded by her family, sallied forth for a drive to the mushroom forest. Alexis sat on the box with Ethim the coachman, Tchaikowsky sat in the phaeton and Leon, the old servant whom Nadejda had appointed as second valet to Tchaikowsky, rode on the footman's box behind.

The carriage rolled merrily along woodland roads, across a stream and around a field; Tchaikowsky sitting quite silent, unaware of anything save the sweet summer air and the shadowed tracery of leafy branches across the road ahead. Suddenly another carriage approached—a whole cavalcade of carriages which must pass slowly on the narrow road; Peter heard laughter and voices which evidently did not belong to peasants or servants. The first carriage drew alongside, Tchaikowsky looked up and met Nadejda face to face, her eyes level with his. He was dreadfully confused, he wrote Anatol afterward. He bowed, but Nadejda seemed even more at a loss. For one long moment a dreadful tension reigned, and then, returning his bow, Nadejda ordered her coachman to drive on.

Peter Ilyich continued his drive, saying nothing to the servants, but he was quick to write his hostess:

To Nadejda Philaretovna

August 30, at 8 P.M.

"I have just got home. For God's sake, Nadejda Philaretovna, forgive me for miscalculating the time so carelessly, and meeting you. Now I have no doubt provoked renewed questions from Milochka and new complications for you in explaining why the mysterious inhabitant of Simaki farm enjoys your hospitality but refuses to visit you at your house. Instead of walking out at four as I usually do, I left home a little earlier.

"How charming Milochka is!

"I have worked so hard that I have nearly finished the first half of the last act."

As for the widow, her reaction to the meeting was not at all like Tchaikowsky's, nor did she trouble to pretend that it was:

Nadejda Philaretovna to Peter Ilyich

Brailov
Thursday

"You apologize, dear friend, because you met me, while I am delighted to have met you! I cannot tell you how comforting it was to meet like that. It convinced me of the reality of your presence in Brailov. I don't seek any close personal relationship with you, but I love to be near you passively, tacitly—to be under the same roof with you, as in the theatre in Florence, and to meet you on the road. To feel you, not as myth but as a living man whom I love sincerely and from whom I receive so much—this give me greatest delight. To me these occasions are extraordinary good fortune.

When first we met I did not realize who it was, as we often pass carriages and I exchange bows without inquiring as to the person. This time, looking neither at the driver nor the horses, I merely noticed a bow—which I learned later came from your Alexis. I returned it, and only when my eye fell upon Leon riding behind did I realize whom we had met, and I felt so gay and splendid that tears came to my eyes and I myself asked Milochka if she knew whom we had passed. She did not, but a long conversation arose about you. Don't think though, dear friend, that her questions or pleadings trouble me. When she asks why we don't exchange visits, I tell her it is because you are composing beautiful music and must not be disturbed. This always quiets her and she asks merely what you are composing at the moment. Our meeting reminded her how she had met you in the street at Florence—she added, 'but he did not see us.' She told me that her German governess often asks why we never go to Simaki any more, and that she has to run away to avoid telling a lie! She is well able to keep a secret."

Neither of them ever mentioned this episode again; Tchaikowsky's apprehension of danger was acute, and the widow took her tone from him.

Like most artists, Tchaikowsky craved solitude and was vociferous about it, but like most artists he was very particular about the kind of solitude he required; just any old solitude would by no means do. The surroundings must be quite perfect, not in the sense of luxury but of natural beauty; also, a companion must be within calling distance. One day at Brailov, for instance, Peter Ilyich, in search of solitude, launched himself into the forest and got lost. In some agitation he found his way into sunlight and broad field—but he had left his *pince-nez* at home, and stare though he would, all four points of the compass remained but forest and green field. So Peter did literally what he had so often done figuratively when in a bad place, he stood still and shouted for rescue. He shouted loud, until he was hoarse, and at last Ethim came running. . . .

When he got home he sat on the verandah, resting and thinking about his nearly completed orchestral suite. How had he been so unobservant as to write the first five movements in four-four rhythm? It would be intolerably monotonous. . . . The summer air was soft, the bells of the monastery carried sweetly across the fields, and suddenly Peter heard a new melody in his head—in three-four time. He hurried inside and set to work, and before two days were gone he had added a redeeming sixth movement to the suite, a *minuet* which he called (by want, he told Nadejda of a better name) *Divertimento*.

And while her guest wrote and rested and hunted the elusive mushroom, Nadejda up at the big house gloried in his proximity and devised further means for his happiness. Taking tea on the river bank one afternoon, watching her boys row vigorously up stream, a splendid thought occurred to her, a plan for bringing herself and Peter Ilyich closer without violating sanctuary. Why not marry one of her boys to a Davydoff, to any one of the Tchaikowsky nieces?

Casually then, Nadejda inquired the age of Natasha, the youngest Tchaikowsky niece. He told her and she thanked him. "Guess why I want to know!" she challenged.

Peter Ilyich replied that he had guessed already, and that nothing would please him better than such a match. His letter provoked a long correspondence on the subject of marriage.

Only one thing troubled her. Reminding Peter Ilyich that she, as mother-in-law, had never met her son-in-law's parents, had even stayed away from her favorite son's wedding for fear of the in-laws—what, she asked, would the Davydoffs think of such a queer, ridiculously shy woman?

Tchaikowsky's reply was soothing. Surely these two children would be happy together, and as to Nadejda's shyness, let it not trouble her at all. Already, the Davydoffs knew and loved her, through him. But let us wait, dear friend, he cautioned. Let us not be in haste; after all, these are but children.

Very well, she would wait, the widow replied. But oh, Peter Ilyich, suppose she should die before the plan took effect? With characteristic despotism she proceeded to plan for that eventuality also. This time her assurance seems a little ingenuous, perhaps even a little pathetic:

"If I should not live until that day, I shall will my plan to Julia,* who upon my death will be entrusted with all my interests, affections and desires—I am convinced the matter will be in good hands. My love and friendship for you I entrust to her also, and I will you, my dearest friend, to transfer to her the relationship between us, which is so dear to me. She and I will talk it over with you further at the proper time."

Tchaikowsky was always agitated by the thought of death, not because he feared it but because he loved to work. He did not want to die while music remained in him. The moment he had Nadejda's letter, he replied to it. He was anxious, he wrote, to live a long time; it would require many years for his musical ability to reach its full peak. But the thought that he might outlive his friend was unbearable. "But let us have an end to this conversation!" said Peter Ilyich. "Let us live, my dear good friend. We shall always have time to die!"

But in Tchaikowsky's letter, one phrase blinded the widow to all the rest. "My dearest friend," she replied, "I cannot resist telling you of the deep ineffable gratitude inspired in

* Nadejda's daughter.

me by one of your sentences, 'But the thought that I may outlive you is unbearable.' *Mon dieu*, how I thank you for those words, and how precious they are. If you could imagine how I love you! It is not only love, but worship and adoration. If I feel sad or painful or afflicted, a few kind words from you can make me forget and forgive everything. Then I know I am not alone in the world; there is a heart that feels as mine feels, a man who understands and is in sympathy with me and who speaks of me in such a kind, human way. How grateful I am, and how dear you are to me! I have read that sentence scores of times each day since it came, and from the fullness of my heart unconsciously pressed the letter to my side."

Sometimes, reading these outbursts of Nadejda's, the reader trembles, wondering if Tchaikowsky will be equal to such emotional assault. Will he flee? Will he simply pack up and leave, instructing Anatol by mail to "arrange matters" for him? Will he answer Nadejda at all?

But of course he answers, and in kind! Her letter, he vows, gave him infinite joy. He knows it is wrong for him ever to doubt her love, and yet he does doubt; he needs the assurance of her word. But when this dread comes, when he darkly knows that she is far above him and all her love undeserved, then he has but one consolation—his music. Whatever its merits or demerits, his music is real, it has been wrought in deepest sincerity; may it lift him, then, to that high place on which Nadejda stands by her very nature.

And now especially, he needs her. Again the Certain Person is on his trail. She has repudiated all their agreements, she refuses a divorce and wants more money. What will be the end of it, God only knows. . . . Furthermore, today he finished proof-reading the piano arrangement of the third act of *Jeanne* and the *Marche Slav*, and now he has no work even should he desire it.

"In spite of the pleasure of knowing I have earned the right to idleness, I prefer that other more salutary condition, when serious work absorbs one's every thought and feeling. Sometimes this is upsetting, but on the other hand it has power to lift one out of any temporary dissatisfaction, whether one's own, or due to a care for one's fellow men. No sooner am I idle than thousands of disquieting thoughts rush upon me, as though glad I was free to welcome them."

Now that his orchestral suite was completed, Peter Ilyich accepted his hostess' oft-repeated invitation to visit her house. Elaborate plans were made so that they should not meet, and this time nothing miscarried. Tchaikowsky spent two hours roaming around the big house, upstairs and down.

"How I love this house!" he wrote. "Especially the rooms on the ground floor, yours and the ones I had when I was here before. I spent most of the time sitting in your room, and it would be hard to tell you how confident and happy I felt, there in a room you had just left and which was still so full of you. All the new furniture is most attractive, the cupboards and tables and the antique clock with its figures of knights. You can never guess which of all the familiar objects I like best: the embroidered bandit in my room! I myself can't imagine why that terrible man is dear to me; nothing is in fact, more inartistic than an embroidered human figure.

"I played your piano and pianino, had tea, went through Mr. Pahulsky's rooms and walked in the park. I came away in the pleasantest frame of mind, one reason was that in your album, among the cards of your closest friends I came upon my photograph—twice. It touched me to discover myself the only person in the book who is not a member of your family."

Tchaikowsky had called himself idle; as a matter of fact, when the Suite was done he kept right on working at Simaki to finish orchestrating the *Maid of Orleans*; this was accomplished the first week in September. As it was, Tchaikowsky had gone too fast with this work; conceived nine months ago in Florence, its composer had written another big work along with it—the First Orchestral Suite. The *Maid* was a four-act, six-scene opera; whether excessive haste or an unfortunate subject defeated him, something did. From the whole opera only one song survives: Jeanne's lovely aria, *Adieu forêts*.

Tchaikowsky finished with *Jeanne* on a day of annual festivity for Brailov manor-house. It was young Alexander (Sasha) von Meck's name-day. In the afternoon Peter Ilyich saw the procession of flower-garlanded boats float down the stream, and in the evening went again to the summer-house by the pond to watch the fireworks and the little regatta of lantern-strung boats. Twice, Nadejda passed close to him where he stood hidden by trees.

And now into paradise, into this quiet heaven under the ancient lime trees, came disquieting news. From Petersburg, Anatol telegraphed that he had lost his job, owing to "an unpleasantness" in his department. He was most anxious, said the message, to talk with Peter. Dreadfully distressed, Tchaikowsky ordered Alexis to make ready for immediate departure. Into the carryall went the comfortable country clothes, notably the cool wash suits of heavy rough silk imported from China—so much enjoyed by Russian country gentlemen. Into the carryall went also the First Orchestral Suite and the *Maid of Orleans*, both works fully orchestrated and ready for printing press or public stage.

Good-bye and good-bye, my kindest hostess!—cried Tchaikowsky. And good-bye, my incomparable, my precious friend!—replied the widow. May we meet again very, very soon....

21

*Nadejda's confession. Tchaikowsky's fame
begins to spread in Europe*

Tchaikowsky went back to Petersburg, homesick for Brailov the instant he left it and feeling, here in the city, dazed and unhappy as if he had been struck, he said, butt-end on the head. As to Nadejda, down in Brailov alone, something epochal had just occurred. Jurgenson had sent her Klindworth's long-delayed piano arrangement of the Fourth Symphony—"our" symphony. Over and over she had played it and as a result had lain awake for two nights in fever and

224

in frenzy. In this music she vowed she heard the whole story of her life; had she been condemned to die for listening, she would, she protested, have listened just the same.

So completely did the symphony disarm her that Nadejda wrote an extraordinary letter, revealing not only her emotion of the moment, but the long pent-up reality of her suffering at the time of Tchaikowsky's marriage two years ago.

Nadejda Philaretovna to Peter Ilyich

Brailov
Sept. 26, 1879
Friday at 8 A.M.

"How sorry I am, my dearest, that you feel so badly in Petersburg, but—forgive me—I am glad you are homesick for Brailov. I doubt if you could ever understand how jealous I am of you, in spite of the absence of personal contact between us. Do you know that I am jealous in the most unpardonable way, as a woman is jealous of the man she loves? Do you know that when you married it was terribly hard for me, as though something had broken in my heart? The thought that you were near that woman was bitter and unbearable. And do you know what a wicked person I am? I rejoiced when you were unhappy with her! I reproached myself for that feeling. I don't think I betrayed myself in any way, and yet I could not destroy my feelings. They are something a person does not order. I hated that woman because she did not make you happy, but I would have hated her a hundred times more if you had been happy with her. I thought she had robbed me of what should be mine only, what is my right, because I love you more than anyone and value you above everything in the world. If this knowledge bothers you, forgive my involuntary confession. I have spoken out. The reason is, the symphony. But I believe it is better for you to know that I am not such an idealistic person as you think. And then, it cannot change anything in our relationship. I don't want any change. I should like to be sure that nothing will be changed as my life draws to its close, that nobody . . . But that I have no right to say. Forgive me and forget all I have said—my mind is upset.

"Forgive me, please, and realize that I feel well and that I

am in need of nothing. Good-bye, dear friend; forget this
letter, but do not forget your heartily loving,

"N. von Meck

"P.S. Would you mind, please, acknowledging the receipt
of this letter?"

This was the first and last time that Nadejda ever asked
to have a letter acknowledged. And mark this: She wanted
to be sure that nothing in their relationship would change,
"that nobody . . . But this I have no right to say." Did
Nadejda mean that she hoped Peter Ilyich would never take
another wife, that no woman would come between them
again? If so—and what else could she have meant?—she
must in truth have been totally ignorant of one dominant
trait in her friend's nature.

Answering Nadejda's reckless confession, Tchaikowsky
did the wise thing and the only thing he could have done.
He ignored all that had been said about Antonina and about
jealousy, and gave expression to his very honest pleasure in
Nadejda's reaction toward the symphony.

To Nadejda Philaretovna

Grankino
Oct. 10, 1879

"It is impossible to say how glad I was to see your handwriting and to know we were again in communication.
Jurgenson forgot to tell me that the piano arrangement of
our symphony had at last been published, so your letter was
the first news I had of it. I am tremendously elated that you
are satisfied with the arrangement, which in truth is well
and skillfully done.

"As for the music itself, I knew beforehand that you would
like it; how could it have been otherwise? I wrote it with
you constantly in mind. At that time, I was not nearly so
intimate with you as now, but already I sensed vaguely that
no one in the world could respond more keenly to the deepest
and most secret gropings of my soul. No musical dedication
has ever been more seriously meant. It was spoken not only
on my part but on yours; the symphony was not, in truth,
mine but *ours*. Forever it will remain my favorite work, as

the monument of a time when upon a deep, insidiously-growing mental disease, upon a whole series of unbearable sufferings, grief and despair, suddenly, hope dawned and the sun of happiness began to shine—and that sun was embodied in the person to whom the symphony was dedicated.

"I tremble to think what might have happened if fate had not sent you to me. I owe you everything: Life, the chance to pursue freedom—that hitherto unattainable ambition, and such abundance of good fortune as had never occurred to me even in dreams.

"I read your letter with gratitude and love too strong for expression in any medium but music. May I be able some time to express it thus!

"Dear friend, may you keep well. I wish it for you more than for myself. Reading how our symphony caused you sleepless nights, I felt my heart constricted. I want my music henceforth to be a source of joy and consolation, and with all my strength I desire for you a spirit well and calm."

Nadejda did not forget herself again. If music was indeed to be all the food of love, why then, she would have more nourishment and more! Why should not Colonne, who had played the *Tempest* in Paris last winter, play the Fourth Symphony, she, of course, to supply the funds? Tchaikowsky received her suggestion in Kamenka and wrote to thank her:

To Nadejda Philaretovna

Kamenka
Oct. 12, 1879

"Concerning the performance of our symphony by Colonne, first let me thank you, my dear kind friend, for your care concerning my glory! Certainly, I should like extremely to have Colonne play the symphony, although I know beforehand that it can meet with no success in France. I don't feel at all sure of what Colonne will say to your suggestion. It is considered a great opportunity to be on one of his programs, an honor that even the Parisian composers solicit in vain. It may easily be that Colonne could not dare play a whole symphony written by a foreigner; it was an act of great civic courage in him to play my *Tempest*, which consists of only one movement. Whether or no the fact that you offer him money will be a deciding factor I cannot say, but anyway, dear friend, I warn you not to be surprised if Colonne turns down your proposition quite politely and firmly."

As soon as she had Tchaikowsky's approval, the widow, who by now had, as usual in autumn, left Brailov for the continent—"for the West"—the Russians call it, and hurried to Paris to set the musical wheels in motion. Tchaikowsky's warning had not been unwarranted. Nadejda found that the names von Meck and Tchaikowsky, which opened wide every musical door in Russia, in Paris fell on unresponsive ears.

A gentleman could elbow in where a lady could not, suggested Pahulsky, all afire for action. Suppose the three of them went to Colonne's concert next Sunday at the Chatelet? Afterward he, Pahulsky, could waylay the grand vizier at the stage door. . . .

Next Sunday the grand vizier (so Nadejda called him in her letter to Tchaikowsky) was bearded as per schedule. After some trouble Pahulsky succeeded in seeing Colonne alone and telling his story. . . . So Russia would like to have Tchaikowsky's Fourth Symphony played at the Chatelet? said Colonne dryly. . . . Not Russia, explained Pahulsky, eagerly. A lady, a great admirer of Monsieur Tchaikowsky's talent. A Madame von Meck who knew that M. Colonne appreciated the Russian maestro's compositions.

"Ah, a lady!" said Colonne, with eloquent inflection. And who, he inquired blandly, would pay the expenses of all this? Tchaikowsky's publisher? It cost money to produce a symphony.

Pahulsky was indignant. He flushed. By no means the publisher. The *lady* would pay. M. Tchaikowsky was far too famous to need any such stimulus to the sale of his works; publishers all over Europe were fighting for his name on their lists. Besides, M. Tchaikowsky was a gentleman born, with a good position in society. . . .

M. Colonne's tone changed. He smiled. He made an appointment to discuss the matter further with M. Pahulsky next day. And when tomorrow came, Colonne agreed to play the symphony, provided that after two rehearsals the usual committee of musicians approved the score. Nadejda, waiting in her hotel for this news, rushed off and telegraphed Moscow for the score of the symphony. Then she wrote Tchaikowsky the whole story, half in triumph, half in derision.

The committee passed favorably upon the score when it came, and Nadejda was beside herself with delight. Tchaikowsky was in Kamenka; Nadejda kept her letter, knowing that Peter Ilyich was coming abroad very soon, and would stop in Paris. Meanwhile, in Kamenka, Peter had had depressing musical news from Moscow. His professional objectiveness—the only objectiveness he possessed—did not fail him, however, and he was able to criticize his opera *Vakoula* (written in 1847) as severely as the audience apparently had criticized it.

Vakoula's reception in Moscow was poor. However, only a day or two later the composer heard that Nicholas Rubinstein had played his new piano sonata superbly, and that Moscow had received it well. Tchaikowsky went to Moscow on business and then up to Petersburg to take train for Paris and Nadejda. They had planned another fortnight "together." From Petersburg at two in the morning he wrote one of the most blandly self-critical notes ever penned from gentleman to lady at that time of day:

To Nadejda Philaretovna

Petersburg
Nov. 10, 1879
Two A.M.

"My dear, kind friend,
"The journey was not unpleasant. I spent two days in Moscow proof-reading and saw all the Conservatory people, including N. G. Rubinstein who wanted me to hear how he plays my sonata." (This was the G major Sonata written in the spring of 1878.) "He plays it wonderfully; I am sorry you could not hear it. I was astonished at the amazing artistic effect he got from that rather dry and complicated piece."

And now once more, the cold Warsaw Station at night, the

long journey to Berlin and Paris. Then the Gare du Nord early on a November morning, with Pahulsky bowing eagerly from the platform, Nadejda's letter in his hand. But Pahulsky could not wait for Peter Ilyich to read the news; in the cab rattling over cobblestones to Tchaikowsky's hotel, Pahulsky related all the Colonne story. As soon as he reached his rooms, Tchaikowsky wrote Nadejda: "Thank you, dear friend, for this new proof of your sympathy with my music. You have rendered great service to the cause of spreading my music beyond Russia. I know the public will be hard upon our symphony, but its performance will excite interest, and this is what I need most just now."

Pahulsky went home and told Nadejda that Peter Ilyich had promised to write his thanks to Colonne. The widow was pleased, but she cautioned Tchaikowsky to come right out and tell Colonne that his admirers, not his publishers, were behind this project.

Tchaikowsky replied that he would be only too glad to do so; it was what he himself had desired. After this exchange the two were silent concerning the symphony; the performance was not to take place for over a month, and Tchaikowsky busied himself with other work. He settled down easily in Paris; by now, he and Nadejda were so used to living in the same city that they accepted the situation like any old married couple reunited. Tchaikowsky began work at once, sketching the first rough draft of a new piano concerto (his Second Piano Concerto, to be dedicated to Nicholas Rubinstein).

During this November and December in Paris, Nadejda provoked from Peter some interesting critical opinions concerning his own early works.

"You ask, dear friend, if I wrote any early works that were never published. Indeed I did, and many of them! And how I bless the Fates that did not permit me to find an amateur who might have been willing to publish all that infantile lisping, which at the time I considered serious composition! A few of my early things have been preserved, most of them I burned. Among these, *Voyevoda*, from which the dances were saved, and *Undine*. The latter was rejected by the directors of the Petersburg theatres in 1868, at which I was much offended, but later I was thankful enough that the directors had rendered me this service. It was an atrocious opera, and I threw it in the fire without a regret."

Curiously enough, Tchaikowsky's criticism of his own work was frequently more objective as well as more just than his criticism of his contemporaries. He was quite right in recognizing that his highest powers were symphonic rather than operatic. Nevertheless the drama had for him a fascination that drew him again and again to the stage, with all its panoply of costume and color—and all the hateful wire-pulling necessary to achieve operatic production.

Nadejda was persistent in urging Peter Ilyich to give some of his compositions to a French or German publisher and thus advertise himself abroad in a legitimate and dignified way. From the rest of Tchaikowsky's letter it will be seen that Nadejda was not the only tempter to woo him thus. His refusal and his reasons for it are proof enough of why Jurgenson, Tchaikowsky's Russian publisher, remained a lifelong friend. There is loyalty here as well as independence and the warm quality of gratitude which was, with Tchaikowsky, a never-failing trait:

"By the way, yesterday I had an offer from Furstner, a Berlin publisher, for all my future works. He asks me to name my terms, and this is not the first such offer I have had from German publishers. It is all very flattering but I refused, and this is why: Long before I enjoyed any musical reputation, Jurgenson willingly undertook to publish my things, at first free of charge and then at a very reasonable fee. Later, he began to publish anything and everything I wrote, and as you know, I write a lot. Up to now, owing to slowness of recognition where music is concerned, I have not earned him a cent, because while a few of my things sell well, others lie forever on the shelves of his warehouse. He bases all his calculations on the hope that some day my reputation will cross the frontier and my works will move in a free European market.

"So doesn't it follow that just now when my name is becoming known in Europe, it would be unfair to confine

Jurgenson's profit on my works to Russia? Besides, I don't want to cater to the German prejudice against Russian music. For a long time now, the Germans have sent their own musical goods to Russia and refused to export anything therefrom. They actually prefer to pirate an edition—as they did with my short pieces and romances—rather than buy the music from a Russian publisher. Probably Jurgenson will be the first Russian publisher to have his editions ordered from abroad. I believe it is the duty of every honest Russian to refuse relentlessly any such German offers.

"So yesterday I wrote Furstner a polite but decisive refusal."

It was nearly Christmas when Tchaikowsky wrote this in Paris. Nadejda was planning to leave France immediately in order to spend the holidays at home in Brailov, and Peter Ilyich, whose nomad life was to continue for some six years before he would see fit to find himself a homestead in Russia, was well content to celebrate Christmas in Rome with Modeste and his pupil and of course, the ever-faithful Alexis. This time his farewells to Nadejda were not so ardent. He was not to be left completely alone and moreover, a heavy program of work lay ahead. Here in Paris he had finished the rough draft of the new (and second) piano concerto. His farewell letter does not omit the usual inexorable summing-up of work accomplished during the Paris visit. In Rome he hoped to rewrite the Second Symphony. His notebook, he said, was filled.

Fortunately, Nadejda was one of those rare women who are capable of feeling that a man's work is more important than any personal attachment; indeed, for her the two things were in this case synonymous. And curiously enough, when the Fourth Symphony was finally played by Colonne, both Nadejda and the composer had left Paris.

The symphony was received rather coldly. Yet the venture was well worth while; Nadejda had done her friend a service. This performance marked the beginning of Tchaikowsky's recognition in Europe. A few days later his finest string quartet, the third (E flat minor) was played in Paris, together with his B minor Serenade for violin, with orchestral accompaniment. In Berlin, Budapest and New York the brilliant, staccato B Flat Minor Piano Concerto (over which Tchaikowsky and Rubinstein had quarrelled) was performed with great success, and Leopold Damrosch wrote that New York had enjoyed the (first) orchestral suite enormously. This of course, was the suite upon which Tchaikowsky had worked so hard at intervals during the past year, and had finished upon his last visit to Brailov in August—the one to which he had with so much satisfaction added a sixth movement in slow waltz time, conceived upon the verandah of Nadejda's Simaki farm-house.

22

Rome—Russia—A present from Nadejda

Tchaikowsky went down to Rome at Christmas-time, and found Rome overpowering. There were too many things in this city, he complained. He envied Nadejda the stillness of Brailov. All this *sehenswürdigkeiten*—museums, ruins! What he craved was a quiet room and plenty of blank music paper.

Modeste Ilyich was an inveterate sightseer and a real lover of painting. He tried to convert his musical brother, but among all the magnificence, ancient and modern, that Modeste dragged him out to see, only one painter truly stirred and refreshed Peter Ilyich—Raphael—"that Mozart of painting," Tchaikowsky called him.

In truth Peter Ilyich was a man of but one language. His letters from Rome remind one of the letters written from Italy by his idol, Mozart. One of Mozart's biographers complained that it was always thus with musicians—blind, single-minded folk that they were. During his visit to Italy, Mozart never mentioned the Vatican or the Colosseum. All he talked about was the street singing, the dancers, and the opera.

It would seem that Tchaikowsky translated all esthetic emotion into musical terms. Not that he was incapable of experiencing emotion through the other arts; literature— Rousseau, Dickens, Dostoyevsky—moved him profoundly.

He loved poetry, that sister art to his own. But for sheer, pure esthetic experience, for the complete losing of himself —or finding of himself—he must needs turn to music. Even when, in the presence of some great painting or sculpture, Tchaikowsky felt emotion, he could express it only in terms of comparison to music. Standing, hat in hand, before the *Moses* of Michael Angelo, man was magnified to heroism. Trumpets crashed the note of victory—where before had Peter heard this glorious, exalted symphony—Beethoven!

Tchaikowsky returned his hat to his head, his *pince-nez* to his pocket, and turning reluctantly from *Moses*, went home to his hotel. He spent a bad night; his description of it and the day following could have been written by none but a Russian pen. How strange, to the Anglo-Saxon, reads this quite simple, candid admission of a grown man's tears as catharsis.

To Nadejda Philaretovna

Rome
January 30, 1880

"I spent a terrible night, my nerves as bad as they used to be. I thought I was dying, so dreadful were my sensations. In the morning I fell into a troubled, restless sleep . . .

"Anatol's letter came just now, with the details of my father's illness and death, a very touching story. Reading, I wept copiously, and it seemed to me that those tears, shed in farewell to a good man, a man who was truly pure in heart, had a healing influence upon me. My confession disappeared and in its place came resignation. Anatol says my father was conscious of approaching death, but that he accepted it bravely and cheerfully."

A few days later, with the revision of the Second Symphony completed, Tchaikowsky began a new composition.

To Nadejda Philaretovna

Rome
February 17, 1880

"I am still nervous and irritable, sleep badly and in general am out of order. But I have been working, and during the past few days have sketched the rough draft of an Italian capriccio based on popular melodies. I think it has a bright future; it will be effective because of the wonderful melodies I happened to pick up, partly from published collections and partly out in the streets with my own ears."

Peter's hotel was next door to the barracks of the Royal Cuirassiers, Italian cavalrymen; how surprised their plumed and resplendent bugler would have been had he known that a Russian barbarian in the Hotel Constanzi, listening every evening to his call, had copied it down for the opening fanfare to a piece for full orchestra! It is a brilliant piece of music, and still popular today. Like other of Tchaikowsky's works that are supposed to reproduce Italian or French scenes, the *Capriccio* is strikingly Russian.

Tchaikowsky's sudden nervous depressions are unchartable. Here in Rome, for instance, he should have been content; Modeste was with him, the weather was glorious, and he was working.

"And yet," wrote Peter Ilyich, "a worm gnaws at my heart; I don't understand why, being quite well physically, I cannot sleep and feel this lassitude. *Dieu*, what an incomprehensible and complicated machine is the human organism! The closest self-examination does not explain the phenomena of our spiritual and material life. And how can one draw a line between the mental and the purely physical? Sometimes I believe myself suffering from some mysterious, purely physical illness that is responsible for my changes of mood. Lately I have thought my heart was out of order, but only last summer a doctor pronounced it in perfect condition. So the blame must rest with the nerves—but what are the nerves? Why, on the same day, without apparent reason, do they behave normally and then lose their elasticity and energy, become unreceptive to artistic impressions, incapable of work? It is all a riddle."

Besides the symphony revision and the *Capriccio*, Tchaikowsky worked in Rome at his Second Piano Concerto which he had conceived in Kamenka and had sketched out in Paris. It was to be dedicated to Nicholas Rubinstein—partly in gratitude for his splendid playing of the B Flat Minor Piano Concerto at the Paris Exposition and partly, perhaps, in the hope that Rubinstein would do as well by this one. But even Rubinstein's glorious playing would not be able to make the Second Concerto into something as brilliant and vital as the First.

At intervals all during his life, Tchaikowsky received orders from Jurgenson or a Grand Duke or one of the conservatories, to write some kind of a *pièce d'occasion*. He always balked, but the professional artist in him would never let him turn down a commission.

To Nadejda Philaretovna

Rome
February 8, 1880

"My dear and kind friend:

"Yesterday Davidov" (Director of the Petersburg Conservatory) "wrote informing me there is to be a big pageant of tableaux with music on March 2nd.* All the Russian composers are contributing something and I was imperatively requested to write music for the seventh tableaux. I couldn't refuse, so wired Davidov my acceptance. My tableau represents 'Montenegro receiving the Russian declaration of war.' You can imagine what an inspiration this will be! However I shall do my part, though reluctantly, and I spent all today at it. It can't possibly result in anything good, and the vexing part is that I have no idea how the other composers will treat their subjects. Something tells me they all chose what they wanted and then I was sent the left-over. However there is no time to get in touch with Petersburg, so I set to work as hard as I could. If I don't satisfy them they have no right to complain.

"Yesterday I had your letter, and am tremendously happy that you like my suite" (the First Orchestral Suite, which had just been published). "I believe, dear friend, that when you become better acquainted with the suite, you will like the *Andante* best; I wrote this with real warmth.

"P. Tchaikowsky"

Nadejda was much agitated over this commission. Was he actually going to execute it? What for? *Must* he write this horrible thing? What was the use—she implied—of her

* Celebrating twenty-five years of Alexander II's reign.

sending registered letters every quarter if Peter Ilyich was not to be freed of musical orders from outside? From first to last, this was Nadejda's reaction to Tchaikowsky's commission-writing, and it was in very essence the attitude of the amateur.

But Peter himself was not worrying about his musical honor. Montenegro and a few boomings and bangings had nothing to do with music. It was a job, and he was a musical craftsman who had long ago learned to do a job when necessary. Before Nadejda's protest reached him, the work was already done and forgotten.

"I mailed Davidov's music long ago," he reported to Nadejda. "I wrote it in frank disgust, knowing it could not possibly result in anything good. But then I don't see how the best-intentioned composer could find anything intriguing in the subject of 'The Impression produced in Montenegro by the Russian Manifesto.' I made a great noise with drums and trombones—and that was all."

But the drums and trombones remained forever silent. That same month, an attempt was made on the Tsar's life; national celebrations became, of course, impossible. Tchaikowsky's manuscript disappeared and has never been found; the composer himself, who owed much to royal patronage, was terribly distressed at the news of attempted assassination. "Whose fault was it?" he demanded. "Is there no strength or loyalty left among those whose duty it is to guard our Emperor? The picture this conveys of the awful disorder at home has driven music and indeed all other interests from my mind."

These letters were addressed to Nadejda in Russia; she was in Brailov for Christmas, surrounded by her children and grandchildren. It was unfortunate for the widow that her generation did not yet, in tubercular cases, connect cause and effect; here in Brailov where the southern sun caressed her, Nadejda was happy and her headaches were infrequent. But always she returned North to hurl herself against the Moscow winter. That shimmering snow so beloved by Tchaikowsky was relentless to the widow; it drove her indoors where she remained for months at a time in rooms overheated by huge porcelain stoves, while day by day her strength diminished and her nervous depression increased.

Then in spring—Brailov again and recovery, then Italy in autumn, with continued health until it was time for Moscow. Now, late in February of 1880, she was again on the Boulevard Rojdèstvensky, again she endured agonizing three-days' pain in her head; she could not lie down, and wrote Peter Ilyich standing, she said, against a desk.

But whenever Tchaikowsky's music was played in Moscow, Nadejda, sick or well, managed to be at hand. This month she heard his old opera, *The Oprichnik*, and found it delightful. The composer had completed this opera in 1872 and the censor had straightway, after the well-known lunacy of censors, forbidden its performance, deeming the subject revolutionary—the plot centered around Ivan the Terrible and his notorious bodyguard, the *Oprichnik*. The widow went on to say that Tchaikowsky's ballet *The Swan Lake* had also been performed in Moscow; Rubinstein had had a pupils' recital and a boy of sixteen had played the piano marvelously; his name was Siloti.

But best of all, went on Nadejda, was Tchaikowsky's new orchestral suite; it had had a brilliant success both in Petersburg and Moscow. Peter Ilyich was especially pleased at this news because not two months since, Jurgenson had written that Rubinstein considered the suite much too difficult for any orchestra to play. "Either Rubinstein is mistaken," Tchaikowsky had replied, "or I must give up composing. I try my very best to write simply and easily, and the more I try, the less I succeed. It is terrible." He had asked Taneyeff to write him in detail just what Rubinstein objected to, and Taneyeff did so, an enormous letter filled with technical argument, complaining in particular of the flute and oboe passage. Tchaikowsky was indignant; he could blow a flute himself, he replied, and those passages were child's play—certainly in comparison with *Francesca* or the Fourth Symphony.

Nadejda, however, knew nothing of this controversy. She had merely heard the Suite under Rubinstein's baton and was stirred. Before it was published, she and Tchaikowsky agreed that to dedicate it "To my best friend," like the Fourth Symphony, would be a reckless invitation of gossip, so the dedication remained a secret between them. But hearing it played, Nadejda conceived a vigorous idea. Why not have Colonne perform it in Paris? Even if the Fourth Symphony had not taken these stubborn French by storm, it had been excellent advertising for Peter Ilyich. What more reasonable than to hammer in one impression by another before Tchaikowsky's name was forgotten in France? She was writing Colonne now, she said, suggesting that he perform the suite at the Chatelet. . . .

But this time the widow's zeal had led her astray. She had stepped upon forbidden ground, the ground of professional self-respect. Any rich amateur can stage his own opera or symphony, but this kind of bribed performance means less than nothing to a serious musician. Tchaikowsky wrote the widow what amounted to a sharp rebuke, addressing her as his dear, kind and benevolent friend, he said he could not endure the humiliation of having Colonne paid again to play his music. To do it once had been splendid; as a single generous gesture, Colonne could understand it. As far as they both knew, Colonne had not divulged the financial side of the transaction, but "one can never be sure of anything. Should the news leak out that my symphonies are being played in Paris because they are *paid for*, oh, what a *coup* for all my enemies who write for the newspapers!

"And so I take the liberty of requesting that if you are going to recommend my further works to Colonne, you do it without supporting your recommendation with any pecuniary reward. But still I thank you once and again, my dear friend, for wanting to help me."

Reading this, Nadejda was horrified. She had sinned innocently and she implored forgiveness. But on the other hand, when, she asked, had anyone been able to bribe his way into the good graces of the Parisian public? All Parisians, including Colonne, were hard as brass. Here she was, dying to hear Tchaikowsky's music played, and here was a man who could play it. And Peter Ilyich asked her to sit supinely while opportunity walked by with its hand out!

Peter Ilyich read this letter in Rome just as he was leaving for Russia; in Moscow and Petersburg his operas were in rehearsal and his presence had been demanded. Spring was nearly here and it was good to be going home. Perhaps Nadejda Philaretovna was right and he had been too straight-laced in this Colonne matter. Peter got out his pencil and scribbled a letter, asking forgiveness for his harsh words and consenting to Nadejda's plan. But nevertheless, he would trust Colonne's motives only when he should hear that the gentleman had agreed to play his music without compensation.

And now Petersburg once more, and Moscow—letters, greetings, telegrams, evening parties and morning parties and all the dizzy routine of success. Up and down Peter travelled in train and cab through the spring mud and the spring rains, met at the station by his brothers and escorted to where celebration waited. Rehearsals to attend, singers to interview (A pest on all temperamental tenors and sopranos!). And always musical proof to correct, always those fat envelopes from Jurgenson. His eyes hurt, his head ached, and he knew that nobody cared except Nadejda. Letter after letter Peter sent frantically to Moscow; and soothingly, from her boudoir the widow replied.

In April Peter left glory behind and went out to Kamenka to assume once more the congenial role of Uncle Petia.

Here in Kamenka, he wrote, the children are everywhere; they run in and out his little garden at will, and as long as he has no responsibility toward them, they do not disturb his work. He is orchestrating the *Italian Capriccio*, also, he is reading proof—hateful task!—on the first act of the *Maid of Orleans*, in hopes it will reach the Petersburg stage next August.

This was late May. "Lilac is in full bloom," wrote Peter. "The bushes remind me constantly of Brailov, where for two years in succession I saw the lilacs in bloom. How lovely it must be there now!"

When Uncle Petia was at Kamenka, his sister and her husband often availed themselves of his presence to go away for a week. "Small anarchies occur," the composer reported to Nadejda, and although he enjoyed the children, his work suffered. During any enforced separation from music paper, Tchaikowsky's head seemed suddenly to teem with melody and musical ideas; a furious restlessness possessed him until he could transmit the ideas to paper. Lacking the regularity of long daily hours necessary for symphonic work, he would write songs and short piano pieces.

But Kamenka, with the "small anarchies," was beginning to weigh a bit heavily on Uncle Petia. As the children grew older and their troubles assumed moral rather than physical proportions, Peter worried overmuch about them. The pretty and self-willed eldest niece Tatiana, in particular caused him real grief. Nadejda, down in Brailov, knew he was overwrought and urged him to come south and occupy her house or the farm at Simaki; she herself was going abroad again, to Switzerland.

Early in July, therefore, Tchaikowsky and Alexis set forth for Brailov. They were to arrive at ten in the evening, and on the way, Peter's imagination became all too active. It was a year since he had been in Brailov; maybe they would not even recognize him when he got off the train! Some of his misgivings he wrote afterward to Jurgenson, some to his hostess, but the real story went to Anatol Ilyich up in Petersburg.

To Anatol

Brailov
July 18, 1880

"In the train it was very hot, and I was horribly nervous. Would the horses be at the station? I was haunted by all kinds of nonsense. What if N. Ph. had given orders I should be thrown out the minute I arrived? Lately I have been insane over the idea, first, that N. Ph. has changed toward me, and then I persuade myself that her solicitude has increased. So in the train, all the time I kept looking forward to a little sealed package containing several thousands, which I need devilishly.

"I arrive pompously, walk in, ask 'Are there any letters?' —'Yes!'—I go to my study and find two letters and a little sealed box. In much agitation I tear it open, but in place of thousands I find a watch and a note requesting that I accept it as a present! It was ordered during the winter in Paris, and has only just been delivered; it must be worth several thousand francs" (ten thousand, Peter had told Jurgenson). "On one side is Jeanne d'Arc on horseback—on the other Apollo with two muses, done on black enamel with little gold stars. Very delicate, sumptuous work. *Dieu!* but Nadejda Ph. is sweet.

"Just between you and me, I should have preferred the

price to the watch. N. Ph. had spoiled me so with anticipation of my wants and wishes, that somehow I expected her to know instinctively what I needed now. I was wrong though, and see now that I won't have a kopek before autumn."

What could Peter do? Nothing but sit down and write his thanks to Nadejda. There had been a letter with the watch, a short note saying that, as she had not long to live (thirteen years of life were ahead of Nadejda) she wished to leave her dearest friend a token, something he would always carry about his person so that he would be reminded of her very often.

"Do not speak of dying!" wrote Peter Ilyich. "Let us be on earth together as long as possible. Life has held much bitterness for us both, yet we have much to live for. Please God that all you say about *Jeanne d'Arc* may be true; for myself I shall be satisfied if my opera proves, if not great, at least outstanding. I shall carry the watch always, not because I need to be reminded of you—never for a moment do I forget you, nor ever shall, if I live to be a thousand—but because it is sweet to me to possess something etc. etc."

Nadejda was in Switzerland now; she had left Russia on the day she forwarded the watch from Moscow. She wrote as the solicitous hostess: did Peter Ilyich like her parrot and Milochka's poodle, Croquet? Had he driven her Moscow trotters? Why hadn't he mentioned the new furniture in her bedroom and sitting-room, and would he please forgive her for not clearing out all the bureau drawers? She had not realized he would be in the big house at all, but had thought he would go right down to the Simaki farm-house.

Peter Ilyich replied happily to these questions. He liked everything in Brailov, and as to the big grey parrot, she fascinated him. Every morning, composer and parrot sat on the terrace and conversed for hours.

Tchaikowsky's month in Brailov moved now with ever-increasing emotional tempo. He was not working hard, merely correcting proof on *Jeanne d'Arc*, but he could get drunk upon nature and solitude as other men upon applause. He moved into the Simaki farm-house and in the wheat field beyond his garden one day fell on his knees and thanked God for letting him be part of all this summer beauty, this holy country stillness. At night he would sit by his open window hour after hour, watching the moon above the giant branches of the oaks, breathing the flower-laden air and listening, every nerve taut with ecstasy, to the mystic untraceable noises of the night.

And now, into this paradise, this beneficent solitude of forest and stream where Peter Ilyich might stand before his house and watch the sun go down, appeared once more that spectre of his past mistakes, that reminder of the inexorable whip of fate—Antonina. Not in person; only a letter. She wrote that she consented to a divorce, and in the next paragraph swore to repudiate any "scurrilous and improbable papers," meaning that she would never accept adultery as grounds, thereby making divorce impossible!

Analyzed, Antonina's letter was nonsense. Why, therefore, Peter asked Nadejda, should nonsense affect him like a dose of strongest poison? "The mere sight of her handwriting on the envelope, with my address written by her, makes me actually sick, not only mentally but physically. Yesterday, for instance, I had such pain in my feet that I could scarcely move; I am ashamed to confess that the severest nausea and weakness possessed me all day."

Tchaikowsky's physical reaction to emotional strain carries an extraordinarily evident symbolism. Properly to interpret it would require the tools of a psychiatric specialist. These nocturnal tremblings of which the composer complained, these sudden pains in the feet that made movement impossible—were they symbolic of a frustrated desire to escape? The layman dare not say, but common sense makes him hazard a guess. Antonina wrote Peter Ilyich that he was a liar, that he and his cousins had been spreading slander about her around Petersburg. And on the fragrant terrace of Brailov, Peter Ilyich, the letter in his lap, sat helplessly wondering if it had been a lie and slander to tell Tolia the girl was stupid and that he hated her. . . . "If you must gossip about people's faults," went on Antonina's letter—for the life of him Peter could not leave it unread—"why don't you begin with your own terrible vices and tell about them?"

If a man cannot run from danger there is but one alternative: to forget danger. Oblivion comes only in work. In such a state of mind, Peter could not compose music, but he could correct proof. So he finished the proof sheets of the *Maid of Orleans*, then went to Nadejda's piano and played over the first two acts before mailing them to Moscow.

To Nadejda Philaretovna

Simaki
July 30, 1889

"Either I am much mistaken or you, my dear friend, did right in having the heroine of my latest composition engraved on my watch. I don't believe the *Maid* is the best and deepest thing I have written, but it seems to me it is the piece which may make me popular. *Onegin* and some of my instrumental works are children that lie closer to my heart and personality. I wrote the *Maid* with less self-absorption than, for instance, our symphony or the Second String Quartet, but at the same time I gave the opera more care as to scenic-phonetic effects, and this in opera, is the main consideration."

In his estimate, the composer was right indeed in sensing that the *Maid of Orleans* was not so inspired as *Onegin*, but utterly wrong in prophesying that the *Maid* would be the most popular of his operas. Now, except for Jeanne's *Aria*, the *Maid* is forgotten, but Tatiana, singing by candlelight, still writes the fatal letter to Onegin while the world beyond the footlights heaves rhythmical, sympathetic sighs—a world that even as it boasts brave scorn of sentimentality, succumbs in tearful delight, a few scenes later, to the spectacle of love denied by virtuous womanhood.

Tchaikowsky was much nearer the mark in his criticism of *Carmen*. One night in Simaki, in order to rest, he said, from his own music, he played Carmen over from beginning to end. Bizet had written it five years ago.

"To me," Tchaikowsky wrote, "this is in every sense a *chef d'oeuvre*, one of the few pieces which will some day mirror most vividly the musical endeavor of a whole generation.

"It is as though Bizet said to us: 'You are not seeking for something lofty and grandiose; you want something pretty. Well, here is a pretty opera.' And indeed, I know of no music which has better title to the quality I would call pretty—*le joli*. From beginning to end, it is charming and delightful. In it one finds a number of striking harmonies and entirely new combinations of sound, but these do not exist merely for themselves. Bizet is an artist who pays tribute to modernity, but he is warned by true inspiration.

"I am convinced that in about ten years *Carmen* will have become the most popular opera in the world. But no man is a prophet in his own country; in Paris, *Carmen* did not win real success. Soon after its first performance Bizet died, though in the bloom of youth and health. Who knows, perhaps the failure of his opera killed him?"

And now it was August and Peter had no work to do. With idleness, his former contentment mounted now to almost dangerous ecstasy. Ahead of him was Kamenka, with all the family troubles awaiting. Furthermore, Kamenka, for all its romantic history, was far from romantically landscaped; the mills and township ruined both air and scenery. The contrast between this and Simaki made Tchaikowsky even more aware, during these last few days, of the beauty he must leave. This was natural enough; what surprises the reader is Tchaikowsky's own very sane criticism of his too-emotional state; he wrote his hostess that it would be really dangerous for him to indulge himself by staying longer in Brailov.

Nadejda by now had gone down from Interlaken to Arcachon, on the coast of France. Tchaikowsky hated to leave Simaki before hearing of her safe arrival. Was she well— Was she tired—Would he hear from her soon? "My dearest, my blessed friend," wrote Peter Ilyich, "I have been very happy here; I do not know how to thank you. I take leave now of my hostess and wish her good health. . . ."

23

Nadejda's little Parisian pianist.
Tchaikowsky's growing fame

While Tchaikowsky made his farewells to Simaki, his hostess at Interlaken was writing history in her own way; she had, indeed, taken history into her house.

Nadejda to Peter Ilyich

Interlaken, July 22, 1880
"... A young pianist from Paris, who has just finished the Conservatoire course with the *Premier Prix*, has come to stay with us. He was in M. Marmontel's class. I invited him to give the children lessons during the summer, to accompany Julia's singing and play four hands with me. The boy plays well, with virtuosity; his technique is brilliant but his playing carries no expression of himself, absolutely none. He has not lived long enough for that; he says he is twenty, but looks no more than sixteen."

This boy with the brilliant, cold technique was Claude Debussy, who was indeed to mature in time to show plenty of originality. He was destined, in fact, to be the most influential French composer of his generation, the founder of musical impressionism, the man to introduce the artistic conception of "atmosphere." Also he broke, at his convenience, the boundaries of traditional tonality and by his example gave music a wider scope.

But this was all to come much later. In Nadejda von Meck's household that summer of 1880, the young Debussy was exactly what his hostess said he was, a brilliant pianist without depth or maturity. History has proved the justice of Nadejda's criticism. Debussy, who was in fact eighteen at the time, matured, for a musician, very late; he was twenty-eight before he began to write great music. In her first mention of him to Tchaikowsky, Nadejda gave the young man

246

no name; the next time she speaks of him he has become
Monsieur Bussy, this young man who was to push open a
new musical door.

Nadejda Philaretovna to Peter Ilyich

Arcachon, Aug. 18, 1880

". . . I myself have never played Bizet's *Carmen*, but as
far as I can judge from the *musicus*, Bussy, the Parisian
musical world at present holds Bizet very high. Judging also
from M. de Bussy as a sample, I have become convinced
that one cannot draw any parallel between Parisian and
Russian pianists, so incomparably higher are our own as
musicians and masters of technique. And mine is *un
lauréat* — received the *Premier Prix* when he was graduated
this year. Now he is working for the *Prix de Rome* — all
nonsense, those prizes, not worth a rap."

Arcachon, Aug. 19, 1880

"Yesterday I decided to play our Symphony with my
little Frenchman and as a result I am in a terribly nervous
state. I cannot play it without fire darting through my every
fibre! It took twenty-four hours for me to recover. My partner did not perform the symphony well, but sightread wonderfully. It is his only — but very great — talent, he reads
compositions, even yours, *à livre ouvert*. His second virtue —
a reflective virtue, so to speak, is that he is delighted with
your music. He is a pupil of Massenet's in theory, so of
course Massenet is his hero; but yesterday he and I played
your suite and he was delighted with the fugue and said,
'Among all the modern fugues I never found anything so
beautiful. M. Massenet could never have equalled it.' He
does not like the Germans and says, 'They have not our
temperament and are too heavy, possessing no clarity of
utterance.' On the whole, he is purely a product of the Paris
Boulevard."

Tchaikowsky made no reply to this. He had gone up from
Brailov to Kamenka and was extremely busy as Uncle Petia;
the nieces were planning another fête with an operetta and
he had been to Kiev to find a libretto.
From Switzerland, that autumn of 1880, Nadejda went

247

to Arcachon on the east coast of France and thence to Florence, taking her little Frenchman with her. She was to occupy the same Villa Oppenheim out among the hills, and no sooner had she arrived — at seven on the morning of September 20th — than she partook of some hasty breakfast and drove to the Villa Bonciani. It was a sad pilgrimage. Nadejda, setting off eagerly down the road, was not the first woman to meet bitter disappointment at the revisiting of an abandoned trysting place. "That small house Bonciani," she wrote Peter Ilyich, "so dear to me, so filled with tender reminiscence — how happy I was when you were there and when in passing I could sense your invisible presence and hear the sound of your fingers on the piano! Today, driving by that cherished spot, tears came to my eyes, and my heart constricted with a pain that became fury the instant I saw that someone else was living there. What a vile thought! I wanted to evict this person immediately and rent the house myself so nobody could live there. But I forebore because I am considered queer enough already!

"By night, when the moon was up, I went again. The Villa was all lighted from within and I could hear someone playing the piano; I felt even sadder and more disappointed. Oh, my dearest, matchless friend, why are you not here? If only you could see how nice it is, the green is so fresh and the countryside so charming. . . ."

Nothing could console the widow but music. It was fortunate that she had her little Bussyk from Paris. She sent Tchaikowsky an opera of Ponchielli's for criticism, adding to the parcel "a little composition, one of many completed by my little pianist, Bussy. The boy is preparing to be a composer and writes very nice little things, but it is all an echo of his professor, Massenet. He is now writing a *trio*, also very good, but redolent of Massenet. He reads music and accompanies a singer perfectly."

Tchaikowsky replied that he would look over the opera and Bussy's composition with the greatest interest. Meanwhile Nadejda had enlarged her household orchestra.

Florence, Oct. 11, 1880
"Another musician has arrived at my house — Danil-

248

chenko"—(a cellist). "He finishes at the (Moscow) Conservatory this spring and planned to go abroad; my engagement with my little Frenchman is drawing to a close. So, not wanting to take a new one—it is annoying to have so many new faces in the family—I wrote to Moscow saying that if Danilchenko was going abroad, to come to me for work. My letter reached him on the eve of his departure for Berlin, so he changed his plan and came to me in Florence. As Bussy is still here and Danilchenko has nothing to do, they play trios every evening. My little Frenchman has written a very nice trio. I regret that I cannot send it to you for criticism, dear friend, because there is not time to copy it, as he is leaving some day soon. I am sorry he is going, because he is such a good partner for four-hand playing; he reads music wonderfully, and as I am constantly playing new things—new to him also—this talent is particularly valuable."

In October Nadejda received the piano arrangement of Tchaikowsky's new opera, the *Maid of Orleans*. In spite of a headache, Nadejda studied an act a day. "It was fortunate," she wrote, "that the opera came while my little Frenchman is still here. He played it to me perfectly. Listening, I was moved to ecstasy. I must admit, dear friend, that I was a little fearful about this opera, and this is why: The chief characteristic of your compositions is their Russian-ness, and I was afraid that, unnoticed by you, this quality might creep into a French opera and then those nasty Frenchmen would raise a shout about it and laugh, and I am terribly sensitive to every criticism of you, terribly jealous for your reputation."

The widow's fears were justified; the opera is a very samovar for Russian-ness. But Nadejda, carried away as her little Frenchman proceeded with the playing of the opera, soon declared the music possessed a scope, a grandeur that overrode all national boundaries, all limitations of time and place. "And how good the love scenes are!" the widow exclaimed, adding with one of her characteristic jibes at love: "In these scenes you are always higher than the subject." Might she be permitted to give her little Frenchman a copy of the opera, and might she have Bussyk make a four-hand arrangement of the dances from *The Swan Lake* and then have them published? Another thing, many private persons have orchestras of their own, as witness the *Orchestre de M. Derwiss*, in Nice, and the Helmeberger Quartet in Vienna. Why should she not have a *Trio de Mme de Meck*? So she has had a photograph made of her trio and is sending Peter Ilyich a copy.

Tchaikowsky enjoyed the photograph. "Bussy's face and hands," he wrote, "bear an indefinable resemblance to Anton Rubinstein's in his youth. God grant Bussy's fate may be as fortunate as that of the Tsar of pianists. Please give Bussy's arrangement of my opera to Jurgenson, no other publisher. I shall be very glad to let your little Frenchman have the *Maid of Orleans*."

But Nadejda decided not to let Bussy carry away the opera score, after all. "I am afraid," she wrote, "that these knavish French composers—Massenet, Delibes, Godard, etc. —will steal whole handfuls from your opera and present them to the Parisian public as their own. I assure you, Peter Ilyich, they steal from you constantly; the other day when we were playing your First Symphony, four hands, I realized it. I too noticed Bussy's resemblance to Anton Rubinstein. I believe in his future because of his devotion to his chosen work; it is his only interest in life. He has a very frivolous nature, quite French, but his heart is very kind. I am sending you his arrangement of your dances from *The Swan Lake*, to give to Jurgenson for printing. Please don't put M. de Bussy's name on them, because if they fell into the hands of Jules Massenet, my young man might be scolded."

Florence
Nov. 15, 1880

"My little Frenchman has left, and it is very annoying that I can no longer hear your piano sonata and other charming compositions, of which I adore especially the F minor Waltz, which Bussy played very well. My trios are ended too. Imagine, Peter Ilyich, the boy wept when he left. It truly touched me deeply; he has such a loving heart. He would not have gone at all, but the directors of the Conservatory were already annoyed because he had postponed his return these two weeks."

Perhaps all of Bussyk's tears were not for his kind hostess. Nadejda's daughter Sonia was fourteen now, extremely pretty with her red-gold hair and velvety brown eyes—and well aware already of the use and value of these weapons. Debussy gave her a piano lesson every day, and long before it was time for him to return to Paris, he was utterly vanquished. He was however, still master of his feelings enough to deceive Nadejda; he hoped to be invited back next year. He would be nineteen then and Sonia nearly at marriageable age. He was poor and he was nobody, but there was power within him and he knew it—and at nineteen a man will aspire to anything. Before he was halfway to Paris, Bussyk was mentally imploring Mme von Meck to let him return next summer and play duets with her.

Mme von Meck did let him return, not only next summer but the summer after; she greeted him affectionately and wrote Tchaikowsky how glad they all were to see little Bussyk. Sonia's eyes were deeper now, brown velvet under the gold of her hair, and Sonia knew more than one way to play duets. Bussyk's hands upon the piano keys were cold no longer; even the widow admitted that his *Premier Prix* virtuosity had caught flame somewhere....

And then one summer's day Bussyk came to her. Perhaps the widow was not altogether surprised at his confession of love; young men were always sighing after Sonia. What truly astonished her was that the boy actually asked to marry Sonia. A von Meck and a Bussy, penniless minstrel from the Parisian boulevards! The interview was brief. The widow smiled, pressed Bussyk's hand and Bussyk found himself on the train for Paris, every kind, inexorable word of Nadejda's more bitter in his heart than if she had denounced him. Why, she had scarcely taken him seriously....

Little Bussyk, as the world knows, became famous. In after years, when he had become one of the first musicians of Europe, the von Mecks still spoke of him affectionately, and with Sonia safely married would have been glad to welcome him back. But a great man can go or stay as he chooses, and Claude Debussy never revisited the scene of his defeat.

All this of course, did not take place at once. That autumn of 1880, when Bussyk in Florence first played trios for Nadejda von Meck, assuring her that nobody living could write a fugue to equal Monsieur Tchaikowsky's, Monsieur Tchaikowsky himself was in Kamenko reading proof, caring for his sister's children, struggling with nervous fatigue. "There is a republic here," wrote Uncle Petia one night—at two A.M. "Master and mistress of the house are away and chaos reigns. The children are more than usually mischievous and I tremble to think what may happen before their parents return. Yesterday Volodia fell off his horse twice and only luck kept him from being smashed to bits. Mitia, however, gives me most anxiety; he is terribly mischievous. Brother Anatol is still here . . . Our fête with the operetta took place last week amid much excitement; afterward I went to bed with a nervous fever, as always when my routine is broken by contact with strangers."

Tchaikowsky's work progressed; three parts of a brand new orchestral suite were finished. (Suite Number Two, in four movements, not completed until 1883.) The *Maid of Orleans* was to be performed in Petersburg simultaneously with *Eugene Onegin* in Moscow. There was no longer any question as to who was the most popular musician in Russia; Peter Ilyich was famous and knew it. Nadejda knew it too, and in her villa among the Tuscan hills had been pondering the subject of fame.

"Fame?" cried Peter Ilyich, in reply. "Glory? What contending feelings the word raises! I desire it, I struggle desperately for it, and yet it is hateful to me."

And how he longs for his music to be known!—the letter goes on to say. If a wider musical audience is the meaning of fame, then with all his soul he desires fame. But when he realizes that in proportion to musical fame a personal notoriety will develop, raising the curtain between himself and the world—then he wishes for everlasting silence instead of more music. . . . Or if not silence everlasting—he adds with characteristic honesty—at least a *little* silence until the world forgets him. . . . "This is not because I fear exposure. I can state frankly that my conscience is clear and I have nothing to be ashamed of."

Coming from a man who suffered intermittent terror lest his wife blackmail him for sexual abnormality, this is the kind of statement the biographer would prefer to omit. Yet who can condemn the disabled man for not naming his disability a vice? Peter Ilyich was indeed humiliated that he was not as other men; had he not, again and again, confessed that only his music redeemed him for manhood? But this statement was not the voice of the wrong-doer telling his remorse; it was rather the voice of the cripple who in agony cries out his shame, hoping that his own voice or another's will refute him and give him leave to live on an earth so implacably reserved for normalcy.

Also, Peter Ilyich was well now, and writing music furiously. What he said to Nadejda concerning publicity was true enough at the moment; with Antonina temporarily out of the way, Peter did not dread publicity for his conscience' sake but simply because he hated to be stared at.

"There is," he wrote Nadejda, "something almost tragic in this struggle between one's desire for fame and disgust at fame's consequences. Sometimes I am seized with a longing to hide, to be buried alive that I may forget everything and be forgotten by these strangers. Alas! I return to the fire and burn my wings anew.

"And my wings will soon have to suffer singeing through the performance of *Jeanne d'Arc* in Petersburg. I shall have to plunge headlong into the nauseous waters of theatrical and bureaucratic tittle-tattle, to breathe the rotten atmosphere of intrigue, small but venomous ambition, every kind of chicanery and conceited stupidity. However, either I stop writing operas or prepare to face all this, I really don't believe I shall ever write another opera, but shall keep exclusively to the domain of symphony and string quartet. When I remember what I had to endure last spring in staging *Onegin*, I feel as if I never wanted to write for the theatre again. Soliciting is really awful.

"All this time here I have been very busy correcting proof for my" (second piano) "concerto and the *Italian Capriccio*. The latter is easy enough to play."

253

Nadejda however, was delighted with every word Tchaikowsky said. She loved his independence of all fawning and solicitation. "Is there another man," she exclaimed, "as sincere as you? Peter Ilyich, you are nothing but your music, while your music is nothing but you, your very self."

And Tchaikowsky? Each time he tried to separate himself from music, to "rest" from it, he was a lost soul; to cease creating music was for him a stoppage of the very rhythm of living, as though his breath—his essential connection with life—had been cut off. He was well aware of it.

To Nadejda Philaretovna

Kamenka
Sept. 21, Tuesday

"How fickle my plans are, whenever I decide to devote a long time to rest! I had just begun to spend a series of entirely idle days, when there came over me a vague feeling of discomfort and real sickness; I could not sleep and suffered from fatigue and weakness. Today I could not resist sitting down to plan my next symphony—and immediately I became well and calm and full of courage. It proves that unless I am travelling I cannot exist for two days without work.

"Lately, I have tried to plan some other interesting work to divert me from music. Alas! Nothing can divert me. There is no Russian textbook on the history of music, and it would have been well for me to busy myself writing one. But this would have meant renouncing all musical composition for about two years—too long a time. Well then, what remains? To set about translating someone else's history? Not interesting enough. To write biography? Much has already been written about the European artists. I cannot write with enthusiasm about Glinka, Dargomisky and Serov, because in proportion as I admire their music, I dislike their personalities.

"So it seems there is no way to occupy myself and satisfy my inward craving for work, except musical composition. I am already planning a symphony and a string quartet! I don't yet know which I shall choose."

A few days after writing this, Tchaikowsky was informed that the *Maid of Orleans* had been accepted by the directors of the Imperial Theatre in Petersburg, and would be performed in January. And now his troubles began. With the letter of acceptance was returned his libretto from the Board of Censors, marked with that red pencil which was the despair of opera writers in Imperial Orthodox Russia. The slightest criticism of monarchy or religion was enough to outlaw any work from the State theatres; the censorship followed no law of rationality; simply, what was sacred must not be impersonated on the stage. Across Tchaikowsky's score the censor had written: "The archbishop in this production must be called 'pilgrim,' not archbishop. All conversations concerning the Cross must be omitted, nor may any cross be permitted on the stage. . . ."

"How stupid it all is!" raged Tchaikowsky. "At the end of the opera when Jeanne is led to the stake, she asks for a cross, and one of the soldiers ties two sticks together in the form of a cross and gives it to her. The whole scene has to come out. . . . The silliest thing of all is calling the archbishop a pilgrim; it makes no sense. Who would believe that such commands issue from a state institution that supervises every printed thing in Russia, and which should therefore consist of educated men? There is nothing to do about it however, and I have had to comply."

Nadejda was furious. Those idiots! she cried. Those *bashibazouks!* Why didn't they make Jeanne herself into a pilgrim, while they were about it? To add to her indignation, Peter was at work on another commission, this time from Nicholas Rubinstein. There was to be an Exhibition in Moscow and the Chief wanted a large piece for choir and orchestra, or simply for orchestra. Either way, it had to be "big." Tchaikowsky was given three choices of subject: (1) The inauguration of the Exhibition. (2) The twenty-fifth anniversary of the Coronation of Alexander II. (3) The inauguration of the Cathedral of Christ the Saviour. . . . Loathsome, impossible themes! cried Peter Ilyich, and before his complaint was fairly silenced, had set to work. Twelve days later he wrote from Kamenka:

"Just think, dear friend!—My muse has been so kind that in a short time I have got through—before my sister's illness—two pieces: A big solemn overture for the Exhibition, and a *Serenade* for stringed orchestra in four movements. I am busy orchestrating them both. The overture will be very showy and noisy, but it will have no artistic merit because I wrote it without warmth and without love."

This "exhibition piece" was the *Overture 1812*— Need more be said? Damnably inseparable from Tchaikowsky's name, it is fully as noisy as the composer declared; certainly, it contains little of that quality called by Peter Ilyich "love" or "warmth."

Tchaikowsky's attitude toward commission writing, as we have seen, never varied. Upon receiving an order, he complained bitterly, set eagerly to work, wrote something "noisy," as he called it, and presented it promptly to the authorities, with a sardonic grin—as sardonic, that is, as Peter's smile could be. His commission dealings can have no better illustration than a letter he was to write later to Jurgenson, upon being commissioned to arrange for chorus and string orchestra Glinka's famous *Slavsia*, from his *Life for the Tsar*; 7500 voices were to sing it at a big Imperial celebration. After finishing the job, Tchaikowsky sent it to Jurgenson with the following note:

"As far as original composition goes, there are only a few new measures in the work, so the City of Moscow, which you say is prepared to surrender me a mountain of gold, owes me only as follows:

For the simplification of the choral parts and instrumentation of sixteen measures, repeated three times
.... 3 roubles
For the composition of eight measures leading into the anthem... 4 roubles
For adding four lines to the third verse, at forty kopeks per line.., ... 1 rouble, 60 kopeks

Total ‾8 roubles, 60 kopeks

"These 8 roubles, 60 kopeks I present to the City of Moscow. But seriously, it is ridiculous to think of payment for such work; it would be offensive. Such things should be done without payment or not done at all."

Nadejda von Meck, of course, hated all this business even more than Peter Ilyich. He knew she hated it and, that autumn of 1880, tempered his official news with something more personal. Along with the noisy Exhibition piece for Rubinstein, Tchaikowsky had said he was orchestrating a new composed *Serenade* for strings; the two works presented a complete contrast. "I wrote the *Serenade* on impulse," he told Nadejda. "I felt it deeply, from start to finish, and therefore I dare to believe it will not be without merit. As always, in the best places in the music, you were in my mind as I wrote."

Whatever his inspiration for the *Serenade*, it proved to one of the loveliest things Tchaikowsky ever wrote; tender and melodious, it charms each hearer anew. Nadejda was madly happy that she had been part of the inspiration for a piece Tchaikowsky believed in; from Florence she told him so, and she did not spare paper to say it. At the end she asked: "Why, Peter Ilyich, have you never written a trio for piano and strings? Every day I regret it, because I hear so many trios and then I sigh that you have not written one."

To Nadejda Philaretovna

Kamenka
Oct. 26, 1880

"You ask why I never write trios. You will have to forgive me, my friend, but this is something quite beyond my power. There is some arrangement of my auditory organs that simply will not accept any combination of piano with single violin or 'cello. To me the different *timbres* of these instruments are at war, and I assure you it is real torment to listen to a trio or sonata with violin or 'cello. I cannot explain this physiological fact, I can only state it. Quite otherwise is the combination of piano and orchestra; here also

257

the *timbres* cannot fuse—moreover the piano is incapable of merging with the rest; the elasticity of its make-up causes it to bound away from any other phonetic mass. *But* there are here two balancing forces; namely, the mighty, inexhaustible richness of the colorful orchestra, set against a small, plain but spirited rival who emerges victorious—provided the performer is talented.

"In this battle is much poesy and, for the composer, many tempting combinations of sound. But what could be more unnatural than to combine three such definite personalities as the violin, 'cello and piano? The merits of all three are lost. The warm, wonderfully sustained sounds of violin and 'cello lose all their value in competition with the kings of instruments, while the latter tries in vain to sing as its rivals can sing! In my opinion, the piano is of value only: (1) as solo, (2) with orchestra, (3) as accompaniment, meaning as background to a picture. A trio, however, presupposes equality and similarity, and how can this ever be achieved between fiddlestick instruments and piano? It cannot. Therefore a piano trio is an artificial thing, each instrument playing, not what is natural to it but what the author has forced upon it because of difficulty in distributing the voices in accordance with his musical idea."

Tchaikowsky was not the first artist to repudiate an idea and then be roused, by the very force of his own negation, to an interest in the thing he had condemned.

It was nearly December now, of 1880, and daily the voice of the world penetrated more insistently to Tchaikowsky in Kamenka. Theatre and concert stage called loudly for his music—and called for the composer to direct rehearsals and conduct orchestras. The time was soon to come when a deeper retreat than Kamenka would be needed; Tchaikowsky could no longer afford to play, in his rare leisure moments, the strenuous role of Uncle Petia.

24

Fame. Farewell to the Chief

Tchaikowsky went up to Moscow and found himself head over ears in work. He loved to work, but this was something different. Whereas an obscure man may create symphonies alone in his room, flooded with the peace and joy of inspiration—fame requires him to sit proof-reading in a glass cage, with all the world pointing its finger.

On December 3rd, 1880, he wrote Nadejda at four in the morning:

"Next week the Musical Society will play my *Italian Capriccio. Oprichnik*"—(the opera written in 1872) "is being performed today at the Grand Theatre. . . . From all sides my music is received with sympathy. All morning I spend reading proof, and as I finish the sheets they are handed to the printer."

From Moscow, Tchaikowsky went up to Petersburg. The autumn fog, the damp and the darkness did not improve his spirits. At eleven in the morning, although his room had good exposure, he had to write by candlelight.

To Nadejda Philaretovna

Petersburg
November 27, 1880

"I arrived here this morning and hasten to talk with you a little, my dear, best friend. For God's sake do not be angry with me for writing you so little from Moscow. My life there was nothing but forced labor, and because of eye-strain in proof-reading, my neuralgic headaches came back and I had to leave Moscow without finishing the work I had planned. I thought it best to change my routine and see if I could get some rest. So I came to Petersburg strictly incognito, and hope to keep this except for one or two close relatives.

"In Moscow I had the strangest sensation; in spite of

everything, my love for that ancient city did not decrease. On the contrary it grew stronger and stronger, but in the most painful way. It seemed to me I had been dead for a long time, that all my former life had dropped to oblivion and that I was quite another man, living in another world and another age. It would be hard to tell you how or why this sensation was so painful, but it was. I could conquer it only by excessive work or excessive libations to Bacchus, and I had wide recourse to both remedies. The result was extreme fatigue.

"There were, however, happy moments. The Directors of the Moscow Musical Society became much interested in my *Liturgy*" (Saint John Chrysostom) "and one of them—Alexiev—gave the best choir in Moscow a generous fee to study the music. As a result, my *Liturgy* was performed in the concert hall of the Conservatory last Friday. The choir sang perfectly and I experienced one of the happiest moments of my life as a composer. Everyone who was there seemed as pleased as I. The Musical Society has decided to perform it again at a special concert. So at last my *Liturgy*, which has suffered much persecution, will become known.

"And on that same evening the professors and students of the Conservatory played, as a surprise for me, the *Serenade* for strings which I just wrote in Kamenka. They played it well, and it gave me the greatest pleasure. At the moment, I consider this the best thing I have written. And have I told you, my dear, that *Eugene Onegin* will be staged at the Moscow Opera? Beviniani will see that it is well done, and this makes me very happy. . . ."

As to the *Liturgy*, when the special concert took place the hall was crowded, largely owing to the fact that the *Liturgy* had formerly been forbidden performance by the censor. As applause was prohibited for church music, it was impossible to tell which parts made the most favorable impression. Modeste Tchaikowsky reported that opinion was divided everywhere except amongst the numerous clergy and church officials present. These condemned the whole performance. Why, they asked indignantly, should M. Tchaikowsky clamber into church music? Let him stick to his waltzes, polkas and operas.

Most of all, the clergy were annoyed by the enthusiastic ovation given Peter Ilyich at the end of the concert. Again and again he was called to the stage and finally presented with a lyre made of laurel leaves. What, asked the clergy, had the blessed Liturgy to do with personal applause and laurel leaves? Bishop Ambrose wrote the newspaper *Rus* about it. This, said the Bishop, was the Liturgy of Saint John Chrysostom, and it had appeared upon the program as the *Liturgy* of P. I. Tchaikowsky! Church music is meant for church, not the concert hall, nor is a liturgy a folk legend to be used as a libretto. Applause—laurel leaves? Let the Orthodox rejoice that this time the Liturgy had fallen into the hands of a reputable musician and was well written and well performed. Let them beware of the time when the sacred Mass would be produced under the name of Rosenblum or Rosenthal, and be received with hisses and catcalls. . . .

Tchaikowsky was genuinely hurt by this criticism. He had written the music not as a musical "piece" at all, but with deepest religious and artistic spirit, in an endeavor to purge church music of modern dilutions and cheap substitutes for the old musical modes. He was not the first man nor the last to fight a losing battle with the church—whether Catholic or Protestant—over the restoration of the ancient dignity of its music.

As to the *Italian Capriccio,* it blew its cavalry call in Moscow under Rubinstein's baton that same December, also in Petersburg under the direction of the faithful Napravnik—and received its just deserts. What really occupied Peter Ilyich this month was the operatic stage. With the *Maid of Orleans* in rehearsal in Petersburg and *Onegin* preparing for performance in Moscow, December rapidly assumed nightmare proportions. Travelling up and down between the cities, Peter watched jealous sopranos fight for the part of Jeanne d'Arc; as for *Onegin*, Moscow gave it a bad press after the first night, added to which the prima donna fell ill and the opera had to be laid aside. Never another opera! cried Peter Ilyich. Never let me put pen to paper where opera is concerned! Roars of protest, vows that he would not bear another such child—and all the while he knew, like a mother in the midst of her worst agony—that he would give birth again and yet again.

"Are you surprised, Nadejda Philaretovna," he wrote, "that a man enjoying success in his career, should complain of fate? Well, my success is not as great as it may seem, and anyway, success could never compensate for the unbearable suffering I experience when coming in contact with human beings, compelled forever to parade as a spectacle, robbed of hope of living as I wish, with no time for reading or writing—pushed about senselessly, as in a ball room. A month of this is ahead of me. I think of it with horror, and wonder where I shall find strength to sustain it."

In Petersburg, Napravnik performed the Second Symphony as revised by Tchaikowsky in Rome a year ago; the first movement was completely new, and sweeping changes had been made throughout. After the performance, the newspapers were most laudatory—but not one critic had noticed that the symphony had been rewritten or changed at all! No wonder Peter Ilyich grew indifferent to professional criticism. . . .

Nadejda was in Brailov now with her boys for the Christmas season, but Tchaikowsky was travelling so busily that he seldom heard from her. In the midst of the Bishop's protest and Petersburg rehearsals of the *Maid of Orleans*, came a few words from Brailov that were to Tchaikowsky, he confessed, as heavenly manna. He needed such spiritual nourishment; everyone, including the newspapers, was prophesying failure for the *Maid*; also, Peter's enemies seized upon the dedication to Napravnik, calling it a piece of shrewdly managed flattery on the composer's part—a mean charge, considering that Napravnik had long been one of Tchaikowsky's best friends, and also that toadying was one fault of which Peter was never guilty.

When the *Maid* was performed late in February, Tchaikowsky had a great personal success—twenty-four times, he was called before the curtain. Nevertheless this ovation gave him no real pleasure; Tchaikowsky knew that the directors of the Maryinsky Theatre were hostile to the opera, and that the singers themselves were angry and dissatisfied with their parts. Next day the press tore both opera and performance to shreds and the *Maid* was crossed from the Maryinsky repertory.

Tchaikowsky shook the Petersburg dust from his feet and entrained for Italy. From Florence he wrote Nadejda a quiet happy letter and then went on to Rome, incognito, as he thought, and looking forward to rest and freedom. But no sooner had he registered at the hotel than Grand Dukes and princesses besieged his door. "I simply have not the strength to refuse these invitations; I am pursued by a false fear of offending people." Baroness Iksul, wife of the Russian Ambassador, invited him to dinner, and Lady Hamilton. What do they want of me? he fretted. "I am not a pianist, and cannot entertain them!" But on March 14th, news came of the assassination of Alexander II, and Tchaikowsky, terribly distressed, and shocked that social festivities should continue under such circumstances, fled from Rome.

But a more personal grief awaited. In Nice, Peter found a letter from Anatol, saying that Nicholas Rubinstein was on his way from Moscow, travelling for his health. Before leaving home, Peter had known the Chief was ill and needed a rest; he and Nadejda had discussed it. The Moscow physicians were at their wits' end; Rubinstein was seriously ill—whether with liver or kidney condition they could not decide—but they knew he ought to be in bed, and bed was the last place Rubinstein would consent to occupy.

"Nicholas Grigorievitch cannot rest," wrote Tchaikowsky. "He is a perfect contrast to you and me. In proportion as we love seclusion, he loves to walk about the world and roar. He simply cannot live without excitement and rushing about; it is life to him. He dislikes reading, to walk bores him and he even has no pleasure in making music for himself—others must be there to listen. What can rest and tranquillity give such a man? Nothing but torture."

And now, in Nice, Peter Ilyich heard by telegram from Jurgenson that the Chief was in Paris, terribly ill, in danger of his life. Peter wired for news and received an answering telegram with the one word, "Hopeless," followed by a second which announced simply: "Rubinstein is dead."

The funeral was held in the Russian church in Paris, the coffin being brought down to the lower chapel to rest in state. Here, for the last time, Peter Ilyich looked upon the Chief's face. The dreaded moment proved even more terrible than in anticipation; the familiar face was almost unrecognizable. Peter stood there, among the candles, the full-skirted priests, the chanting, the incense that should disguise the hideousness of man's mortality—and he was not deceived. Looking down at the bier, wave after wave of terror and grief passed over Peter Ilyich. This shrunken mask that had been a face, these grey claws crossed upon the breast. . . . Oh, above all, these colorless, motionless hands proved Nicholas Grigorievitch was no more! Standing beside the body of his Chief, doubt swept over Peter Ilyich. In that moment, and indeed for days to come he lived in a painful confusion, engrossed in the desperate search to which every sensitive man is propelled by the sight of death. "I long to believe in a future life," he wrote Nadejda. "When I can say the longing has become belief, then I shall be happy."

Rubinstein's body was sent home to Russia for burial. Tchaikowsky went to the station and watched the coffin put on the train. "I am crushed with grief," he wrote Nadejda. "My God, my God, how terrible are such moments in our lives."

Nadejda had not much comfort to give. "Poor, poor Nicholas Grigorievitch!" she wrote. "Or rather, poor we who have lost him! Now who will be able to play your music so well?"

25

Good-bye to Brailov. Antonina disposed of

Tchaikowsky did not accompany the Chief on this last journey home, but he planned to return to Russia none the less. The Moscow Conservatory was without a director; whether or no Peter Ilyich accepted the position (he knew it would be offered him), duty and common decency required that he be in Moscow to help choose Rubinstein's successor. Also, Nadejda had written him vague but extremely alarming letters concerning financial losses; if she were indeed on the verge of bankruptcy, as she intimated, Peter would have to go back to teaching. This, and the sad fact of Rubinstein's death brought Peter, so he said, face to face with changes that would affect his whole life.

Peter went home by the northern route that landed him in Petersburg. He wrote often to Nadejda, reminding her that now she was in trouble, it was good he need be a burden to her no longer. "I am absolutely secure now from poverty and even from financial discomfort; I have only to say the word to be admitted to either conservatory with an excellent salary. The fact that if I take up a professorship it will be done for necessity, and without any pleasure whatever, is not worth thinking of."

Arrived in Moscow, he found this indeed to be the case. Moscow without Rubinstein was a ship without a helmsman and everyone—even Rubinstein's enemies—admitted it. The heads of the Musical Society implored Tchaikowsky to accept the Directorship of the Conservatory. It required all his strength, Peter wrote Nadejda, to refuse. His own choice as Director was Taneyeff, whom later he hoped to see appointed. Such matters move slowly; meanwhile, Tchaikowsky went out to Kamenka where the children gave him a touching welcome. Their parents were away and Uncle Petia assumed charge.

"I was with them the whole day and am so tired I can write only these few lines. It made me sad to see old Madame Davydoff, my brother-in-law's mother, who is nearly blind. She is the last of the wives of the Decembrists who followed their husbands to Siberia. Last year she lost one eye and now she is losing the other through the many tears she has shed over family troubles and the Tsar's death. But such is her religious faith that she bears her misfortune calmly, fully resigned to God's will."

Nadejda von Meck replied to Peter's letter in a tone quite remote from the resignation he had commended in

Davydoff. Things were going from bad to worse, wrote Nadejda. So much so that she feared for the proposed union of the families von Meck and Davydoff. Her money seemed to be dissolving; would Leo Davydoff want a pauper for son-in-law? — "It may seem strange to you" — so ran her letter — "for a woman to worry about money when she owns a railroad a hundred and sixty miles long, leading to one of the best seaports in Russia, also an estate of twelve thousand acres" (Brailov), "the most luxurious house in Moscow and a huge collection of diamonds and every kind of *objet d'art*, etc. But my children, although possessing all this, may very well have no money to live on, because, although every one of these properties is sound and should bring in a return if properly handled, I have no one capable of this management. Volodia cannot do it because he bears the von Meck name and everyone tries to exploit him — as they do me — in each and every matter. No one has ever tried to help us with our affairs; on the contrary, people have tried to obstruct us. The envy and wickedness of the world is incredible."

As to Peter Ilyich, he was at present engrossed in Davydoff family troubles and had no spirit to comfort Nadejda. . . . Tatiana, his beautiful eldest niece, once gay and fairylike as her name, had got herself engaged to a gentleman of noble blood who had behaved far from nobly. Uncle Petia tried to distract her. For hours on end the two played duets on the piano or read aloud from a book in the garden. But all to no purpose. Tatiana had recourse to morphine and refused to rally. Uncle Petia wrote page after page about her to Nadejda in Moscow, but Nadejda, who never had much sympathy for love's alarums, merely replied that the girl was well rid of a bad bargain, and Peter Ilyich had better leave Kamenka if he was going to be so disturbed. . . . "I want so terribly to be useful here," wrote Peter, "but every day convinces me that I am powerless to do anything really valuable for any of them. I feel no desire to write music; I have never been this way for such a long time before. I ask myself if inspiration is gone forever, and then I recall other periods of equal flatness and hope that when my moral horizon clears, my desire to create will dawn once more. . . . Jurgenson wants me to come to Moscow and talk over some work he has for me."

What Jurgenson really wanted was for Tchaikowsky to edit the works of the late Bortniansky, who had arranged much music for the Church. Jurgenson forwarded the Bortniansky material to Peter, who pronounced it a mass of rubbish, advised his publisher to abandon the plan and then, after examining what he called his "finances," and finding them far from satisfactory, plunged into the job. All through July and August he worked at Bortniansky—"a loathsome task," he wrote Jurgenson, "which I shall finish because I always finish what I have begun. But one of these days I shall burst with sheer irritation."

When Nadejda von Meck heard about Bortniansky, she was furious. Must the composer of the Fourth Symphony be compelled to deaden his inspiration with such nonsense? "If you have contracted with Jurgenson to do this work, you will have to finish it, but can't you do it at intervals, spread it out and work on your own music in between?"

A check fell out of the envelope; Peter looked at it and looked back at the long letter that accompanied it. Nadejda was offended, she said, because in money difficulties Peter Ilyich had gone to Jurgenson. "Do as you please, of course," she wrote, "but surely, you cannot refuse me this time?"

Tchaikowsky did not refuse her. He was completely worn out with this Bortniansky. What with the sheer tedium of the work and worry over Tatiana, he had been ill for two weeks with a heavy fever. Diphtheria, he called it, quite calmly, adding that everybody in Kamenka had been down with it. The minute he got out of bed he went doggedly back to Bortniansky. . . . Now he could pay a hack Moscow musician to do half the work. But he is ashamed, he tells Nadejda, to have whined; if ever again he gets into money difficulties, let his friend remember it is nobody's fault but his own, and he can very well expiate it in uncongenial work. What happens is—says Peter—he gets hold of some money and then needy people ask him for it. What can he do but give the money away? It makes the family angry; here in Kamenka they tell him he cannot afford this role of benefactor. "But I have so much money! Thanks to you, Nadejda Philaretovna, in the last four years I have attained to riches such as I never dreamed of. Not just enough, but far in excess of my needs."

It is easy to see why the widow—so suspicious of the world where her fortune was concerned—loved to give money to Peter Ilyich. Here was a man who not only was worth supporting as an artist, but who did not seem to know the meaning of the word greed. Six thousand roubles a year was a fortune to him. Unfortunately for the widow, the rumors that had gone round Moscow in the spring concerning the von Meck properties were true; she had lost a serious amount of money. Not enough to interfere with Peter's pension, but enough so that immediate funds must be raised if Nadejda were not to lose her capital.

Ensconced in what she had called "the most luxurious house in Moscow," the widow sat at a desk that was deep in bills, financial statements. . . . Something must be sacrificed to meet these demands. *Brailov!* All the time, Nadejda had known Brailov was the solution, but she had not liked to face it. Brailov had never paid as an estate; in spite of enormous outlay on the latest scientific equipment for farm and beet-sugar factory, each year had seen a deplorable financial deficit. Peter Ilyich had expressed himself distressed and puzzled over this and had offered in all seriousness to send his brother-in-law, Leo Davydoff, down from Kamenka to interview Nadejda's steward. Surely, Peter had said, Nadejda Philaretovna was being badly cheated somewhere. Kamenka, with only old-fashioned equipment, brought in more revenue.

But Nadejda had refused Leo Davydoff's help. Such an investigation would hurt her steward's feelings, she said. And now, this August of 1881, a buyer had appeared for Brailov, offering 1,440,000 roubles ($720,000). A shocking loss of course; the property was worth twice that sum. . . . So Nadejda, with a sad backward glance, sold Brailov and bought a less elaborate estate. "We shall have to forget Brailov now, my dear friend," she wrote Peter; "put it forever from our minds and imagine it as occupied by strangers. . . ."

This advice was characteristic of Nadejda, who believed that by saying she had put a thing from her mind, she had actually done so. Again and again the widow played this dangerous part, and again and again it recoiled upon her with the deadly spring, the powerful inevitable blow of heaven and law defied. This was the trait which, pathologically multiplied, in the end was to separate Nadejda forever from Peter Ilyich.

But when Tchaikowsky heard that Brailov was gone, he offered no comfort and no system of philosophy. He had best not tell Nadejda how he felt; let his dear friend go away somewhere, said he, and try to forget. Could she go to Italy now, in the autumn? Perhaps he could join her there. Meanwhile he went up to Moscow for the month of September, living with Anatol quite happily, as fashionable Moscow was still in the country for its summer vacation and the two could roam the streets undisturbed. Then he went again to Kamenka, where he was harried by the appearance of another young man asking for help. Peter, of course, emptied his pockets into the boy's and then wrote Jurgenson, imploring him to take the lad at once into his publishing house.

And this was not the only good turn Jurgenson did his famous client this summer of 1880. Carefully tracking Antonina, Jurgenson discovered something unpleasant but important. As long ago as the winter before last, Antonina had taken a lover and had had a child by him. She had placed the child in a foundlings' home, and she herself was now in Moscow, living with the child's father. There was no uncertainty about any of it. Jurgenson had been at pains to collect positive evidence. "She will leave me in peace now," wrote Peter Ilyich, a little wearily.

Antonina was not out of his life, however; she would always remain his responsibility and he would pay her an allowance. The mere sight of a letter in her handwriting would continue to prostrate him, make him physically ill. Jurgenson remained go-between and Tchaikowsky's valuable protector; no publisher wants his best author incapacitated by a woman, and anyway, Peter Ilyich was Jurgenson's very good friend.

Thus, except for a few harried allusions in Tchaikowsky's diary later on, we take leave of poor Antonina. She was born to be a victim, and perhaps it is the worst tragedy of the born victim that the pity they win from us is tinged rather with impatience than with liking. Her mania that the world of men was in love with her mounted until in 1896 she was put in an insane asylum in Petersburg, where she remained until her death in 1917. During the progress of her insanity, Antonina went right on having children and placing them in the foundlings' home; none of the Tchaikowskys ever knew who the father was nor did they see the children, but everyone was grateful to Antonina that she did not give them the Tchaikowsky name, as she might have done—never, of course, having divorced Peter Ilyich. The Tchaikowskys were grateful also that Antonina did not seek them out; they tried to forget her—if her name was mentioned, cold silence met the question and the conversation shifted quickly.

And now the Bortniansky edition was finished, thanks to Nadejda's check earlier in the summer. Tchaikowsky started north to Petersburg; he was planning to go to Rome with Modeste. Nadejda was in Florence. At Kiev, Peter stopped off for a fortnight, becoming engrossed once more with church music as heard at the Lavra Monastery. Here the ancient chants were sung in the ancient manner, preserving the original harmonies. Tchaikowsky was much impressed, and angry with a stupid public that spurned this traditional singing, preferring the doctored and sweetened music of the more modern churches.

"It outrages me," he wrote, "and I cannot bring myself to admit that I am powerless to do anything about it. All my efforts to work for Russian church music have met with persecution. My liturgy has been forbidden by the authorities. Two months ago, when Mass was held for the soul of Nicholas Rubinstein, those in charge of the funeral asked that my liturgy might be performed. Alas! I was deprived of the pleasure of hearing my liturgy sung in church because the Moscow diocesan authorities absolutely forbade it; Bishop Ambrose called it Roman Catholic.

From Kiev, Tchaikowsky went to Italy. Nadejda was still in Florence, but the composer stopped there only for a day or two; Modeste with his young pupil wished to be in Rome,

270

and Nadejda seemed to understand that the brothers needed some time in Rome together. Also, Nadejda was happy now in her Villa Oppenheim because her favorite grandson, Volichka, was with her. She wrote glowing descriptions of him, sending his latest photograph. During this December of 1881 the two exchanged easy conversational letters.

Tchaikowsky, who usually complained about Rome because there were too many things in it, wrote now in great content.

"Rome is like Moscow," he said. "The more one knows the city the more one loves it." At Saint Peter's they had sung Palestrina *a capella*—a cheering occasion for a man who loved church music performed in its original purity. "My room is very comfortable," wrote Tchaikowsky, "and the minute I arrived I began to compose. I don't know how it will turn out, but I am writing music for the scene between Mazeppa and Maria from Pushkin's *Poltava*. If I become really fascinated by it, perhaps I shall write a whole opera on the subject!"

This from the man who not six months ago had declared he was through with opera forever. He did write the opera *Mazeppa*, completing it the following year. It was not performed until 1884, and had only a moderate success. It has since gone into complete oblivion.

Disquieting news reached the composer now from Petersburg: Napravnik had resigned his leadership of the Musical Society because he could not weather the quarrels and intrigues. He is too honest! cried Tchaikowsky. Davidov, Director of the Petersburg Conservatory, was to conduct the orchestra in Napravnik's stead. Also, from Petersburg, Leopold Auer declared he would not perform Tchaikowsky's Violin Concerto because it was too difficult, too startling in its harmonies and effects. Adolf Brodsky, a violinist who had taught for a time at the Moscow Conservatory, had courageously championed this piece ever since its appearance (Tchaikowsky had written it in the spring of 1878 when Nadejda sent him to Switzerland to recover from his marriage). Now, on December 4th, 1881, Brodsky played the concerto in Vienna at a Philharmonic concert—and fury broke over his head. Hanslick, the famous German critic, attacked it viciously, and Peter Ilyich, picking up the *Neue Freie Presse* downstairs in his hotel, came upon a savage paragraph which he repeated in a letter to Nadejda.

"All my compositions, Hanslick says, are 'uneven, coarse, savage and in bad taste.' As for the violin concerto, the beginning is tolerable, but the further it goes the worse it gets. At the end of the first movement, says he, the violin does not play but roars, shouts and bellows. The Andante begins pleasantly, but soon plunges into the atmosphere of a Russian feast, where everybody is drunk and the faces of the people are brutal and revolting. 'A critic,' Hanslick goes on to say, 'once called a picture so realistic that it stank; when hearing Tchaikowsky's concerto I realized that music also may stink.'

"Isn't this a strange criticism? I have no luck with critics. Since Laroche left Russia there isn't a person at home who has a friendly word for me on the printed page. And now in Europe my music is called 'stinking.'"

Peter Ilyich was not the man to be crushed by criticism; the very next paragraph of his letter—pausing not a moment to revile the critic—describes his newest musical venture.

"My dear, what do you think I have begun to write? You will be astonished! Maybe you will remember suggesting to me once that I write a trio for piano, violin and 'cello, and maybe you remember my answer—in which I told you plainly how I disliked that combination of instruments. And now, in spite of this antipathy, I have decided to make a trial with that kind of music. I have already written the beginning of the trio; I don't know whether it will be successful or whether I shall ever complete it. But I want to finish at least as much as I have sketched.

"I hope you will believe me when I tell you that my chief reason—or rather my sole reason—for reconciling myself to this combination of strings and piano, which I never liked, is to give you pleasure."

Nadejda was actually embarrassed by this. Could it be that she had forced Peter Ilyich into work uncongenial to him? Of course the music would be wonderful, but how very distressing to think of her dear friend struggling with unsympathetic material just for her sake!

Peter Ilyich replied instantly that Nadejda must not think it tiresome for him to work on the trio.

"At the beginning, it was a real effort to reconcile myself to this combination of instruments, but now the work interests and intrigues me, and again I love to think it will give you pleasure. As to the violin concerto, I was awfully touched by Brodsky's courage in making his very first Vienna appearance with a work so intrinsically difficult to play, and moreover, Russian, which the Viennese don't like. It is however very strange to me that Auer, to whom the concerto was dedicated in token of his former public championship of my music—and Davidov, my good friend, refused to play the concerto in Petersburg."

Tchaikowsky changed the dedication of the concerto after this episode, substituting the name of Adolf Brodsky. Meanwhile Nadejda, true friend that she was, searched the newspapers until she found a favorable Viennese review of Brodsky's performance. She sent it to Peter, followed next day by still another. "You see?" she wrote triumphantly. "I was right, Vienna has other men than Hanslick. Let them curse your music if they will—only let the music be performed! It will find more admirers than abusers. . . . And now I see that Damrosch played your concerto two years ago in New York. What a brave fellow! The Lord give us more such men."

So much for the violin concerto, reviled so bitterly, and now a popular part of every violinist's concert repertory.

As for the trio in process of composition in Rome that January of 1882, it did not prove quite the matchless music Nadejda had anticipated. It was dedicated, as all the world knows, *À la mémoire d'un grand artiste* (Nicholas Rubinstein), and Tchaikowsky's fears as to its form were in some measure justified. Requiring an hour and a quarter to play— tremendous length for a piece of chamber music—it attempts too often to burst the confines of its medium and soar unsuccessfully into symphony, a lack of discipline happily not so discernible in the composer's string quartets. The second movement is a long set of variations on an andante theme in E major, intended, says Rosa Newmarch, as recollections of Rubinstein and his musical characteristics at various times of his life. The elegiac bits of the *Trio*, where one definitely feels Tchaikowsky's grief at the loss of his friend, are eminently successful and touching. But all the way through, Peter veered startlingly from the elegiac strain; lively mazurkas, gay waltzes alternate with rapidly varying rhythm until the last page, marked *"lugubre,"* recalls to us the fact that Rubinstein is in his grave.

And now, as the New Year—1882—arrived, Tchaikowsky, from his little room, which he had said was so comfortable, wrote further that he was "filled with ideas and plans and I am much disposed toward writing music. I think, my dear friend, that I shall write better than I used to, or else it will prove that although my cartridge has grown bigger, I have no more powder. I have grown cold to my former music; all of it, without exception, seems immature, imperfect as to form, and empty. Reason tells me I exaggerate my defects, yet I cannot force myself to look on any of my music with pleasure. In brief, either my song is done, or henceforth I shall sing a better one."

26

1882–1890. The Fifth Symphony. "Do not forget . . ."

In truth, Peter's song was not done and he was to sing a better one. The Fifth and Sixth Symphonies were as yet unwritten, as were the *Nutcracker Suite, Hamlet* and the opera *Pique Dame*. Peter was forty-two now, he had definitely "arrived," he was a musical lion, the most popular musician in Russia. With Antonina in abeyance, with money worries gradually vanishing as his music began bringing in a securer income, Tchaikowsky found himself strong, healthy and surprisingly adequate to the world's demands.

He came out of his neurotic shell, emerging consciously, confessing that he had resolved to show himself to the eyes of the world.

Nevertheless, the pension from Nadejda continued to arrive with quarterly regularity. Nadejda clung to her "right," as she called it, to "watch over" Peter Ilyich. The pension was to her a symbol of Peter's dependence, and the widow dispatched it eagerly, awaited eagerly the acknowledgment, which reached her now from increasing distances—from England, Bohemia, France—wherever Peter travelled on behalf of his profession. Nadejda herself lived abroad nearly all the year now, reluctantly following the sun from season to season, outlawed for increasingly longer periods from her beloved Moscow.

Brailov was gone, but when he needed retreat, Peter went down to Plesheyevo, the new von Meck country estate south of Moscow where Nadejda spent a month or two each summer. Plesheyevo was a beautiful old place, built in the eighteenth century before Russia's bad period of architecture had set in. When Nadejda bought it the house was filled with magnificent old furniture. Characteristically, Nadejda threw it all out, replacing it with the plush-and-gilt Parisian atrocities she loved. Between herself and Peter Ilyich, the technique of invisible intimacy and invisible guestdom was by now comfortably established; the widow's proximity caused Peter no alarms.

Meanwhile, music flowed unceasingly from the composer's pen. Between the years 1882–1885 he wrote the opera *Mazeppa*, which has since found oblivion; the second and third orchestral suites and the *Fantasia Concerto* for piano and orchestra, which followed soon afterward, met with instant success. The performance of the Third Orchestral Suite in Petersburg in 1885 marked a period in the composer's career; von Bülow's skillful baton rendered it Tchaikowksy's greatest triumph to date. It was followed by another triumph, when *Onegin* was performed soon afterward for Tsar Alexander III. Peter was summoned to the Imperial box, a long and friendly conversation was held, and forever after Tchaikowsky was assured of Imperial patronage—no small matter to a nineteenth-century Russian musician whose career could be made or marred by royal patronage. Tchaikowsky's music, so Russian yet so cosmopolitan and easily comprehended, comprising none of the wild dissonance, the strange distastefulness (to Imperial palates) of a Moussorgsky or a Borodin, suited the Imperial family perfectly. In truth, they adored Tchaikowsky's music and said so. The Grand Duke Constantin wrote often to Peter Ilyich, obviously eager for the friendship of Russia's first musician.

What might be called Peter's Kamenka period ended about this time, 1885. By then his sister Alexandra Davydoff was launched into the long illness which was to end in her death, the children were grown, Kamenka was a quieter and a sadder place. Anna Davydoff was by now married to Nadejda's son, Nicholas. The lovely Tatiana upon whom Uncle Petia had spent so much time and pity, was at Kamenka no longer; she had met a death as dramatic and swift as her brief young life. Peter grieved deeply and looked about for another home, one that would be his own and would be permanent. He found it in Maidanovo near Klin, a small village easily accessible to Moscow and Petersburg.

Peter's manner of settling into his new house was very characteristic. He entrusted the whole thing to Alexis, who rented the house, purchased all the furnishings, arranged them in the rooms, and when all was ready notified the master he could move in. Peter himself bought nothing except an antique English clock that would not go and two horses which he had a hard time getting rid of afterward. Alexis' taste was deplorable and the place was truly hideous, but Peter loved it, pronouncing himself pleased and proud and often speaking with obvious pleasure of "my table linen, my silver, my cook, my dog." (Alexis hated dogs, so his master dared not have more than one.) As soon as he moved in, Tchaikowsky began work on the symphonic poem, *Manfred*. He wrote Nadejda about *Manfred* and his new house and she replied with sympathy for the music and misgivings as to Peter Ilyich as landlord. The following September when Peter reported that he had not only finished *Manfred* but had completed also the first act of a new opera, *The Enchantress*, Nadejda was again in a skeptical mood. "I like your uncompromising statements regarding my opera," Tchaikowsky replied. "You have a good right to look with suspicion upon this insincere form of art." But opera, Peter went on to say, was a serious composer's only means of reaching the mass of people. Symphony was no doubt a higher, purer form of art than opera, but to refrain from writing the latter, to resist the glitter and attraction of the stage, required the soul of a hero. "Only one such hero," continued Peter, "is alive today—Brahms." Both as man and artist, he wished to say that Brahms had never deviated from the highest ideals. "Unfortunately," finished Peter, "Brahms' creative gift is meagre, unworthy of his aspirations."

So frequent, by now, were Tchaikowsky's trips abroad, that when he found himself, happily, in his country home, he asked nothing more than to be let alone that he might write his music in peace. *Manfred* was the last composition he wrote in anything but completest solitude. Peter liked *Manfred* at first, but three years after its composition he wrote the Grand Duke Constantin that *Manfred* was a "repulsive work, and I hate it heartily, all except the first movement. In the near future, I plan to destroy the three last movements, which musically are simply trivial (especially the final movement which is impossible). So, from a piece of music that is much too long for a symphony, I shall make a symphonic poem. Then and then only I feel sure my *Manfred* will please. The first movement I wrote with delight, the rest with such effort that I was quite ill for a time afterward."

Previous to the composition of *Manfred,* Tchaikowsky had been very communicative about what he was writing, but from now on he became extremely reserved about his work, never discussed it or mentioned it to the many friends who came out from Moscow to see him. This is not to say Peter did not enjoy his friends' company; on the contrary, he often invited friends to stay with him in Maidanovo, but the unbidden guest had need to beware. Not for nothing did Peter tack a placard on his garden gate:

"Peter Ilyich Tchaikowsky. Receives Mondays and Thursdays from 3 to 5. Not at home. Please do not ring."

1886 saw the completion of *The Enchantress,* an opera in

four acts which failed completely when produced the following autumn in Petersburg. Tchaikowsky was much humiliated and wrote Jurgenson how ashamed he was to have exposed his publisher to such a financial loss. His publisher, however, sustained the loss quite philosophically, knowing he would soon be recompensed by new Tchaikowsky successes. Orchestral suite number four, called *Mozartiana,* was already in the printing press. This suite was an arrangement for orchestra of some of Mozart's smaller, less known works. In his preface to the score Tchaikowsky said he had arranged the suite in order to bring these gems of musical literature to the attention of the public. Never did he forget his god, Mozart, "that Christ of music," Peter called him. Even during this period of strenuous activity and achievement he took time off to remind Nadejda of his and the world's debt to the great, the gay master of form in music. Peter was forever conscious that a lack of form was his own worst musical defect; he confessed it in a letter to the Grand Duke Constantin:

"All my life I have been much troubled by my inability to grasp and manipulate form in music. I fought hard against this defect and can say with pride that I achieved some progress, but I shall end my days without ever having written anything that is perfect in form. What I write has always a mountain of padding; an experienced eye can detect the thread in my seams, and I can do nothing about it."

This letter was written in 1888, and with this date Tchaikowsky found himself at the peak of his fame, a peak which he was never to descend and one which was higher than he himself had ever dreamed of climbing. One thing that hitherto had hampered Peter greatly was his inability to conduct an orchestra. His old stage fright had hung on, vaguely and dreadfully reminiscent of the days when he had conducted with one hand to his chin so his head would not fall off. But just before the New Year of 1887, Tchaikowsky decided to try to conduct his revised opera, *Les Caprices d'Oxane,* and wrote Nadejda von Meck about it from Moscow.

To Nadejda von Meck

Moscow
January 26, 1887

"My sweet, dear, priceless friénd:

"For a week, now, I have enjoyed your hospitality. I live in your house as in Christ's bosom. I can't say enough about the care your servants show for my comfort. Unfortunately I can be at home very little as we have rehearsals daily. Every morning I take a walk, and by eleven o'clock I am seated before the orchestra at the conductor's desk. The rehearsals are over at four and I am so tired that when I get home I can only throw myself down and sleep. By evening my strength returns and I can eat something.

"Certainly, conducting is hard for me and takes a great toll of my nervous system, but I must admit it gives me real pleasure. (1) It is pleasant to know I have conquered my in-born timidity. (2) It is extremely pleasant for the author of an opera to conduct his composition himself, and not be forced to keep approaching the conductor with requests to change this or that. (3) Everyone who takes part in the production shows me such sincere sympathy that I am deeply touched.

"And, dear friend, in truth I am much less worried and anxious now than when I used to have to sit passively at rehearsals. I believe that if all continues to go well, the after-math will be favorable rather than unfavorable to my sick nerves."

On the day of performance, Peter woke feeling, he wrote, "really ill," convinced that a horrible nightmare was about to be enacted. All day he endured agonies, and when evening came could barely walk onto the stage at the appointed time. The curtain rose, and Peter found himself almost smothered with wreaths of flowers presented by the chorus, the orchestra and friends. This gave him, he said, time to recover, and from then on the evening rang with applause. Peter was a bit skeptical about Moscow applause. The theatre being at least half full of his friends he could not tell if the compliment was for his work or himself. "I shall con-

279

duct twice more," he wrote, "and the third time should tell me for certain how much all this noise has been worth."

The third time was a success, convincing Tchaikowsky that from now on he could conduct without, figuratively or literally, losing his head. The news spread, and from that evening Peter Ilyich was in great demand as a conductor of his own works. Concert tour followed concert tour; even Paris was conquered, and as to Prague, it went wild over *Eugene Onegin*. Tchaikowsky wrote Nadejda a bit ruefully that he had left Prague "laden with laurels—but only laurels. I don't know how to look after my pecuniary interests." Anton Dvorak especially had been entranced with the opera.

Anton Dvorak to Tchaikowsky

Prague
January 14, 1889

"Dear Friend,

"When you were in Prague, I promised to write you about your opera *Onegin*. But now I write, impelled not only by your request but by my own feelings when I heard your work. I joyfully confess the great and deep impression your opera made upon me. I always expect work of genuine artistic value from you, and I do not hesitate to say that not one of your compositions has pleased me so much as *Onegin*.

"That beautiful composition, so rich in warmth and poetry, shows mastery in every detail; in short, this is music that calls out to us, and that enters so deeply into our soul we can never forget. Listening and watching, I felt myself transported to another world.

"I congratulate you—and all of us—on the existence of such a composition. God grant you may leave many more such to the world.

"In sincere greeting,

"Your devoted friend,
"Anton Dvorak."

In between all these triumphs and activities, Peter Ilyich had moved again—or rather, Alexis had moved for him—while the composer was down in Tiflis visiting his brother

Anatol, the brother whose duties as a district attorney had taken him to this southernmost border of Russia. Peter's new country home was not far from the old one, in the village of Frolovskoe. It was an extremely simple, unpretentious little place, built like a bungalow, with a little terrace containing a pond. In the middle of the pond, to Peter's vast delight, was an islet. From Frolovskoe, on his return from Tiflis, Peter wrote enthusiastically to tell Nadejda he was planting a garden. He went at it with a furious delight that was equalled only by his horticultural ignorance. On these cold June nights he would not sleep, he said, for fear the frost would kill his seedlings.

To Nadejda Philaretovna

Frolovskoe
June 10, 1888

"I shall work very hard now for a while. I want terribly to prove not only to others but to myself that I am not yet played out. Very often, doubt seizes me and I ask myself, Isn't it time to stop writing music, haven't I overstrained my imagination, hasn't the wellspring itself dried up? This must happen sometime if I live on for ten or twenty years, and how do I know that the time is not arrived when I should lay down my arms. . . . I don't remember if I told you I have decided to write a symphony. When I began it, composition came hard, but now it looks as if inspiration had come. ... We shall see."

This was to be the Fifth Symphony. It was completed in two months, the composer maintaining, during his work, quite strict silence concerning his progress. The first performance took place in Petersburg under the composer's baton a couple of months after the score was completed, and fell rather flat. Considering the Fifth is now Tchaikowsky's best, or second-best loved work (many persons prefer it to the *Pathètique*) the indifference with which it met must be attributed to poor performance. Also, even though Tchaikowsky succeeded in staying on the podium without accident, he was anything but an inspired conductor. His modesty stood hopelessly in his way and time after time, works that later became famous met with failure or indifference when conducted by himself. Concerning the Fifth Symphony, Peter wrote Nadejda von Meck in December, 1888:

"Having played my symphony twice in Petersburg and once in Prague, I have come to the conclusion that it is a failure. There is something repellent in it, some over-exaggerated color, some insincerity or fabrication which the public instinctively recognizes. It was clear to me that the applause and ovations referred not to this but to other works of mine, and that the symphony itself will never please the public. All this causes a deep dissatisfaction with myself. It is possible that I have, as people say, written myself out, and that nothing remains but for me to repeat and imitate myself. Yesterday evening I glanced over the Fourth Symphony, *our* symphony. How superior to this one, how much better it is! Yes, this is a very, very sad fact."

Few people today would admit that Tchaikowsky's Fourth was superior to his Fifth Symphony, and no one at all would declare that the man was played out who was to write the *Nutcracker Suite*, the *Hamlet Overture*, and the Sixth Symphony. Perhaps such periods of profound dissatisfaction are necessary to the artist; Peter himself suspected as much. Anyway, in the midst of this attack of melancholy, Tchaikowsky set to work to compose one of his gayest, most popular works, the ballet, *Sleeping Beauty*, written from sketches he had made one summer at Kamenka for a little holiday play staged by his Davydoff nieces. This was the ballet that was destined to be a favorite with two Tsars in turn. Peter worked at it easily, with an enthusiasm he had not felt in composing, he declared, since the days of *Eugene Onegin*. He did it in six weeks, at Maidanovo, and in the midst of it he had a pleasant surprise. At Christmas, Alexis brought to his study a tiny Christmas tree, all decorated, and with it a complete edition of Mozart, with Jurgenson's card enclosed.

And now, in January, 1889, Tchaikowsky embarked on another concert tour. From Berlin to London the plaudits rang and Peter should have been content. Yet strangely enough, it was now that his peace of mind, the healthy objectivity he had possessed for the past five years, began to crumble. Perhaps crumble is too strong a word. Peter remained well and active; but in every letter we find a note of doubt and bitterness—the old note, and somehow, endearing. This furious travelling, this rushing from city to city in pursuit of fame: what was it for, his heart asked him? Would he not do better to stay at home and write his music? In the midst of rehearsals and concerts he was "doing nothing," he wrote Nadejda. "I say doing nothing because my real mission is to compose, and all this other activity is incidental and useless and will only shorten my days."

Leipzig, Berlin, Hamburg, Prague, Paris, Dresden, Geneva, London. . . . Brilliant public successes, accompanied by devastating homesickness and gloom. And all the while, when he had a few days' respite, he wrote music. The opera *Pique Dame*, second only to *Onegin* in charm and still very popular.

Pique Dame was finished in the spring of 1890. Peter went to Italy for a rest and took with him the opera score in order to make the piano arrangement. The moment he returned to his country home at Frolovskoe, he wrote Nadejda that he had commenced a new work, a sextet for strings.

"Knowing your great love for chamber music, I rejoice that you will surely hear my sextet. You won't have to go to a concert because it will be quite easy to arrange a good performance at home. I do hope this music will please you. . . . I wrote it with the greatest pleasure and enthusiasm, and no effort whatever."

In truth, Nadejda Philaretovna was by now in need of music that could be heard easily, and at home. During these years while Peter had been so active, so outward-going, while he had been saying *Yes* to life, Nadejda had been saying *No*. Tuberculosis, that her strong constitution had resisted for so long, was laying now its wasting hand upon her. Daily, yearly she sank backward, downward along the path of illness and decay. Quite early in the eighties, Modeste Tchaikowsky had written his brother that he had met Nadejda Philaretovna in Rome one day, out walking; the letter had exclaimed upon her altered appearance: "How old she has become, and how queerly she dresses!"

Her high-handedness, her lavish manner of living, continued unabated; when she was abroad and wished to hear the music of her adored Peter Ilyich, she simply went to Paris and commanded Colonne to teach his renowned orchestra to play it, and Colonne, well fortified by crackling French banknotes, complied. Not one soul did the widow invite to share these performances—except young Vladimir von Meck, her favorite grandson. Alone in a box above the darkened empty theatre the two sat happily, sharing a secret joy. . . . .

Writing to Peter Ilyich, Nadejda seldom mentioned her illness except as explanation for occasional lapses in her correspondence. We do not know exactly what form her tuberculosis took; she mentions her cough, her frequent "colds," her dread of snow and dampness. Also the painful migraine attacks arrived with increasing frequency, followed by several days of prostration during which the victim could not sit up to write. Peter always grieved for Nadejda's suffering, but, himself accustomed to indifferent health, was not alarmed by his friend's condition; never once had she spoken the word *consumption*. Therefore he had no warning of what was to come that autumn of 1890. From Peter she had concealed only too well her increasing fear and depression. Peter thought he was secure in this friendship; indeed, he would have called this friendship the one secure spot in a life that he had himself described as having "no haven." "You are the only person in the world," he had written Nadejda, "who can make me deeply, profoundly happy. I am infinitely grateful, and hope only that what inspires your feeling for me will never end or alter, because such a loss would be unendurable."

In September, 1890, Peter went down to Tiflis to conduct a concert of his works, staying, as usual, with Anatol. Peter loved the Caucasus. Tiflis was in the mountains, on the River Kura, and it was more Persian than Russian; the brothers roamed the strange foreign streets and walked the fertile valleys beyond the town, Peter never ceasing to marvel at the luxuriance of the verdure, the profusion of flowers and the glorious heat of the sun. And here, in the midst of beauty, came a letter that put happiness from Peter's mind. Nadejda's fortune, she wrote, was on the edge of collapse and she could send Peter Ilyich no more money ever, from now on. It was not this statement that frightened Peter so much as the tone of the letter which was curt and strange and unlike any words Nadejda had written him during all their long intimacy together. The whole letter was tinged with inexplicable, ominous finality. . . . As for the money, this was not the first time Nadejda had cried wolf, wolf!

But this time, somehow, her statement about money losses carried conviction. How, wondered Peter, could ruin have come so swiftly? The von Meck fortune was too public an affair to dissolve thus secretly and suddenly; there had been no such rumors around Moscow, and Moscow always seemed to know von Meck family business as soon as the von Mecks knew it. Perhaps illness had depressed Nadejda, perhaps she was having one of her migraines and exaggerated her troubles. Also, when people lost their money they often lost their friends with it. Rich people especially seemed to think friendship depended upon money, and Nadejda was an avowed skeptic where human nature was concerned. Only to Peter Ilyich had her skepticism never applied. How many times had she not assured him that among mankind he was the only soul she could trust?

Peter read the letter and re-read it, and, profoundly troubled, took up his pen:

To Nadejda Philaretovna

Tiflis
October 4, 1890

"Sweet, dear friend of mine :

"Your letter just came; what you have to say grieves me deeply — not for myself, but for you. I say this with utmost sincerity. Certainly it would be false to pretend that such a radical change in my budget will not affect my material welfare, but it will affect it far less than you probably think. In the last few years my income has markedly increased, and there is no reason to doubt it will continue so to increase, and rapidly. So if among your many troubles you are troubled also a little about me, I pray you be assured that I

285

have not felt even the smallest passing grief at the idea of this material loss. Believe me, this is absolutely the truth; I am no master of those phrases intended to deceive. Therefore, the point is, not that for a while I shall have to curtail expenses, but that you, with your habitual large scale of living, will have to endure privation. This to me is a terribly offensive and vexing thought.

"The last words of your letter (Do not forget, and think of me sometimes) offended me a little, but I tell myself you could not really have meant them. Is it possible you think me capable of remembering you only when I use your money? Could I forget for one second all you have done for me, all that I owe you? Without exaggeration I can say that you saved me, that I would surely have gone mad and perished had you not come forward with your friendship and sympathy. With the money you gave me as safety anchor, you rallied my expiring forces and gave me back my ambition to continue on the road of music. No, my dear friend, be assured I shall remember you and bless you to my last breath. It makes me happy to know that now, when you can no longer share your wealth with me, I can let myself go and express the whole strength of my warm and un-limited gratitude. Probably you yourself do not realize the extent of what you have done for me. If so, you could never have said what you did—that now you are poor you hope I will think of you 'sometimes.' Never for one moment have I forgotten you, nor will forget you, because every thought I have concerning myself, concerns you also.

"I kiss your hands with all the warmth my heart contains, beseeching you to realize, once and for all, that no one has greater sympathy for you, no one feels himself more truly part of your troubles or shares them more than I.

"Some other time I will write about myself and what I have been doing.

"Forgive this hasty scrawl. I am too upset to write clearly."

Peter had said he no longer needed Nadejda's money, and it was true that his own earnings had greatly increased during the past few years. But, characteristically, he had taken on a whole list of pensioners. Modeste alone received two thousand roubles a year and Peter supported his servant

Alexis' wife and family, besides countless young musicians who appealed to him for help and were never refused. At the moment, therefore, his funds were low, and for Peter the present, *le moment qui passe*, always represented eternity. From Tiflis he wrote Jurgenson that he would have to start life anew on an entirely different scale; he would have to go to Petersburg and look about, actually beg for a salaried position in the Conservatory—the thing he had avoided and scorned a dozen times in the past.

On his way north from Tiflis, Peter stopped in Moscow, and the first thing he learned was that there was nothing wrong whatever with the von Meck fortune. The railroad was as good as it had ever been and so were the other properties. Nothing had been sold, nothing confiscated. Bewilderment was followed by profound depression: Nadejda then had never really loved him. He had been her hired man, her toy; she had sent him money lightly, as the caprice of a rich woman and he had never truly earned his pension by the music he wrote. She had tired of him now and of his music; and to rid herself of him she had invented the flimsy excuse of financial ruin—an excuse that she well knew circumstance would soon disprove.

Truly this was the bitterest blow that Fate had dealt to Peter; he would not accept it, he told himself, arguing in his friend's behalf even as the facts arrayed themselves against her. He would not accept the fact of her cruelty, her light abandonment of this long friendship—until he gave her more time. Perhaps she would even yet reply to his letter from Tiflis; after all, very little time had passed since he had written, and Nadejda was probably getting ready for her autumnal migration to Italy or France. Peter shook his head and went about his business, fortunately unaware that six months would pass before a word of news would come —and that when it came, it would be bitter news.

Externally his life moved rapidly and brilliantly during the six months. Petersburg went wild over the first performance of *Pique Dame*, and Tchaikowsky's empty pockets were filled beyond any need of a salaried job. In Kiev the opera had even greater success; but Tchaikowsky, depressed and skeptical of applause, wrote to no one and told Modeste that *Pique Dame* was a failure. He accepted several big commissions and went out to Frolovskoe to work on them. First, the *Hamlet Overture*, prepared for a benefit entertainment for Lucien Guitry (father of Sascha Guirty). "I am very tired," he wrote Modeste in January, 1891. "My uncertainty as to the future weighs on me. My brain is empty; I have not the least pleasure in work. *Hamlet* oppresses me terribly."

Nevertheless *Hamlet* was written, and the world is still grateful for the professional conscientiousness that would not let Tchaikowsky leave a piece of work unfinished. No sooner was it done than the Imperial Opera in Petersburg commissioned an opera and a ballet. *King René's Daughter* was chosen for the opera, and for the ballet, the *Nutcracker* legend. *King René's Daughter* became eventually, the one-act opera, *Iolanthe*; Modeste prepared the libretto and was a long while doing it.

Meanwhile, Peter received an offer to go to America on a concert tour. On the way thither he was asked to stop off in Paris and conduct a whole concert of his works played by no other orchestra than Colonne's own, at the famous *Concerts Populaires* series. All these offers were accepted, and in March, 1891, with the completed first act of the *Nutcracker* ballet in his pocket, and with grief still heavy at his heart over Nadejda Philaretovna's continued silence, Peter set forth on his travels.

27

New York. Nadejda accepts a strange guilt

The Paris concert was a decided success and Tchaikowsky should have rejoiced that at last he had taken so difficult and scornful a musical citadel. But he seemed totally indifferent to triumph, and the instant the concert was over, fled to Rouen to wait for sailing time and to work on his ballet. The day before he embarked for New York, he picked up a newspaper and read the news of his sister Alexandra's death in Russia, the sister he loved best and whose house at Kamenka had for so long been home to him. It was too late now to cancel the American contract and, numb with grief and the bewilderment which always beset him on a long journey, Tchaikowsky boarded the *Bretagne* for what he thought would be strange, unfriendly shores.

Peter remained in America about a month, giving six orchestral concerts, four in New York, one in Baltimore, one in Philadelphia—and had, in spite of himself, a good time. He visited Washington and Niagara Falls and professed himself duly, though vaguely, impressed with both. He found himself, as he wrote Modeste, "much more important here than in Russia," and kept a diary, part of which has been translated into English by Rosa Newmarch.* The diary is an amazingly naive document. The bathtubs of New York and the tremendous buildings on Broadway— actually thirteen stories high, some of them!—impressed Peter profoundly, as did the hospitality of the Americans, their frankness and ingenuousness. Accustomed when abroad to look behind every overture of friendship for some reason, some *arrière pensèe*, Peter found to his amazement that here was no *arrière pensèe*; these people came to his hotel door and asked if there was anything they could do for him, anything he needed—and when he said no, and waited for them to ask him a favor, they merely said, "Have a drink?"—and paid for the drinks, and laughed, and shook his hand and went away. It was, Peter wrote Modeste, unbelievable, and if he had not been so hideously homesick he would have fallen quite in love with these people. One of them at whose house he dined, a Mr. Carnegie, who owned thirty million dollars (in his next letter Peter called it forty million)—this singular, warm-hearted character who had once been a telegraph boy, adored Moscow and looked just like the dramatist Ostrovsky. At the dinner party Mr. Carnegie had whacked Peter on the back, called him the uncrowned king of music, hugged him heartily (without kissing, Peter added. Men did not kiss in America). This Mr. Carnegie had given a pantomime representation of Peter on the conductor's box which had been simply wonderful and had made everyone roar with laughter.

The Americans ate so much, said Peter. And so extrava-

* *Life and Letters of P. I. Tchaikowsky*. The Bodley Head, London, 1906.

gantly. Why, at Mr. Hyde's, in the middle of dinner, ices were served in live roses. . . . Everywhere, his music met with enthusiasm, but it was disconcerting the way the newspapers commented more on his personal appearance and characteristics than on his music. Why did they do this? They said he was "stout, with greying hair, well built, an interesting-looking man of about sixty. . . ." And here he was just turned fifty! They said he was timid on the stage and responded to applause with short, sharp bows, and that only with baton in hand did he regain his assurance. Everybody in this strange cordial country seemed to want his autograph. On Sundays one could not buy a drink without plotting; some remnant of English Puritanism caused them to close all the cafés. Negro faces were everywhere; the porters on the trains were Negroes and were such kind, nice men! On the train to Baltimore when he had been so dead tired the Negro had made his bed for him and helped him into it and waked him next morning in time to get off. Before one big dinner party in Peter's honor, the host had turned suddenly solemn and closed his eyes and said the Lord's Prayer! The steamer was awful, going and coming, rolled and plunged and Peter was sure he would perish; the fog horn emitted "terrible roars like a colossal, enraged tiger." Nerve-racking in the extreme, wrote Peter. The passengers discovered his identity and tried to make him play the piano. A mademoiselle sang Italian songs all evening in an excruciating voice, but nobody was rude to her. How strange! Somebody stole 460 francs from his stateroom. . . .

Nothing mattered, however, except that the steamer should get quickly back to Hamburg. Until it did, Tchaikowsky would be in a daze, as he had been since the moment he left Russia. And when finally he felt German ground beneath his feet, the composer fled swiftly eastward to Petersburg and thence to his country home. Before sailing for New York, disgusted with Frolovskoe since his landlord had cut the forest down, Peter had ordered Alexis to move back to the old house at Maidanovo. So it was at Maidanovo he settled again in June of 1891, working hard at the *Nutcracker* ballet and the opera, *Iolanthe*. Still no letter came from Nadejda von Meck, and after a few days Peter went to Moscow. Here at last he found an envelope postmarked Plesheyevo—but it was not from Nadejda. It was from Vladislav Pahulsky, and it was short and polite and non-committal; it was, in fact, more damning than no letter at all. Pahulsky, it will be remembered, was the Polish violinist—more gentleman, perhaps, than violinist—who had lived for so long in Nadejda's house and who by now was married to Nadejda's daughter, Julia.

Tchaikowsky wrote an instant reply.

To V. Pahulsky

Moscow
June 18, 1891

"Your letter has just come. You say that Mme Nadejda Philaretovna is ill, weak and so nervously upset she can no longer write me as before. Truly, not for anything in the world would I be the cause of adding to her suffering. What hurts, troubles, and, I may say, offends me deeply, is not the fact that she does not write, but that she has lost all interest in me. If she wished to hear from me without writing, it would be quite feasible; you and Julia Karlovna could be constant intermediaries. Yet not once has she requested either of you to find out how I am living or how my life is going. I tried, through you, to re-establish a correspondence with N. Ph., but your every letter put off politely my attempts to preserve even for a little, the shadow of what had been. Surely you know that last September, N. Ph. informed me she was ruined financially and could render me no more material aid. You probably saw my reply. What I urgently desired was that my relationship with N. Ph. should not change, now that I no longer received money from her. Unfortunately, that seems to be impossible because N. Ph. has evidently become quite cold to me. As a result, I stopped writing to N. Ph., and every connection between us was severed as soon as the money ceased coming. This is terribly humiliating; it makes the realization that I accepted a pension from her an unbearable worry and torment.

"This autumn while I was in the country I re-read all N. Ph.'s letters. Not illness nor anxiety nor financial troubles could, I thought while reading, alter the feelings expressed in those letters. Yet those feelings have changed. Perhaps it

291

is because I never met N. Ph. that I always idealized her. In such a person, half-divine, I could not imagine such a treason; it seemed to me the earth would fall to pieces under my feet sooner than that N. Ph.'s feelings toward me would alter. But it has happened, and all my faith in people, all my trust in the world has turned upside down. My peace is gone and whatever happiness fate intended for me is poisoned.

"Without meaning to, N. Ph. has surely behaved very cruelly toward me. Never before have I felt such humiliation or suffered such a blow to my pride. And the hardest part of all is that because of N. Ph.'s weak physical condition, I dare not risk grieving or disturbing her by telling her how all this troubles me.

"Therefore it is impossible for me to speak out frankly — the only thing that could give me relief. But enough of this. Perhaps I shall regret writing, but I could no longer resist the impulse to pour out somehow, somewhere this bitterness that has accumulated in my heart. Of course, not a word of it to N. Ph.

"If she asks about me, tell her I returned safely from America and have settled in Maidanovo to work. My health is good.

"Do not answer this letter."

Pahulsky did answer it. He returned Peter's letter, repeating what he had said before: that Nadejda Philaretovna was sick, physically and mentally. Severely ill, and her apparent indifference came from illness and nothing else. In her heart she still loved her old friends, said Pahulsky, but he dared not, in her present condition, show her Peter's letter.

This was the end for Peter Ilyich; it was his last attempt to re-establish communication. His best friend was gone, lost to him forever. What he had considered an ideal relationship had been then, he wrote Jurgenson, nothing more than a "commonplace, meaningless farce, which fills me with humiliation and disgust." Phrases of Nadejda's early letters leaped tauntingly to his memory: "You are life itself to me," she had written from Brailov. "I wandered today through the rooms you have just left, sat in the chair at your writing table and felt your dear presence. Peter Ilyich, my best of friends, how can I express my gratitude for what you are?"

Those were not words inspired by caprice. But if love such as that could fail without a reason, what then, in the world of human beings, remained for a man to believe in? The anger and indignation that for a time had upheld him, now deserted Peter Ilyich; a deep hurt remained, a wound from which he was never to recover. He was not a young man, to recoil easily from such a blow—a blow not only to his self-esteem but to his belief in human nature. He was fifty-one and he was tired, too tired to make new friends or to wish for them.

This was June of 1891. Scarcely more than two years of life remained to Peter Ilyich.

And Nadejda von Meck—did she know what she was doing, what pain she was causing? Peter was aware that his friend was very ill, but he knew also that illness alone was not sufficient cause for her sudden cruelty. What he did not know and was never to discover was that something outside of her illness, outside of herself, had caused Nadejda's change of heart. Something had risen to break, once and for all, that proud fierce spirit, something which had nothing to do with Peter Ilyich. Yet it was upon Peter, ironically enough, that the widow let the consequences fall.

From time to time, in these pages, mention has been made of Nadejda's eldest son, the handsome, brilliant, lavish Vladimir, who once defied the House of Rothschild with twelve manufactured secretaries. Vladimir's life had continued as recklessly as it had begun and now, in 1890, he fell mortally ill of a slow disease against which medicine had then no weapon. Day by day, herself fevered, coughing, Nadejda watched her son, this charming, invincible creature, decay before her eyes, mind as well as body.

Nadejda watched, and there came an hour when she could accept this thing no longer. Here was nothing to fight, and Nadejda, who had confessed that resignation had no part in her nature—Nadejda had to fight or perish. So she groped for an enemy, for something she could come to grips with, something she could withstand and battle every waking moment.

She found it in a sense of her own guilt. She had neglected

her son, the widow told herself. All these years, these thirteen years, she, a mother, had been interested in but one thing, but one person — and that person had been far outside the province of motherhood: *Peter Ilyich Tchaikowsky.* Daily, nightly Peter Ilyich had occupied her mind; his music, his letters, her replies to his letters. In secret she had had this joy; she had told no one but Julia and Julia's husband. Vladimir had not known. She had thrust her son from her and had set up a secret idol in his place, and thereby she had destroyed her son. . . .

Sitting alone in the garden at Plesheyevo, gazing into the hot summer sunshine, the picture of her guilt rose sharp before the widow's eyes, fierce and sure as the devils that had beset the saints of old. Fiercer even and surer, for Nadejda, still an atheist, lacked all trust in divine forgiveness. She could suffer punishment, but she could never achieve the reward of punishment. She would hasten now to punishment, hasten to put from her this evil thing that she had cherished as holy and had called by the name of love — or art, or music. This thing that had caused her to deceive those closest to her, to sit for hours alone with her pen and writing paper, to snatch whole weeks in Florence, Paris, Rome — weeks that should have been devoted to her son.

Impossible to tell all or any of this to Peter Ilyich. Impossible to attempt any explanation whatever, or indeed, to confide in anyone except, perhaps, Julia. But she would not tell even Julia until later, much later, when she had safely put this wickedness from her.

Nadejda rose and went into the house. Slowly, her hand on the banister, she made her way upstairs to her writing desk. Unfaltering, her pen went down the page. Only at the end, it weakened. "Do not forget," wrote Nadejda to her once beloved friend. "Do not forget, and think of me sometimes."

This was the letter addressed to Tchaikowsky at Tiflis in September, 1890. After it, Nadejda von Meck lived nearly four years. She died far from home, in Wiesbaden, January 13, only three months after Tchaikowsky himself had died in Petersburg. She was buried in Moscow, the city she loved, in the cemetery of Saint Alexis Monastery, by the side of her husband, that valiant knight, Karl George Otto von Meck.

Thus ended one of the strangest intimacies in all history, and its end was as inexplicable as its course. Nadejda's final letter was, on the face of it, as utterly cruel as Peter said it was: to refuse a man's friendship the instant she ceased sending him money, to refuse, in other words, to admit him on terms of equality, was the apotheosis of arrogance; it was outright denial not only of everything Nadejda had herself promised and written, but of the most elemental structure of friendship itself.

On his death-bed, delirious, Peter was to call again and again upon the name of Nadejda Philaretovna.

Perhaps the sharpness of this blow to friendship, the unbearable heaviness of it, was due mostly to its total unexpectedness. During thirteen years there had been no hint, late or early, of distrust or estrangement on the widow's part. On the contrary, Nadejda had set Peter very obviously on a pedestal of her own making; she had stood below and looked up to him, a creature incomparably higher than herself. Had she not confessed again and again her pride in being permitted to foster genius, to be humbly, indirectly instrumental in the creation of music that would belong to the whole world? Never was relationship more seemingly selfless on a woman's part; Nadejda gave and gave and in return asked for—what? For nothing except that the man to whom she gave should continue to live as his best self, should continue on the road he desired most to tread, continue to be what his whole spirit and every beat of the blood along his veins told him to be—a good composer.

From the beginning, no one can doubt the sincerity of the widow's attachment. Even her most high-flown letters carry conviction.

No more than Peter Ilyich, can we condemn Nadejda for her denial of truth and of friendship. She was a sick woman. While we have no record that her mind was actually affected, while the word insanity has not come down to us attached to her name, we know that toward the end she suffered from what her daughter called "a terrible nervous affliction" —and devoted daughters have a right to choose their words. Nadejda Philaretovna, an autocrat, a woman to whom wealth had given a tremendous power over all her surroundings and who for twenty years had exercised this power as though it were her divine right, was visited suddenly by a guest to whom divine right meant nothing. Nadejda could not command this grim visitor, could not buy him off. Her every weapon was powerless. Small wonder, then, that she took refuge in delusion.

One of the most interesting things about the correspondence between Nadejda and Peter Ilyich is the way one's judgment alters, during the years, toward the two. At first one is inclined to admire Nadejda Philaretovna, even while smiling at her extravagant, ecstatic manner of conducting a correspondence. And one is inclined to blame Peter Ilyich a little—even, at times, to suspect him of self-interest. But this is only during the Antonina period, when Peter was ill and distraught and terrified, a man ready to clutch at any straw of escape. Little by little, as Peter regains his strength and comes into his kingdom, as he attains his stature, is set upon his spiritual—and physical—feet, we learn to respect him and to love him. And little by little, while we never lose respect for Nadejda Philaretovna, we begin to understand why, among all the persons of her household, no one loved her except Julia and the tender, gentle-natured young grandson, Vladimir II.

This was a woman too proud, too fiercely independent, to merit love. Toward Peter her generosity was real and it was admirable. She gave all, asked nothing. But against all others the widow protected herself. Wrapped in the armor of wealth and solitude she drew into herself, grew downward and inward.

The truth is, perhaps, that at the time we meet the two, Peter was at his lowest, Nadejda at her highest. And Peter's foot, once it felt solid ground beneath it, climbed steadily, faithfully, persistently upward. The widow, on the other hand, already forty-five when we meet her, carrying within her the germ of disease, fought a valiant fight, but slipped ever downward, toward fear and defeat. Dowered, like Peter Ilyich, with over-emotionality, over-intensity, Nadejda did not say, "This is a curse, let me tear it from me." No, she indulged her nature; we never see her laugh, as did Peter, at her own wild orgies of self-dramatization. "After my usual habit," wrote Peter one day from San Remo, when his brother had been late in arriving from Russia, "I invented a whole drama of horror, and enacted it. I leaped the first train for Genoa, expecting to find the travellers dead or surely dying. And I found Modeste's pupil in bed, sleeping off a cold. . . ."

Peter Ilyich, in short, was not what the world calls a "strong character," yet he possessed one strength Nadejda never had. He knew his weakness and fought it, and for this quality of courage, of honesty toward himself, the gods rewarded him by granting the one gift he desired above all others—the privilege of conscious growth.

28

1891–1893. The Sixth Symphony. Death of Peter Ilyich

That summer of 1891, after Peter's return from America, and after Pahulsky had returned his letter, Peter lived on at Maidanovo, completing *Iolanthe* and the *Nutcracker* suite —this latter being, as the world now knows, one of the most brilliant bits of orchestration the composer produced. In Paris, while waiting for his ship to New York, Tchaikowsky had found a new instrument, the *celesta*, which he now described to Jurgenson as a cross between a piano and a glockenspiel. He urged Jurgenson to buy one and have it ready for the first performance of the *Nutcracker* ballet. Let the instrument be sent from Paris secretly; should Rimsky-Korsakov or Glazounov hear of it they would seize upon it and make use of it first, spoiling the fun.

Jurgenson, that enterprising man of business, accomplished all expeditiously. In the *Nutcracker* suite the celesta, now so popular, had its first and extremely successful introduction as an orchestral instrument.

The suite, however, was not performed for many months. Meanwhile at Maidanovo, toward the end of that summer of 1891, something unfortunate happened, a seemingly trivial incident which under the circumstances, depressed Peter very much. The watch that Nadejda had had made for him in Paris, the black-and-gold 10,000-franc Jeanne d'Arc watch, was stolen. Peter had grown very fond of this watch and proud of it. For years he had worn it as Nadejda had desired him to wear it, over his heart, a constant reminder of his friend. He scarcely let it out of his sight for cleaning and repairs. And now, when any link with Nadejda was doubly precious, Peter went for a walk one afternoon and, by a combination of small accidents, left the watch in his room. Although Alexis was in the house taking his afternoon siesta, a thief must have entered, for when Peter returned, the watch was gone. The police could not find it, but they found the thief and brought him to Tchaikowsky. The man promised to tell where the watch was if they would leave him alone with Peter Ilyich. The two went into the next room, where the thief, in the dramatic manner that seems to accompany even the most trivial Russian incident, went down on his knees and implored forgiveness. Gazing upon him, Peter Ilyich in agitated tones forgave all. Whereupon the man announced that he had never stolen the watch and could not possibly tell anybody where it was. So was broken one more link with Nadejda von Meck.

This autumn Peter Ilyich made his will, and no sooner was it signed than he realized he was almost penniless because he had given away all his money. To crown his irritation he received an offer of a return trip to America at only one-half the fee of the first tour. To Modeste he expressed himself humiliated, and his cabled reply to the agent in New York read merely, "Non. Tchaikowsky."

Pique Dame was given in Prague and Kiev that winter, as well as in Moscow; *Onegin* was performed in Hamburg. Tchaikowsy travelled about, conducting these and other performances of his works, and suffering from a really terrible homesickness. It was to his nephew Bob Davydoff that he wrote his troubles now; Bob was the son of Peter's beloved sister Alexandra, and after Alexandra's death Tchaikowsky and the boy became increasingly intimate. Tchaikowsky wrote Bob from all over Europe and finally dedicated the Sixth Symphony to him. Unfortunately, Bob was a weak reed to lean upon. With none of the inward grace of youth and all of its irresponsibility, he was an example of the Tchaikowskys at their worst. Boasting the Tchaikowsky charm and none of the Tchaikowsky loyalty, his insincerity would have been detected by anyone less ingenuous than his Uncle Peter. Bob took from his uncle all he could get; he was a drug addict who was eventually—long after his uncle's death—to end as a suicide in Tchaikowsky's house at Klin.

Behold Peter Ilyich, therefore, that winter of 1892–1893, travelling about Europe as though pursued and sending frantic letters home to Bob—letters which seemed to give the writer no comfort. Gone were the days when Peter could write his nightmare to Nadejda and, sure of her warm, strong protection, see the nightmare dwindle even as his pen described it. Sometimes, on these European tours, he became so depressed he cancelled his concerts on the spot and fled home to Maidanovo. Even Maidanovo proved unsatisfactory, and the composer moved again, in the spring of 1892. This time the house was in the town of Klin, the last estate on the road to Froloskoe, and like Tchaikowsky's other houses, was in no way distinguished or attractive—typical of the Russian architecture—or lack of architecture—of the 1860's. It was, however, the best house in the village. The first floor was low, made of brick, the second of wood, with higher ceilings; Tchaikowsky slept upstairs and his servant, after the Russian custom, on the first floor. This was Tchaikowsky's last home and the house that was afterward to become the Tchaikowsky museum. There was a big garden round it, whose boundaries adjoined the estate of Taneyeff's brother, an extraordinary man, not at all musical but a great admirer of Tchaikowsky.

The summer after moving into his Klin house, Tchaikowsky suffered from a return of a physical ailment called in the 1890's catarrh of the stomach, and which seemed to be a kind of nervous colitis. Peter had had it at intervals for the last twenty years, sometimes with extreme severity. Once, staying in a Petersburg hotel during the rehearsals for *Pique Dame*, he had sent for Modeste and declared he would not live through the night. The doctors always prescribed the water cure, but Peter hated Vichy. Now, however, in the summer of 1892, he agreed to try it because Bob Davydoff was also in need of a cure. So the two set off together. Peter hated it, even in Bob's company, and cut short his visit to return in July and busy himself with the mountains of proof-reading that had lately become an obsession with him. The older he grew, the more Tchaikowsky hated any mistake of print, however small. He wrote Bob at this time that even in his dreams, sharps and flats rose up before his eyes and refused to do as they were ordered. But the work was interrupted by another concert tour and yet another. Some demon seemed to be driving Peter Ilyich before the public, in spite of his very real desire to remain at home in peace. Honors fell upon him in showers. He was elected a member of the Academie Française, and the University of Cambridge invited him to come to England and receive the degree of Doctor of Music. More concert tours all over Europe, and from all over Europe, letters flying home to say that Peter Ilyich had "nothing to write about but fits of weeping." He was even surprised, he confessed, that this extraordinary homesickness did not drive him mad. Once, in a railway carriage, he was taken so ill he became delirious. He got out at a nearby station, dosed himself with his usual remedies and was, as usual, well the next day.

Peter himself did not know why, considering all this suffering, he continued to travel. "It seemed," wrote Modeste afterward, "that my brother had ceased to belong to himself; some irresistible force had taken possession of him and drove him blindly forward and outward. And that 'something' was not a simple deference to public demand. By now he had learned how to refuse artistic engagements or commissions that did not appeal to him. Nor was it the old restlessness and desire to be on the move, because the old places that he had loved so much had become impossible for him. Kamenka and Verbovka were no more now than the ruins of his sister's memory; even Italy had lost its charm. Paris, now that he was so famous, only frightened him. Simaki and Brailov belonged to strangers. The only thing that took him voluntarily from the seclusion of Klin was the desire to go to Petersburg to see his relatives.

"Nor does vanity explain my brother's persistent wandering on these concert tours. Although he possessed, in common with all artists, the desire for recognition, we know that in reality these ovations gave him more anxiety than pleasure, and the longing to be present at any great success of his works was spoiled by the torment of feeling himself under the eyes of the crowd. As for the money earned on these tours, it was less than negligible; always, Peter Ilyich returned home poorer than he set out.

"No, this mysterious force that drove him was a deep, inexplicable anxiety, a mood of despair that sought forgetfulness in distraction anywhere and everywhere. I cannot explain it as a premonition of death; there is no foundation for such a presumption. Nor have I the right to speculate too deeply concerning my brother's psychological condition during these last years; but I must remark upon the fact that such a period of despondency and bewilderment preceded every decisive change in his life. Before deciding upon a musical career in the early sixties, just before his marriage in Moscow, in 1885 directly before he made up his mind definitely to emerge from solitude and show himself in the eyes of the world — then as now, during this last winter of his life, one had the conviction that things could not go on longer as they were, that a change was coming, that something old and finished would shortly give place to something new and unknown."

And now, in February, 1893, seven months before Tchaikowsky was to drink the fatal glass of unboiled water, now in the midst of depression and darkness, a light broke and, as always with Tchaikowsky, the light came from within. He began to compose the Sixth Symphony, and the work, says Modeste, "was like an act of exorcism, by which Peter Ilyich cast out all the black spirits that had possessed him for so long."

The first mention of the symphony is found in a letter to Anatol, under date of February 22, 1893. Next day, writing to Bob Davydoff, the composer said:

"I want to tell you how contented I feel about my work. You know I destroyed a partly composed, partly orchestrated symphony I wrote last autumn. It was the right thing to do, because there was little good in the thing — an empty play of sound without real inspiration. On the way to Paris last December the idea for a new symphony came to me, this time a symphony with a program, but a program that will remain an enigma to all. Let them guess for themselves; the symphony will be called merely 'Programmatic Symphony' (6). But the program is indeed permeated with subjectiveness, so much so that not once but often, while composing it in my mind during my journey, I shed tears. As soon as I got home I began to write out the sketches, and it went so quickly and eagerly that in less than four days the first movement was done and all the rest clearly outlined in my head. Half of the third movement is ready. Its form will contain much that is new; for instance, the finale will not be a noisy *allegro*, but, on the contrary, a quite long *adagio*. You cannot imagine the joy it gives me to know my day is not yet done, and that I am still capable of work. Of course I may be mistaken, but it doesn't seem so. Please don't tell anyone except Modeste."

This letter is the chief evidence of those persons who think Tchaikowsky committed suicide, who think that seven months later he drank intentionally that glass of raw water. The program of the Sixth Symphony, say they, was *death*, and no wonder the composer refused to reveal it. This is a theory that on the face of it is too ridiculous to need refutation. Concerning the letter above and its mention of tears — surely no one who knows Peter Ilyich, no one, indeed, who is even a little familiar with the artistic temperament — will consider tears shed in the act of artistic creation as anything but happy tears, tears of triumph over the painful, ecstatic labor of giving birth. . . .

His day was not yet done, wrote Peter to his nephew, he was yet capable of work. Sitting in the big, ugly, cluttered room at Klin over his sheets of lined music paper, Peter was once more filled with that furious, mad energy he had once described to Nadejda as the greatest joy life had to offer. Once more, driven by that inner consciousness of the immense value of time, the immense privilege that is man's if he but rouse himself to use it, Peter, bent over his work table, forgot the hours themselves in a realization of life that rose far above any ticking of the clock.

His mood was not, however, one of unremitting inspiration. The symphony progressed, after those first sketches, more slowly. During the spring Tchaikowsky had a letter from Jurgenson saying his presses were for the moment idle, and he would publish as many songs and piano pieces as Peter could compose. A month remained before he must travel to England to receive his Cambridge degree, and Peter made up his mind to write one piece a day for thirty days; the fifteenth day found him three pieces ahead of schedule. He wrote Jurgenson that he could not, however, deliver these pieces at his old fee of 100 roubles, but would have to ask more "in consequence," so the letter read, "of the number of paying propositions made to me lately (I swear it is true)."

Once more we see Tchaikowsky, the workman, settling to his tools with the true workman's pleasure in his craft—and this even in the midst of a far deeper inspiration. It had not been so long ago that he had written the Grand Duke Constantin, "Most of my fellow-workers do not like composing to order; but as for me, I never feel more inspired than when I am asked to write something or other, with a fixed time limit that means somebody at the other end is impatiently awaiting my work." Apropos of this commission of Jurgenson's in the spring of 1893, Tchaikowsky wrote Bob Davydoff:

"I continue to bake musical pancakes. Today the tenth has been tossed. The remarkable thing is that the further I go with this business, the easier and pleasanter it becomes. In the beginning it was very hard, and the first two pieces were the fruits of much effort of will, but now I scarcely have time to get one idea in shape before another follows, and so on the whole day long. So if I could stay a whole year in the country, and if my publisher were willing to print all that mountain of notation and pay for it, I could, working *à la Leiken*, make thirty-six thousand, five hundred roubles. Not a bad idea."

About the middle of May Tchaikowsky threw down this ardent craftsman's pen and went to England for the Cambridge honors. In London he conducted the Philharmonic in a performance of his Fourth Symphony—"our symphony," to which Nadejda Philaretovna was by now as sadly deaf as she was deaf to all the world of reality and health and beauty. The symphony had a truly brilliant success in London, eclipsing even the famous Saint-Saens, who followed on the program with a symphony of his own.

But Tchaikowsky, writing home to Bob Davydoff, merely inquired if it was not strange that of his own free will he had chosen to undergo "this torture?" He could neither sleep nor eat, he wrote; what fiend could have suggested this trip to him? Yesterday he had resolved to throw over the whole thing and turn tail; but he would be "ashamed to come home now with nothing to show for it. . . . I suffer not only from distress that cannot be said in words (there is a place in my new symphony where I think I have expressed these feelings quite well)—but from an extreme distaste for strangers, from some indefinable fear and from the devil knows what. Physically this fear has expression in pains through the lower abdomen and in an aching and weakness in my legs. Well, this is certainly the last time in my life I shall permit such a business, or at least, not except for big money and then not for longer than three days at a stretch. Two more weeks, I have to sit here, and it might as well be for eternity, it looms so long."

The dreaded day arrived, and Peter Ilyich went out to Cambridge to receive his degree in company with the other musicians to be so honored: Saint-Saens, Boito, Max Bruch and Grieg. The festivities began on the twelfth of June, a composition of each musician was performed, Tchaikowsky's being the beautiful *Francesca Overture-Fantasia*. Professors and lords and maharajahs did him honor; a grand dinner followed with toasts drunk and compliments flying high. Next morning the future doctors of music donned huge robes of scarlet and white silk; on their heads—empty now of melody and by their own report filled with astonishment—were placed velvet caps with gold tassels. Thus they walked through town, under what Saint-Saens described as a tropical sun, led by the maharajah in a gold turban and diamond necklace, and cheered all the way by enthusiastic spectators. Arrived upon the platform, Tchaikowsky, who by now was having quite a good time in consequence of having discovered a Cambridge professor and his wife who could speak Russian, stood up and listened to a Latin oration in his honor and received his degree. After a garden party and a dinner in London, he was free to go home, and home he went, via Moscow and a visit to Bob at Grankino.

To Bob Davydoff

Nicholas Tchaikowsky's
Estate in the Government
of Kursk
July 31st, 1893

"I spent two very pleasant days in Moscow after I left you. Tell Modia that the day after he left I was very ill, and they said it was from drinking too much cold water at dinner and supper. Castor oil soon cured me and I left next day. It is so nice here. For the next two days I must write letters, and then I can start again on my symphony."

To Modeste

Klin
August 3, 1893

"I am up to my neck in the symphony. The further I get with the orchestration, the more difficult it becomes. Twenty years ago I would have pushed at it, unthinking, with all the strength of my shoulders and it would have come out well. Now I have become a coward, with no faith in myself. For two whole days I have sat stewing over two pages; they won't work out as I wish. Yet it progresses.

"My house, thanks to Alexey's efforts, has a very coquettish appearance. Everything is neat, the garden is a mass of flowers, the paths are trimmed and we have new fences with gates. I am well served as regards food. And yet, except during working hours, I am bored, and wish myself elsewhere. . . . Still, I have noticed before that after long trips and much society, I am tired like this. Probably it will soon pass. . . ."

To Bob Davydoff

Klin
August 15, 1893

"The symphony that I planned to dedicate to you—I have since changed my mind—is progressing." (Tchaikowsky had not changed his mind, and was merely teasing his nephew.) "I am very pleased with its contents, but not quite so pleased with the orchestration. Time after time, things don't work out the way I want. It will be neither unusual nor surprising if the symphony meets with lack of appreciation and abuse. It won't be my first such experience. But I can say positively that I consider it the best of all my works to date; especially, I know it is the most sincere. I love it as I never loved any of my musical children.

"My life just now lacks all variety; sometimes the evenings bore me but I have no right to complain because the important thing now is the symphony and I can work nowhere so well as at home. My great amusement here is my godson (Alexey's son), to me a wonderfully attractive child."

To Taneyeff

Klin
August 24, 1893

"I have finished the symphony. There remains only to add the instrumental signs and tempo marks. Regarding the former, I want to ask Konius' advice, who will come here shortly for the purpose. He will bring a violin and his youngest brother Leo. I need the latter to play through the piano arrangement which I have just finished making. When you come to Moscow—I ask this very earnestly—will you play over the symphony with Konius and determine all the doubtful places that I can't decide without you? I did not so much as dare to ask you to make the piano arrangement because it would have been the greatest impudence on my part. You have no time for such work now. But I do earnestly beseech you to play it over. What a disgusting business, these piano arrangements! One has to drive oneself to it.

"Take care of yourself. God grant your work goes well.
"Yours,
"P. Tchaikowsky."

On the same August day, Tchaikowsky wrote Jurgenson:

"Dear Friend,
"I have finished the orchestration of the new symphony. Now for about a week I shall busy myself putting in the signs and generally looking it over. I made the four-hand

306

arrangement myself and must play it through, which I shall do when the youngest Konius gets here. As soon as we have gone through it together, I can send it to you, providing you want to publish my symphony. As regards the score and parts, I cannot promise to finish them before the first performance, which will be in Petersburg on October 28th.

"On my word of honor, never in my life have I been so satisfied with myself, so proud, so happy to know that I have made, in truest fact, a good thing."

Thus the summer wore away. In September, Tchaikowsky went to visit his brother Anatol at Mikhailovskoe, and wrote happily to Modeste about the beauty and quiet of the country. Early in October he returned to Klin and busied himself with orchestrating a piano concerto he had made out of parts of the symphony he had written the previous May—the symphony he had written Bob Davydoff about, and had called uninspired. This was afterward published as a piano concerto (Number Three), for piano and orchestra, Opus 75. Early in October he heard of the death of an old friend, Zverev, for whom a memorial service was to be held in Moscow next week. Two friends came out from Moscow the day before to accompany Peter back to town, and on the 19th of October therefore, late in the afternoon, the three boarded the train for Moscow, a two-hour ride. As the train passed the village of Frolovskoe, Peter pointed to the belfry tower and to the quiet, pretty churchyard below. "There," he said, "is where I shall be buried, and passing by, travellers will point out my grave."

He repeated to Taneyeff next day at Zverev's memorial service this wish to be buried in Frolovskoe, but he said it in no morbid mood; it was a natural remark at such a time, in the presence of death. During these days, it is the testimony of all who saw Peter Ilyich that his mood was in no way depressed. On the contrary, he seemed cheerful, filled with faith in himself and in the future. He had brought the new piano concerto with him to Moscow and showed it eagerly to Taneyeff. That honest person, who often called a spade worse than a spade, pronounced the concerto a virtuoso piece, and no real music. There was, as usual, truth in Taneyeff's criticism, but it did not seem to depress Tchaikowsky, nor did he destroy the concerto as he sometimes did with music Taneyeff condemned. Merely, he decided not to publish it. (It was published after the composer's death, and Taneyeff was the first to perform it in public.)

The morning after the memorial service for Zverev, Tchaikowsky went to the Moscow Conservatory to hear a Mozart vocal quartet with piano accompaniment that Tchaikowsky had lately arranged from the Mozart Piano Fantasia (Number Four). It was well sung by some of the Conservatory students and Peter was pleased; he adored that simple melody, he said, and wondered wherein lay its potent fascination. That evening he dined with friends. Kashkin in his memoirs tells how the conversation turned on the sad facts of Zverev's and Albrecht's recent deaths, and how few of the old circle were left. Who would be the next to go? "Peter," said Kashkin, "you will outlive us all." Peter denied this prophecy, but declared he had never felt so well and so happy as at the present moment. The friends sat together until it was time for Peter to take the midnight train for Petersburg. His Sixth Symphony was to be performed in a week's time and he was going up to conduct the rehearsals. Concerning the first three movements of the symphony, the composer professed himself, to Kashkin, well satisfied, but concerning the last movement, the long *Adagio lamentoso*, he was still doubtful, and if in performance it did not work out well, he would perhaps destroy it, he said, and write a new one.

Peter rose to go to the station; no one offered to go with him, as it was known that he did not like to be seen off on trains. He and Kashkin made an appointment to meet in Moscow two weeks later for supper after a concert of the Musical Society. Then they said good-bye, and neither of them dreamed it was forever.

Next morning in Petersburg Modeste and Bob Davydoff met the composer at the station and took him to the apartment they were sharing that autumn. Peter was delighted with their new living arrangements and his spirits were excellent, especially while his presence in town was not known and his time could be his own. Only one thing worried him, said Modeste. At rehearsals, the new symphony seemed to make no impression on the orchestra players and this caused the composer anxiety as well as chagrin; he knew the performance could be ruined by indifference on the part of the musicians. Also, any apparent coldness on the part of the orchestra, a yawn, a bored look, paralyzed Peter Ilyich; he lost all sense of the music's structure, all sense of shading and nuance and hurried through the rehearsal so as to free the musicians from their irksome task of playing his music. And this was usually repeated at the concert itself, resulting, of course, in a performance that lacked all strength and precision and rendered his work insipid and lacking in color. Modeste says this was the case with the Fifth Symphony and with *Hamlet*, both of which did not attain recognition until conducted by someone other than the composer.

But in spite of the orchestra's coolness, Peter did not lose faith in the intrinsic excellence of his new symphony. With other works, his friends had seen him easily elated or depressed by the most casual criticism; this time he remained firm, reiterating his conviction that the Sixth Symphony was the best thing he had ever written or ever would write. On the 28th of October the concert took place and was flatly received, because, Modeste says, of being flatly played. "The symphony was applauded and the composer called before the curtain, but the enthusiasm was no greater than had been shown for other works of Tchaikowsky's. Certainly the symphony did not make the deep impression it made when conducted by Napravnik on November 18th" (alas, too late for the composer to enjoy!). The newspapers were as lukewarm as the public, the critics finding the symphony lacking in originality. "As far as inspiration is concerned," wrote one of them, "this music stands far below Tchaikowsky's other symphonies."

Modeste attributed all this to bad performance, arising from lack of sympathy between conductor and players. But Rimsky-Korsakov, in his memoirs, disagreed with Modeste's judgment, declaring that although the symphony was splendidly played by Napravnik, it had gone very well at the author's hands, too. The public had not fathomed it the first time, and had not paid enough attention to it; precisely as several years earlier it had failed to give due attention to Tchaikowsky's Fifth Symphony.

The day after the concert, Modeste found his brother up and dressed early, sitting at the tea table with the score of the symphony in his hands. He was trying to think of a name for it before sending it to Jurgenson for publication. Somehow, merely *Number 6* did not seem sufficient, yet his first idea of "Programmatic Symphony" would not do. "How," Peter asked his brother over his glass of tea, "can it be called Programmatic when I refuse to give it a program?" Modeste suggested the word "tragic," but Peter shook his head and Modeste went out of the room, leaving his brother frowning indecisively. Suddenly Modeste reappeared at the door. "Pathetique!" he called out. "Perfect, Modia!" cried Peter. "Bravo! *Pathètique*." And he wrote the word on the score and mailed it to Moscow.

But the composer must have felt a bit doubtful, for next morning he wrote Jurgenson:

Petersburg
October 30, 1893

"Please, my dear, put the following on the title page of the symphony,

" 'To Vladimir Lvovitch Davydoff
No. 6
Comp. P. Tch.'

"I hope it isn't too late.

"Something queer is happening with this symphony; we can't say it has displeased the public, but it has perplexed them. As for me, I am prouder of it than of anything I have written. But we can talk it all over soon, because I shall be in Moscow next Saturday."

Next evening Peter Ilyich went to hear Anton Rubinstein's opera, *The Maccabees*. The day following, he was quite well, even gay and bright, records Modeste. That night he dined at Vera Butakov's. Vera was a Davydoff, a sister of Leo Davydoff, Tchaikowsky's brother-in-law, and she was a very old friend of Peter's. Years ago, indeed, Vera, who was older than Peter Ilyich, had embarrassed him greatly by falling in love with him. Peter, much irritated, had fled rapidly. But the breach was soon healed. Vera married an admiral in the Russian army and moved in court circles. It was at Vera's house that Tchaikowsky had met the Grand Duke Constantin, and it was to Vera that Tchaikowsky owed much of the Imperial patronage that had served his music so well.

So Peter dined gayly at Vera Butakov's that November night of 1893. Afterward he went to the theatre and during intermission paid a back-stage visit to the actor, Varlamoff. The conversation turned upon spiritualism; Varlamoff, with sly humor, poked fun at these ghost-raisers. Peter laughed heartily. No use, he agreed, in running after death. "Time enough, before we need meet that ugly snub-nosed one. We can all wait awhile, and as for me, I know I have a long time to live."

After the theatre, Peter had supper with friends at the Restaurant Leiner, eating macaroni and drinking his favorite white wine and soda water. At two in the morning they all walked home, Peter quite well and serene.

Next day was Thursday, November 2nd. Modeste, coming to the sitting-room for morning tea, was surprised to find his brother not there and went to Peter's room. Peter was in bed. "I've had a bad night, Modia," he said. "But it's nothing. Just the old complaint."

Modeste offered to fetch the usual remedy, castor oil, but Peter shook his head. He had to call on Napravnik later in the morning to talk business, and later on he did go out. In half an hour he returned, feeling out of sorts, and Modeste suggested calling a doctor. Not an important, fancy doctor, said Modeste pleadingly as Peter shook his head. Just their old friend, Vasili Bertenson, to look him over?

Peter refused. He would take Hunyadi water, he said. What good could a doctor do? Hadn't the two of them seen him this way scores of times? It was nothing but the usual infernal nervous dysentery. "Go on about your business, Modia," said Peter. And Modia went.

Peter wrote some letters until lunch time, when Mulbach arrived to talk business. The three sat together; Peter did not eat, but seemed in no way indisposed. He would take no wine or coffee, he said; it might be bad for what ailed him.

Peter got up, and pouring himself a glass of water from the tap in the next room, brought it back and drank it before anyone noticed what he was doing.

He set his glass down. "Petia," cried Modeste. "That water wasn't boiled. What crazy folly! It's November and you're in Petersburg."

Peter shrugged. He had never feared cholera, he said. Oh, yes, he knew one shouldn't touch fruit or raw water in the cholera season, but a man couldn't go tiptoeing round in fear of death. Now, about this contract to play the First Suite in Prague; did Mulbach think . . .

Peter's face changed suddenly; he got up from the table, went to his room and was ill. Modeste left him on his bed and went back to Mulbach. Next time Modeste looked into the bedroom, his brother was asleep. Good, thought Modeste. All Peter needs is rest, and Modeste went out with Mulbach. Returning at five he found his brother feverish and suffering from cramps; this time Peter's protest was not heeded and Vasili Bertenson was sent for. "This is a very sick man," said Vasili, and prescribed hot applications on the stomach and feet. Complete rest. Vasili was an easy-going man and an old friend of Peter's; he knew what a high-strung fellow this was.

The word cholera was not mentioned. Nor was it, records Modeste, so much as thought of.

Uneasily, Modeste, as the evening wore on, heard his brother groan in the next room, heard him get up again and again, but always, when Modeste came in, Peter refused help. Modeste called his servant and bade him fetch Vasili's brother, the famous Leo Bertenson, doctor to royalty and all of fashionable Petersburg. By the time Leo came, Peter was screaming aloud, not from abdominal pain, but from a horrible constriction in the chest. "The dry cholera!" whispered Modeste to himself, his face stiff with horror. "Peter will suffocate; in a few hours he will be dead. Oh, impossible." . . . Only the figment of imagination; Peter had often been as sick as this. . . .

Bertenson sent the specimens out for analysis. Waiting, Modeste saw his brother stiffen in the first convulsion, watched him slowly relax, sweating. . . . "Modia," whispered Peter, "is it cholera?"

312

"No," said Modeste. "No, Petia . . ."

At eleven that same evening the messenger returned from the hospital, bringing a male nurse with him. Modeste, watching Bertenson's face as he read the report, needed no further word. The glass of raw water had not been responsible; Peter had probably had the germs of cholera in him when he came to Petersburg; he might have picked them up on the journey. But the raw cold drink, and especially the bitter Hunyadi, had quickly intensified the irritation.

And now, swift action to fight this ancient enemy. White aprons, carbolic soap, antiseptic powders, sulphuric acid for Peter to take, quinine, nitre. . . . Peter turned, half sat up as he saw the men enter the dim room in their white hospital aprons. When he was fourteen, his mother had died of cholera. White aprons, and this sickish pungent odor of carbolic. . . . "Here she is then, the cholera!" exclaimed Peter, and a moment later screamed aloud in pain. . . .

And now the ranks of watchers must be augmented: cholera needs constant nursing, and nursing which is horribly dangerous as well as unpleasant. This ancient enemy of man that came from the East to lay waste to Asia, and that even now can take its toll of eighty deaths out of every hundred stricken—this is a scourge transmitted with terrifying swiftness. One touch of a polluted garment is enough. Peter worried constantly over the care expended on him, thanked his attendants for the smallest service, begged them to go and rest. A small army of men surrounded the sickbed. Nicholas Tchaikowsky, the eldest brother, was sent for; the only woman in attendance was the wife of Modeste's servant. Bob Davydoff was there, young and blond and beautiful in his smart uniform of the Preobashensky Guards—Russia's crack regiment, the Tsar's own bodyguard. Erect, booted above the knee, his fair hair wild, his young face lined with ill-concealed horror, Bob heard his name spoken and sprang to the bedside. Peter put out his hand. "Bob," he said, and smiled. "Bob . . . I am afraid, after seeing this mess, you will lose all respect for me?"

Bob shook his head wildly and turned away. The sick man was in the living-room now, his small iron bed had been rolled out from the tiny bedroom. Even the living-room was dark most of the day, nearly always a light burned. That Thursday night it began to rain, a raw wind blew from the northwest; outside, horses slipped on the cobblestones. How Peter had hated these Petersburg Novembers, and how he had complained to Nadejda Philaretovna about them! . . . During the night his suffering increased and the convulsions were followed by helpless weakness. "It seems to be death," Peter told his brother. "Good-bye, Modia."

But unhappily it was not death. All night the watchers took turns massaging the patient after his convulsions. By five next morning the constriction in his chest had ceased but another suffering came to take its place: the unappeasable, tormenting cholera thirst. Peter called for water, begged for it, bargained with the doctors for it, and when they offered it on a spoon, refused it in disgust. At nine on Friday morning Leo Bertenson went away. Peter was easier for a time, the blueness of his face yielded to a healthier pallor, but cholera spots appeared around his mouth and his lips were dry and black. When the spots disappeared, the watchers breathed more freely, and on Bertenson's returning toward noon, Peter thanked him. "You have rescued me from the claws of death," he said. "I am much better." He held this improvement until nightfall and the watchers were sent off to bed.

But on Saturday the patient woke much depressed. "Leave me," he told the doctors. "You can't help me. I shall not recover." And from now on he continued depressed though quite conscious, ceased his little jokes with Bob, his bargaining for water, and submitted passively to treatment.

And now arrived the most dangerous symptom of cholera: inactivity of the kidneys. The doctors put much hope in a hot bath that was to be administered in the evening, but when they heard the word *bath*, Modeste and Nicholas Tchaikowsky looked at each other and winced: their mother had died when put into this cholera bath. "Will you consent to the bath, Petia?" they asked. "With pleasure," replied Peter wearily. "But when you put me in it I shall certainly die as my mother died before me."

That evening Peter was too violently ill for the bath to be attempted. "You are wasting all this kindness and patience," he told Leo Bertenson again. "I tell you I cannot be cured." He slept now, restlessly, moving his head and lips. Over and over he repeated the name of Nadejda Philaretovna, reproaching her indignantly one moment and the next, smiling quietly, as though listening to a reply. When he woke, consciousness returned slowly so that it was some moments before he recognized his servant and good friend Alexis, who had come up from Moscow on the night train. "I am glad you came, Alexey," said Peter, and smiled. At two that afternoon Leo Bertenson ordered the last extreme measure to be tried: the bath. Peter was asleep, but they carried him to the tub across the room; when he felt the water he roused, pronounced it pleasant but asked to be put back to bed; he was so weak, he said.

From now on, Peter sank rapidly; perspiration was profuse, the pulse weakened, the patient roused to consciousness only for brief intervals. All hope was abandoned, the priest was sent for and read aloud the prayers for the dying without, apparently, reaching the sick man's consciousness. Modeste, dry-eyed, numb with exhaustion, moved about the room, polite as always, but seeming not to comprehend when spoken to. This was more to him than brother, this wasted, suffering figure on the bed. Modeste looked down at Peter's blackened lips, at the fingers shrivelled with cholera. This man had been Modeste's life. Modeste had lived in this stronger life, had moved in its shadow....

On the bed-table, Modeste saw the fat night-candle flutter under its glass hood; windows shook with a hard wind from off the Baltic. . . . How interminable the hours, yet how all-too-quick! Not long now, Bertenson had said. Not very much longer. Bob was asleep in his chair, poor boy, in his dressing-gown with the white apron over it. . . . That dressing-gown would have to be burned.... Modeste looked at his watch. It was Monday morning. A little after three....

There was a slight sound from the bed and Modeste leaped to his feet. Bob woke, too, and got up quickly; Alexis was already there, by his master's side. Peter's face cleared, his eyes opened; he looked in turn at the three men standing by him, then looked upward, in his eyes a clear light which remained for some moments, until without a sigh or a struggle, Peter Ilyich breathed his last.

Contrary to all the rules of cholera hygiene, usually strictly enforced by the city officials, Peter's body lay in state in his brother's apartment. Mourners came by the hundreds, filing through the room, kissing the dead man's hands and face—and the legend goes that not one of these mourners caught the infection. Then, with the coffin closed, the body was taken to Kazan Cathedral for the funeral service. Peter's wish to lie in Frolovskoe churchyard was not realized and he was buried in Petersburg in the Alexander Nevsky Lavra Cemetery. The shock of his sudden death roused the country, and when, not two weeks later, Napravnik played the Sixth Symphony in Petersburg, interest had mounted to furor. People listened avidly to this music which rumor said the author had written as his own requiem. Their biographical curiosity was never satisfied; music is not one of gossip's servants. Nevertheless this curiosity served Peter Ilyich well in sharpening the ears of the world to what the composer himself had been convinced was his best work.

Peter had willed his royalties to Bob Davydoff; the Klin house was not Peter's to bequeath, but the furniture was left to Alexis, who with such devotion and consummate lack of taste had assembled these dreadful chairs and tables and clocks and carpets. Alexis bought the house and began immediately to collect everything he could find pertaining to or belonging to his dead master. When, in 1897, he sold the house to Modeste Tchaikowsky and Bob Davydoff, the two continued Alexis' plan of making the house into a Tchaikowsky museum. Well for Peter that he could not know the fate of those dear ones who lived on in his house; there Bob, the charming, spoiled child of fortune, shot himself; there Modeste, in 1916, knew that he was to die of cancer. . . .

But the Tchaikowsky brothers were not easy to kill. Modeste died, but Hippolyte Tchaikowsky lived on at Klin, old Hippolyte the Admiral, despoiled of his cherished uniforms by a new world that considered epaulets a crime and good manners a nonsense. The revolutionary government let Hippolyte keep his position as assistant curator of the Tchaikowsky museum. Seriously, with his straight old back, his military bows, Hippolyte received museum visitors, showed them Peter's big black piano, showed them the glass case wherein lay the *Pathètique* score, traced with the delicate, precise strokes of his brother's penmanship; seriously bowed them out again into a world so wildly new that even had he been set down in its streets, Hippolyte would have failed to recognize it as the world he and Petia had lived in. . . .

Surely, it was well for Peter Ilyich that he died when he did, died in the very fulness of his time, before a world changed, before an era faded. Imperial thrones were yet secure when Peter passed away. Peter had truly loved his Tsar in the old-fashioned way. When Peter died, anarchy and communism were but theories. Gentlemen still sent pressed violets in letters to ladies, and ladies, when they could afford it, responded with slim enamel watches across which Apollo pranced in diamonds. . . .

Surely, Peter Ilyich would not have been happy in a world that found the waltz a thing to ridicule, a world which with proud defiance put the word sex in place of the word romance. A world that for a time indeed, considered Tchaikowsky — even dead — as outmoded, ridiculous as the waltz-time he had loved. When he died, Peter Ilyich was but fifty-three, still young, as composers go. Yet somehow, the world does not mourn him as a man cut down in his prime. The world does not, sighing, say as it says of Mozart, of Keats, of Schubert, "Oh, had this man lived longer, what still more glorious gifts he might have had for us!" No; there is about the Sixth Symphony something strangely final, something that tells us: This man's cup was full; he had reached his zenith, he had attained that which so often he had told his "best friend" he longed to attain: he had perfected his talent to the limit of his ability, he had fulfilled his urgent duty toward that gift which the gods had given him. . . .

God rest him, then, as the Russians would say. God rest the soul of Peter Ilyich, who worked hard, who sinned and suffered for his sins — who was an artist, and true to himself.

BEST SELLING PAPERBACKS FROM HODDER

☐	12901 8	**THE VOYEUR** by Henry Sutton	8/–
☐	01090 8	**THE INCREDIBLE JOURNEY** by Sheila Burnford	4/
☐	12804 6	**AND TO MY NEPHEW ALBERT I LEAVE THE ISLAND WHAT I WON OFF FATTY HAGAN IN A POKER GAME** by David Forrest	5/–
☐	04359 8	**GOODBYE MR. CHIPS** by James Hilton	4/–
☐	12779 1	**EVERY HOME SHOULD HAVE ONE** by Milton Shulman and Herbert Kretzmer	5/–
☐	15154 4	**THE MUSIC LOVERS** by Catherine Drinker Bowen and Barbara von Meck (The Story of Tchaikowsky)	7/–
☐	12508 X	**LOVE STORY** by Erich Segal	5/–
☐	00892 X	**THE SECRET OF SANTA VITTORIA** by Robert Crichton	8/–

All these books are available at your bookshop or newsagent, or can be ordered direct from the publisher. Just tick the titles you want and fill in the form below.

....

HODDER PAPERBACKS, Cash Sales Department, Kernick Industrial Estate, Penryn, Cornwall.

Please send cheque or postal order, no currency and allow 9d. per book to cover the cost of postage and packing in U.K., 1s. per copy overseas.

NAME ....

ADDRESS ....

....